Enhanced Enterprise Risk Management

Enhanced Enterprise Risk Management

John Sidwell and Peter Hlavnicka

BUSINESS EXPERT PRESS

Leader in applied, concise business books

First published in 2022 by
Business Expert Press, LLC
222 East 46th Street, New York, NY 10017
www.businessexpertpress.com

ISBN-13: 978-1-63742-398-1 (paperback)
ISBN-13: 978-1-63742-399-8 (e-book)

Business Expert Press Business Law and Corporate Risk Management Collection

First edition: 2022

10 9 8 7 6 5 4 3 2 1

Description

The performance and survival of a business in a global economy depends on understanding and managing the risks—both external and those embedded within its operations.

It is vital to identify and prioritize significant risks and detect the weakest points. Adding other elements to an essential ERM program, such as PESTLE and Porter's Five Forces, treatment plans, scorecards, the three lines of defense (3LoD) components, and process improvements (Six Sigma, 8D, etc.) significantly increases the ERM success rate.

The authors outline a comprehensive strategy for designing and implementing a robust and successful ERM program—that is not just successful in implementation but also in yielding enormous returns for the organizations that implemented this enhanced ERM program.

Keywords

Enterprise risk management; ERM; risks; lines of defense; 3LoD; COSO; governance; stress testing; evaluation; measurement; assessment; response; reporting; framework; PESTLE; Porter's Five Forces; internal audit; process improvement; scorecards; heat maps; finance

Contents

Testimonials

"The most useful ERM program I have ever seen. I have asked the other companies on which I am a board member to emulate your exact program." —**Thomas McDaniel, Audit Committee Chairman at SunPower Corporation, former Executive Vice President, Chief Financial Officer and Treasurer of Edison International**

"I have personally served on 12 corporate boards. On two of those companies, I worked with John where he was the chief internal auditor. He was outstanding. In both companies, he put an ERM plan into place that was outstanding. It was well structured, covered all of our major risks and, best of all, it was a plan that management bought into and owned. John is a true expert in designing and implementing ERM plans and, now with this book, in sharing with others what he knows. As I have taught corporate governance, accounting and auditing at three major universities (U of Illinois, Stanford, and BYU), I have learned that there are five key elements to having a successful company: (1) having the right leaders in place, (2) having a strategic plan and mission in place that is bought into by everyone in the organization, (3) implementing processes to accomplish the plans and mission, (4) mitigating the risks that keep you from accomplishing your plan, and (5) excellent communication processes throughout the organization to ensure that everyone in the organization is on the same page. It is often the fourth of these success elements that fails (mitigating risks) that John's excellent ERM work addresses. I strongly recommend this book to anyone interested in understanding and mitigating their risks so their organizations can be more successful."—**W. Steve Albrecht, PhD, MBA, CPA, CIA, and CFE; Professor Emeritus University of Illinois, Stanford, and Brigham Young University**

"While most ERM programs are sufficient in identifying business risks, John's program successfully focused on the Treatment Plans to mitigate the risks. In volatile/dynamic industries and a world of heightened geopolitical risks, this program is excellent and brought life to our risk management process and had a significant impact on the organization."—**Thad Trent, Executive Vice President and Chief Financial Officer On Semiconductor Corporation, former Executive Vice President and Chief Financial Officer Cypress Semiconductor Corporation**

"John was a pioneer and early adopter of the three lines of defense and ERM. He built a framework that involved the leaders and staff across the company to identify risks, both known and previously unknown to the executive team. Importantly, he was able to use a common sense approach to quantify and rank the risks and track the trending of the various risks. With the closed loop process, tracking and managing mitigation plans protects the shareholders and stakeholders."—**Chuck Boynton, Executive Vice President and Chief Financial Officer Poly, former Executive Vice President and Chief Financial Officer SunPower Corporation**

Foreword

As a serial founder, Board Director, Venture Capitalist, and Adjunct Faculty Member, I have spent more than two decades on the frontiers of reputation risk management, cyber risk governance, and Enterprise Risk Management. I've signed off on many variations of ERM programs. Few have served as an orienteering guide to navigate our complex geopolitical, ecological, and social landscape.

ERM failures I have observed in the industry were because the organizations struggled with having a clear ERM objective and structure applicable to the specific needs of their company and industry. Others were due to the leadership taking on too much risk, believing the market would react positively to their message of apparent unbridled commercial growth—at any cost. Their strategies lacked globally responsible leadership, citizenship, board of directors' endorsement, or alignment with executive leadership team support. Others simply tried to implement too many changes at the same time. Especially in these complex times, navigating shades of gray has never been more critical.

Through a journey from conception to birth, the growth and success of an ERM program, John and Peter lay out the path for ERM practitioners to follow—step by step. They provide a robust, practical approach to the discipline, empowering you to identify and quantify your organization's strategic and operational risks. Investing your time in reading this book will provide you with an opportunity to learn from real-life case studies and examples of ERM best practices applicable across all industry sectors and business models.

ERM is core to supporting strategic planning, decision making, and reputation risk management.

If you follow the best practices provided in this book, the chances of establishing and implementing a successful ERM and reputation risk program at your company increase exponentially.

But don't let me hold you off any longer, so go ahead and enjoy your journey.

—Leesa Soulodre, MBA, MiM
Adjunct Professor, Singapore Management University
(SMU), General Partner R3i Ventures Pte Limited

Acknowledgments

We would like to express our gratitude for the help of many individuals who made this book possible, as well as those who guided us and helped us on our journey.

We would like to thank the team at Business Expert Press including Scott Isenberg, Charlene Kronstedt, John Wood, Melissa Yeager, Sheri Dean, and Gunabala Saladi from Exeter for the talented editing and guidance during the production process.

A special thank you to Zara Tadifa, with whom we have worked side-by-side over the past in creating, customizing, implementing, and refining such ERM programs in the technology and solar industries.

John Sidwell—I am immensely grateful to valuable colleagues with whom I have collaborated in the past as part of peer groups and professional organizations (especially NeuGroup) to enrich our message: Tom Austin (Cisco), Marco Loures (Broadcom), Petrie Terblanche (Criteo), Steven Proctor (Lumen), Art Perez (Sales Force), Anna Davis (Qualcomm), Paul Walker (St. John's University), and Ted Howard (NeuGroup). They are genuinely interested in ideas, who render a constructive critique of any material, suggestion, or practice, and who are always eager to test new ideas, new ways of thinking, and new practices. In addition, W. Steve Albrecht (BoD), Chuck Boynton (CFO), Tom Werner (CEO), Thad Trent (CFO), Hassane El-Khoury (CEO) provided incredible support, and valuable guidance in helping to customize the ERM programs to better fit the business environment and drive success. Most importantly, I specifically want to express loving memories of my brother, Richard Sidwell, who influenced me to keep pushing my career goals and motivated me to write this book even though the workload was sometimes overwhelming. He taught me to laugh at the stress points!

Peter Hlavnicka—I would like to extend my appreciation to the extremely talented and experienced team at R3i Ventures Pte. Ltd. led by amazing Leesa Soulodre; to many encouraging and inspirational founders such as Colina Q Tran (CEO, Grandemy), Hami Kim (amazing musician and CEO, Kooky.io), Yun Sil Chu (CEO, Moaah), Bell Beh (CEO, BuzzAR), Anthony Chua (CEO, Stratificare), George Heng (CEO, SenzeHub), and about 30 other founders I had the pleasure to mentor and learn from; and my close friends and trailblazers Howard Kim, Henry Wong, Elena Lim, Chelle Coury, Brett Millar, Louis Lye, WT Soh, Kelvin Phua, Kirti Chandel, and many others. Without their continued encouragement, friendship, and support, my life's endeavor would not be complete.

CHAPTER 1

Introduction

The performance and even vitality of a business today depends on managing both—the known and foreseeable risks. Every business needs to understand the acceptable risks in achieving its objectives, as well as the type and level of risk embedded within its operations. It is vital to identify and prioritize significant risks and detect the weakest points. Managing risks may be in a form of an essential Enterprise Risk Management (ERM) program but can be significantly enhanced by considering other elements frequently present in most companies, such as the Three Lines of Defense (3LoD) components and Process Improvement teams (Six Sigma, 8D, etc.). There are employees within these functions who are aware of and employing resources to address perceived risk areas. To better prioritize and manage risks, it can be helpful to integrate these programs into the formal ERM program. The overall objective should be to apply the limited risk management resources to the highest company risks for strongest payback. In this book we will address the basic ERM program first, then delve into the 3LoD as well as Process Improvement activities.

ERM has been around for some time. There are a few frameworks that influence and address managing risks, such as Committee of Sponsoring Organizations of the Treadway Commission (COSO),[1] National Institute of Standards and Technology (NIST),[2] International Organization for Standardization—ISO31000. The leading practice is to use COSO as the base, but also consider elements of both ISO and NIST as appropriate. We will focus on COSO as the primary framework for managing risks.

---

[1] www.coso.org/

[2] www.nist.gov/

CHAPTER 2

What Is ERM?

Enterprise Risk Management (ERM) is a process reinforced by a set of principles and must be supported by an appropriate organizational structure, which is aligned with the external environment and with other corporate activities. It needs to be comprehensive, ingrained into routine activities, and responsive to changing economic, political, legislative, regulatory, ecological, and other conditions impacting business. A successful ERM program should be proportionate to the level of risk depending on the size and complexity of the business or organization, enabling the ERM to deliver outputs, including compliance with applicable governance requirements and assurance to stakeholders regarding the management of risk and improved decision making. The impact or benefits associated with these outputs include more efficient operations, effective tactics, and effective strategy, and need to be measurable and sustainable.

Committee of Sponsoring Organizations of the Treadway Commission (COSO) defines ERM as:

> *Enterprise risk management deals with risks and opportunities affecting value creation or preservation, defined as follows:*
>
> *Enterprise risk management is a process, effected by an entity's board of directors, management and other personnel, applied in strategy setting and across the enterprise, designed to identify potential events that may affect the entity, and manage risk to be within its risk appetite, to provide reasonable assurance regarding the achievement of entity objectives.*
>
> *The definition reflects certain fundamental concepts. Enterprise risk management is:*

- *A process, ongoing and flowing through an entity*
- *Effected by people at every level of an organization*

- *Applied in strategy setting*
- *Applied across the enterprise, at every level and unit, and includes taking an entity level portfolio view of risk*
- *Designed to identify potential events that, if they occur, will affect the entity and to manage risk within its risk appetite*
- *Able to provide reasonable assurance to an entity's management and board of directors*
- *Geared to achievement of objectives in one or more separate but overlapping categories*

> *This definition is purposefully broad. It captures key concepts fundamental to how companies and other organizations manage risk, providing a basis for application across organizations, industries, and sectors. It focuses directly on achievement of objectives established by a particular entity and provides a basis for defining enterprise risk management effectiveness.*[1]

There are as many descriptions of ERM as there are different ways to apply these principles. But there should be a common understanding of the fundamentals. Figure 2.1 shows what ERM "is" and what ERM "is not." While it may seem basic, it is important that all executives, managers, and employees have a common understanding of these components, and also understand that risk is not inherently bad—managed/calculated **risk** can generate **returns**.

Taking too much uncalculated risk can destroy the value of a company. There is a lot of publicly available information showing examples when risk management failures in some part(s) of a company can be quite costly. The companies shown in Figure 2.2 are from all types of industries—retail, service, banking, technology, and manufacturing. The size of these companies also varies substantially, which means that there is no discernible relationship between the type of industry and between the sizes of

---

[1] COSCO. 2004. *Enterprise Risk Management –Integrated Framework*, www.coso .org/documents/Framework%20Reference%20Secured.pdf (accessed January 10, 2022).

ERM IS:

- A continuous process led by senior leadership
- Built into routine business processes
- Designed to identify and manage current and emerging risks
- Tied to the Company's strategic goals and objectives
- A means to hold leadership accountable for managing risks
- Applied across the organization

ERM IS NOT A:

- Means to prevent all risks
- Program to avoid all risks
- Prescriptive method for managing individual risks
- One-time process
- Tool, system or software
- "One size fits all" framework

Risk is not inherently bad; risk generates return. However, taking too much uncalculated risk can destroy the value of a company. Public information shows examples of company events show that risk management lapses occur from a variety of areas in the company and could be costly.

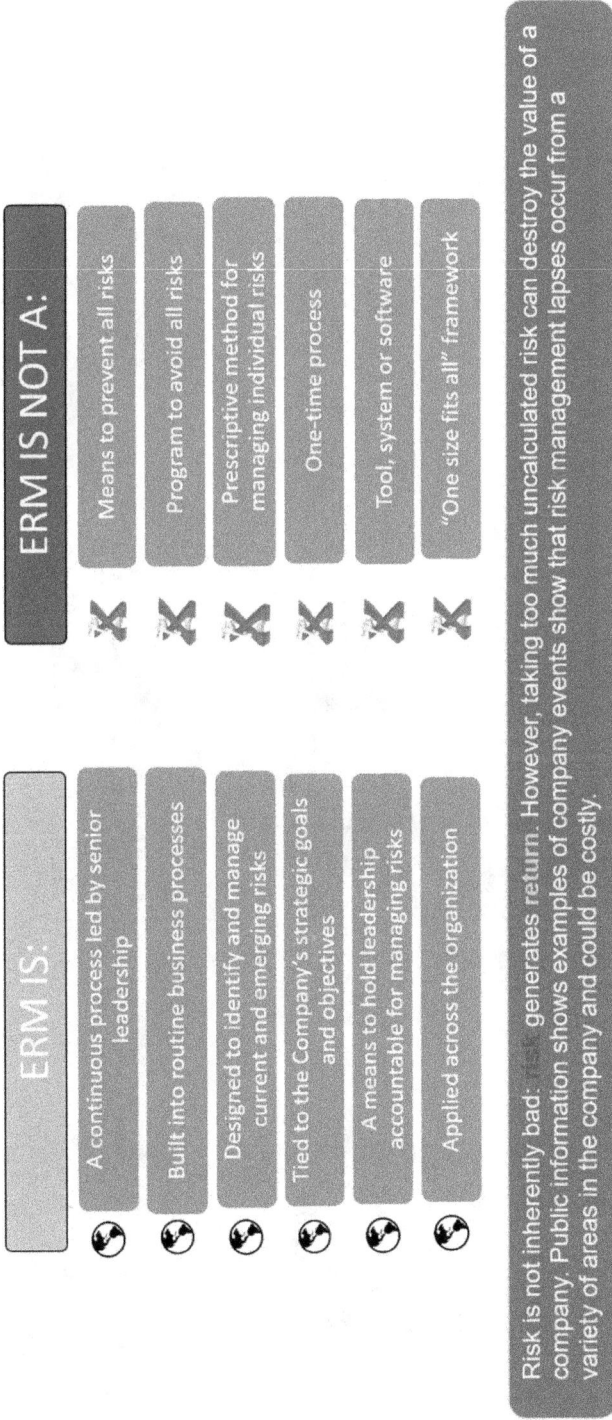

Figure 2.1 ERM introduction

Weak Operating Controls

Cause: Wells Fargo unrealistic sales goals and weak internal controls resulted to creation of up to 3.5M fake accounts, and hitting customers with unfair mortgage fees and car insurances.

Cost: Wells Fargo underwent leadership change (including Board & CEO), downgraded lending rating, settlement payments over $300M and regulatory fines over $1B to date

Bribery of Local Authorities

Cause: Local management in Wal-Mart's Mexico operations bribed government officials to get permits for new stores, with country executives allegedly condoning these illegal practices.

Cost: As of 2014, Wal-Mart has spent $439 million in two years investigating bribery allegations while government investigations are still ongoing

Service Delivery Failure

Cause: Delays in training and vetting staff for 2012 Olympic games had resulted in the company being far behind schedule to provide 10,000 security personnel.

Cost: G4S lost over $140 million.

Lack of Third Party Management

Cause: Leakage of confidential customer data to Cambridge Analytica attracted scrutiny from government regulators both in US and EU about Facebook's privacy measures and enforcement of controls up to third party developers with access to its customer data.

Cost: Facebook market value declined by ~$50B in a week. Facebook also faces a class action suit from its stockholders

Lack of Overarching Governance

Cause: SunEdison lacked management response to missed targets and business risks including substantial decrease in ASP, challenges in raising funds from own operations, delayed execution of projects and too aggressive & unplanned M&A deals. Conflict of interest at the Board level impaired oversight function of the Board.

Cost: SunEdison filed for Chapter 11 bankruptcy in April 2016.

Consumer Safety

Cause: A gas pedal design flaw caused Toyota to recall over 10 million cars. A subsequent investigation found that Toyota lied to regulators and the U.S. Congress.

Cost: The cost of the recalls was estimated at $250–$400 million. Additionally, Toyota faced a $1.2 billion fine by the U.S. Department of Justice.

Customer Data Breach

Cause: Hackers gained access to an estimated 70 million customer credit cards, compromising personal information. Sources suggest managers constantly dismissed cyber security concerns raised by internal experts.

Cost: Target has estimated the cost to shareholders from the breach to be $148 million plus a loss of trust.

Strategic Failure

Cause: Kodak ignored the rise of digital photography at first and corrected too late.

Cost: Kodak lost considerable market value, with annual revenue decreasing from $16 billion in 1996 to $6.2 billion in 2011.

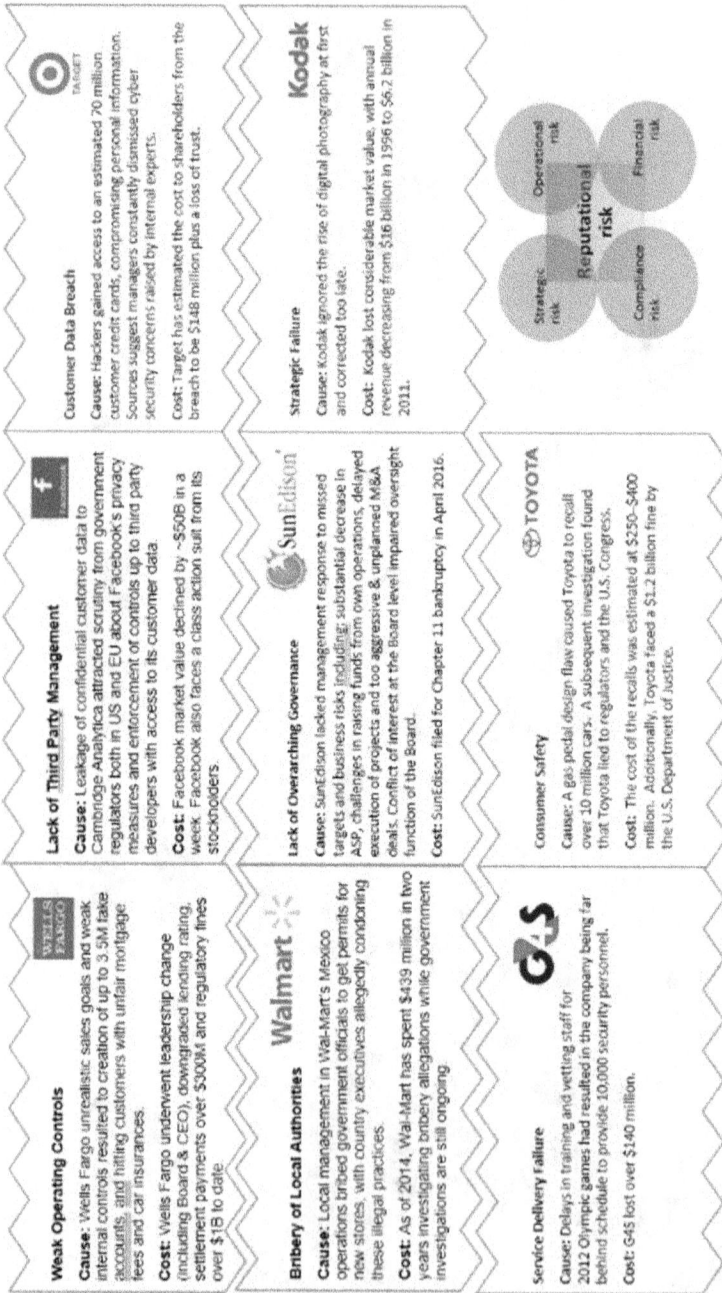

Figure 2.2 Example of various risks

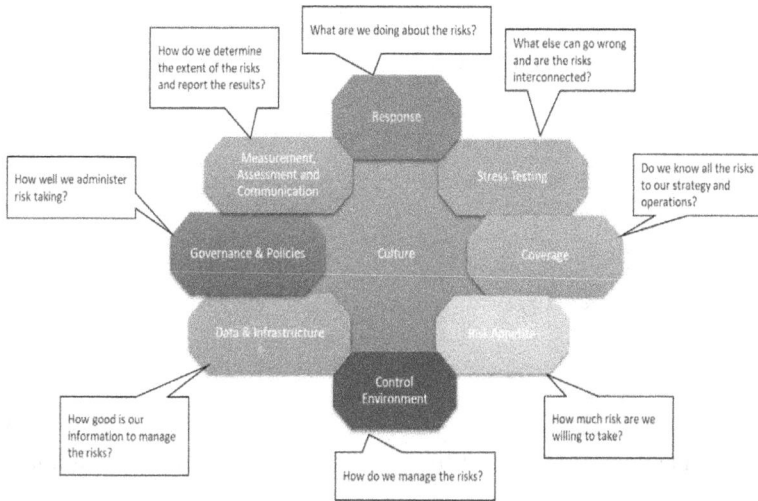

Figure 2.3 ERM in form of questions

company versus the relative degradation of company value. The events shown in Figure 2.2 include all categories of risks (Financial, Strategic, Operational, and Regulatory), and it is apparent how the reputation was negatively affected for a majority of the cases.

Risk management lapses are diverse, and the cost can be great. Regulators and stakeholders are holding the Management and the Board of Directors fully accountable.

Let's summarize ERM in basic terms—ERM is a company's ability to answer the following questions (as shown in Figure 2.3):

Coverage

ERM must be integrated into the overall business strategy because every business needs to answer the fundamental question: *What is our strategy and associated risks?*

Therefore, a business must set its strategy first—defining goals and objectives with respect to products, markets, segments, revenue, profits, and so on. Only then can it assess the risks associated with the strategy and decide what level of risk it is willing to accept in executing the strategy, that is its **risk appetite**.

The minimal set of risks that must be incorporated into a business strategy, and consequently into its ERM program include:

- Liquidity (Financial and Other Assets)
- Recognition and Reputation (Brand and Business)
- Operational
- Suitability
- Compliance (Legal and Regulatory)
- Business Environment (Market, Economy, etc.)

Figure 2.4 depicts a pictorial of the business coverage impacted in a typical manufacturing and distribution environment. Note, the administrative functions occur in all types of companies.

Risk Appetite

Risk appetite **is the level of volatility a business is willing to accept in executing its strategy**. Risk appetite is a crucial tool aiding the Board of Directors and executive leadership teams (ELTs) to understand the essential links between the business strategy and the risk(s). Therefore, ERM has to be an integral part of the overall business strategy and an essential part of the business value creation for investors and shareholders.

It is important to differentiate **risk appetite** from **risk tolerance** (although they are often erroneously used interchangeably). **Risk tolerance** differs from risk appetite and **represents operational boundaries or parameters implemented in the context of the business's risk appetite definition**.

Culture, Governance, and Policies

Culture, governance, and policies help a business to manage its risk-taking activities. Culture is one of the most important aspects of ERM effectiveness, while policies are used to transfer/communicate the risk appetite strategy to the broader audience. They specify *what* the business is willing to do or not do, and the procedures describing *how* to do it.

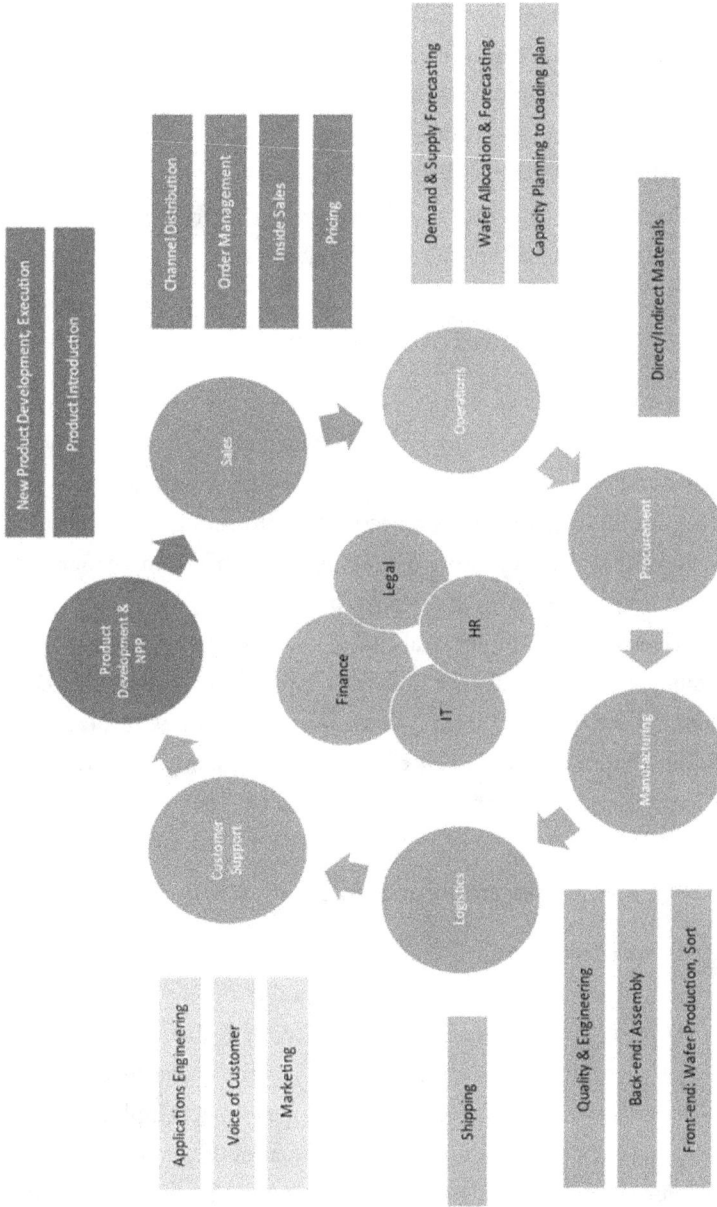

Figure 2.4   Pictorial of the business coverage impacted in a typical manufacturing/distribution environment

Risk Data and Infrastructure

Boards of Directors and ELT accomplish their risk management responsibilities through a deep understanding of a company's risk profile. The risk data and infrastructure refer to how the information is collected, integrated, analyzed, and translated into a cohesive story. This area is probably the most challenging aspect of ERM. Companies have spent between US$200M to US$300M on ERM activities without yielding the desirable business results. An effective risk management infrastructure requires a highly robust management information system.

Control Environment

The internal control environment is one of the most important tools in the management toolbox to effectively manage risks. A well established and functional system of internal control can help safeguard an organization and minimize risk to its objectives by protecting assets, ensuring accuracy of records, promoting operational efficiency, and encouraging adherence to policies, rules, and regulations.

Management relies on internal controls to manage residual risk to an acceptable level. **Residual risk** is defined as **the level of inherent risks reduced by the level of internal controls and processes in place surrounding the risk**. Building an effective internal control environment allows management to control what can be controlled.

Measurement and Evaluation

At any given time, Boards of Directors and management must manage a portfolio of risks (from asset quality, liquidity, interest rate, to business continuity, information security, privacy, etc.). The science and art of measurement in ERM is about concluding which risks are significant and where to invest time, energy, and resources. To accomplish the goal of measurement and evaluation, a company may adopt various models— from color ratings (green, yellow, and red) to a highly sophisticated risk-adjusted models.

Regardless of the method used, measurement, and evaluation help, the Board of Directors and management answer the **so what?** question.

The process of measurement and evaluation must include the system of internal controls and must determine how well the risks can be managed.

Given the importance and complexity of this subject, this book will be devoted to this topic to help risk management professionals choose the right methodology for their company.

Scenario Planning and Stress Testing

The art of ERM is the ability to answer the question, **what can go wrong that will create deviation from expected outcomes?** In that pursuit, management must address risks with known probability distributions (**known unknowns**) from those with an unknown distribution (**unknown unknowns**). Scenario planning and stress testing are tools that focus on the different categories of risks. A robust scenario planning and stress testing discipline is a must when considering both internal and external risk factors.

CHAPTER 3

COSO Evolution ERM Frameworks

Enterprise Risk Management (ERM) has been around for some time. In August 2004, the Committee of Sponsoring Organizations of the Treadway Commission (COSO) issued its "Enterprise Risk Management—Integrated Framework" after completing a three-year long project expanding on previously issued "Internal Control—Integrated Framework" and thus providing more robust focus on ERM. The financial crisis (2008) helped to boost ERM into overall business strategy (see Figure 3.1).

In 2013, COSO upgraded the framework creating the COSO Cube to better align risk management with the way management runs an enterprise and integrates the risk program within the management process (see Figure 3.2).

In September 2017, the "2017 COSO Enterprise Risk Management Framework—Integrating with Strategy and Performance" takes a more pragmatic forward-looking view of ERM. The change from the iconic 2004 COSO Cube to the 2017 Helix structure reflects an evolution for risk professionals earning acceptance at the executive table. The change in focus supported the need to consider risk elements in strategy-setting processes and performance management processes. Historically, ERM programs intended to minimize the erosion of risks to an acceptable level. However, owing to the speed of risks in our fast-paced, ever-evolving global business environment, the updated model changed the direction while also encouraging ERM programs that help the identification of opportunities to create value-add (see Figure 3.3).

Today an effective risk management program is an integral part of overall business strategy as investors, shareholders, and consumers become increasingly concerned about risk(s). Risk(s) can be a determining factor

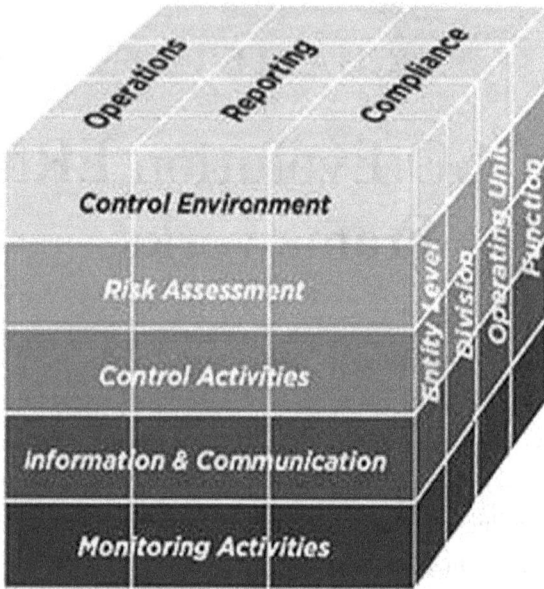

Figure 3.1 COSO *internal control—integrated framework*

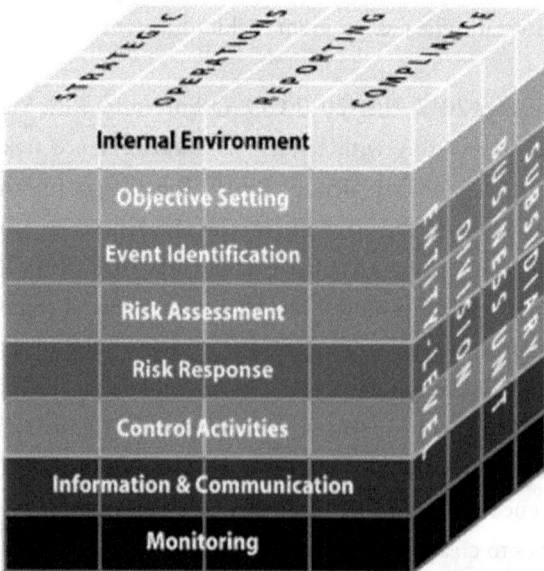

Figure 3.2 COSO *upgraded cube framework*

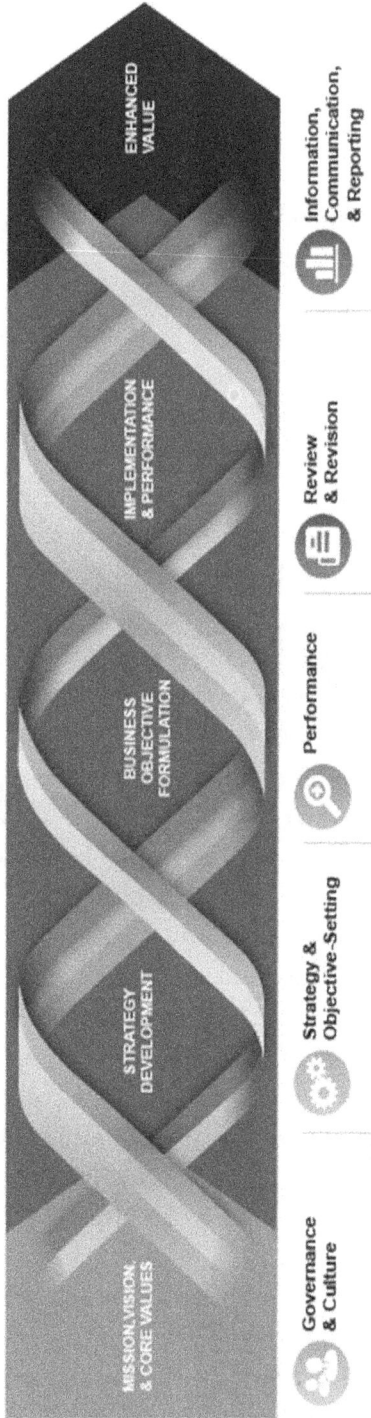

Figure 3.3 COSO helix structure

of strategic decisions and should be embedded in all business activities, or it may just be a basis for an uncertainty the business has to manage. Comprehensive ERM enables a business to assess and address the probable outcomes of all types of risks on its products and services, operations, and stakeholders. This will result in what is commonly referred to as **upside of risk** (i.e., **benefits realized by implementing ERM**).

The expected benefits of the ERM should be formulated in advance. The desired outcomes from successful ERM include stronger compliance (regulatory, Sarbanes Oxley ("SOX"), contracts, etc.), enhanced operational efficiency (reduced product costs, cost of capital, more accurate financial reporting, etc.), tactical direction, strategic alignment, and decision-making effectiveness (resulting in competitive advantage, improved customer perception, increased marketplace coverage, etc.).

ERM, as an integral part of business strategy setting, redefines the value proposition from tactical to strategic. ERM is about managing the risks that matter and viewing them from an opportunistic standpoint. There are volumes and volumes of literature available to discuss theoretical elements of risk; however, in this book, we provide insights into the leading and enhanced practices from some of the most successful and innovative global ERM concepts and practices that organizations can use to their full advantage to compete, succeed, and survive in today's challenging economical, ecological, and geopolitical environment, and ever-challenging global markets.

The new COSO framework structure is made up of five components and introduces 20 key principles collectively among the five components. It encourages the integration of ERM with business practices and strategic direction, which generates more comprehensive, useful information and yields enhanced performance. It also tends to provide a continuum from Strategy to Business Execution to Performance and thus creating more value-add to the exercise or processes (see Figure 3.4).

The five components shown in the helix include:

- Governance and Culture—creates a base setting to exercise general oversight of an ERM program and philosophy;
- Strategy and Objective-Setting—creates a framework to link risk management to objective/goal setting;

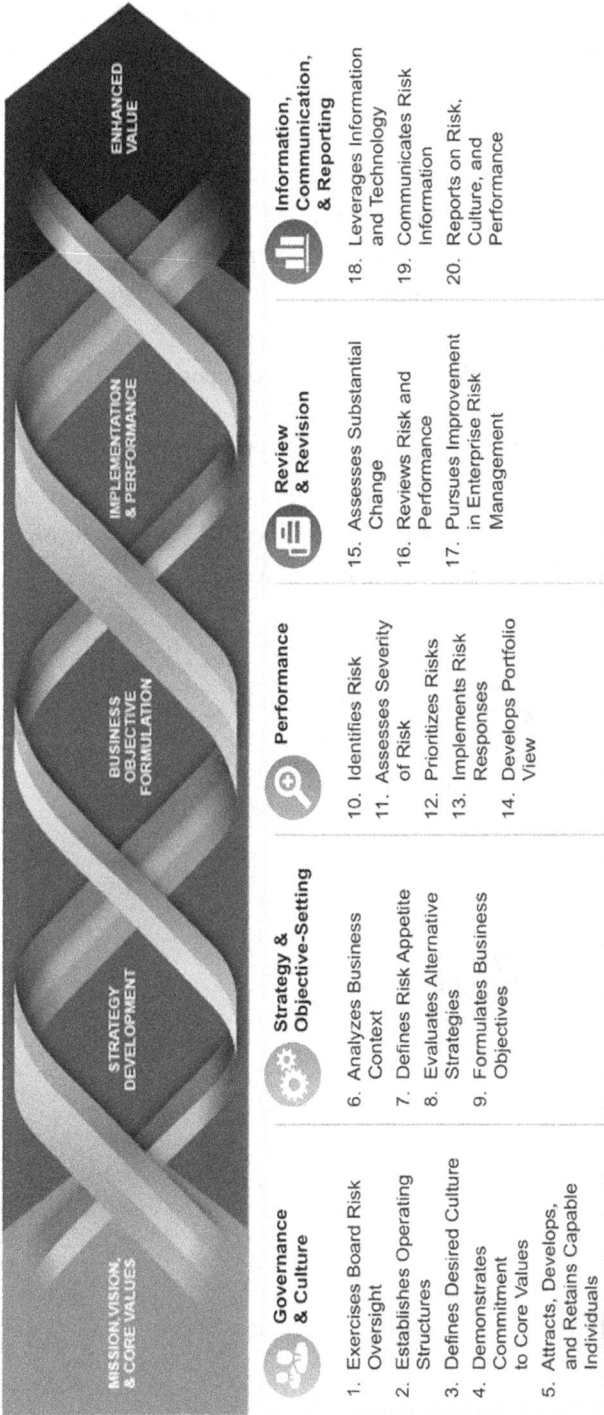

MISSION, VISION, & CORE VALUES

STRATEGY DEVELOPMENT

BUSINESS OBJECTIVE FORMULATION

IMPLEMENTATION & PERFORMANCE

ENHANCED VALUE

Governance & Culture

1. Exercises Board Risk Oversight
2. Establishes Operating Structures
3. Defines Desired Culture
4. Demonstrates Commitment to Core Values
5. Attracts, Develops, and Retains Capable Individuals

Strategy & Objective-Setting

6. Analyzes Business Context
7. Defines Risk Appetite
8. Evaluates Alternative Strategies
9. Formulates Business Objectives

Performance

10. Identifies Risk
11. Assesses Severity of Risk
12. Prioritizes Risks
13. Implements Risk Responses
14. Develops Portfolio View

Review & Revision

15. Assesses Substantial Change
16. Reviews Risk and Performance
17. Pursues Improvement in Enterprise Risk Management

Information, Communication, & Reporting

18. Leverages Information and Technology
19. Communicates Risk Information
20. Reports on Risk, Culture, and Performance

Figure 3.4 COSO helix structure and 20 key principles

- Performance—allows for the identification and addressing of risks pertinent to business execution supporting the strategies;
- Review and Revision—requires the organization to constantly review effectiveness of mitigating risks during the remediation process, and adjusting as necessary to correct efforts; and
- Information, Communication, and Reporting—focuses on gaining, analyzing, and assessing information to report performance to executives and/or Boards.

The 20 key principles within the five components are as shown in Figure 3.5.

Figure 3.6 emphasizes the integration of ERM into the strategic planning for the company. It still uses the same 20 principles but shows a more fluid approach in thinking about the ERM process incorporated with the changing dynamics of an organization.

Governance & Culture

1. Exercises Board Risk Oversight
2. Establishes Operating Structures
3. Defines Desired Culture
4. Demonstrates Commitment to Core Values
5. Attracts, Develops, and Retains Capable Individuals

Strategy & Objective-Setting

6. Analyzes Business Context
7. Defines Risk Appetite
8. Evaluates Alternative Strategies
9. Formulates Business Objectives

Performance

10. Identifies Risk
11. Assesses Severity of Risk
12. Prioritizes Risks
13. Implements Risk Responses
14. Develops Portfolio View

Review & Revision

15. Assesses Substantial Change
16. Reviews Risk and Performance
17. Pursues Improvement in Enterprise Risk Management

Information, Communication, & Reporting

18. Leverages Information and Technology
19. Communicates Risk Information
20. Reports on Risk, Culture, and Performance

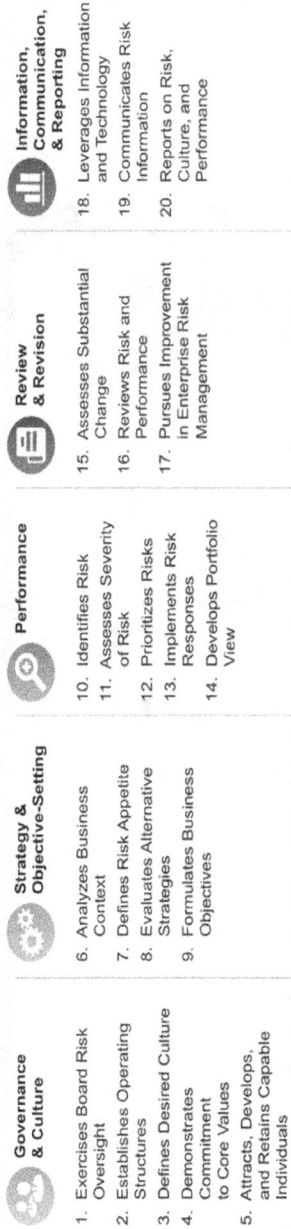

Figure 3.5 COSO ERM—20 key principles

Risk Governance And Culture

1. Exercises Board Risk Oversight
2. Establishes Governance and Operating Model
3. Defines Desired Organizational Behaviors
4. Demonstrates Commitment to Integrity and Ethics
5. Enforces Accountability
6. Attracts, Develops, and Retains Talented Individuals

Risk, Strategy, and Objective-Setting

7. Considers Risk and Business Context
8. Defines Risk Appetite
9. Evaluates Alternative Strategies
10. Considers Risk while Establishing Business Objectives
11. Defines Acceptable Variation in Performance

ENTERPRISE RISK MANAGEMENT

Mission, Vision, and Core Values

Strategy and Business Objectives

Enhanced Performance

Risk in Execution

12. Identifies Risk in Execution
13. Assesses Severity of Risk
14. Prioritizes Risks
15. Identifies and Selects Risk Responses
16. Assesses Risk in Execution
17. Develops Portfolio View

Risk Information, Communication, and Reporting

18. Uses Relevant Information
19. Leverages Information Systems
20. Communicates Risk Information
21. Reports on Risk, Culture, and Performance

Monitoring Risk Management Performance

22. Monitors Substantial Change
23. Monitors Enterprise Risk Management

Figure 3.6 COSO ERM—five components

CHAPTER 4

ERM Structure

The internal risk culture is the combined set of individual and corporate values, attitudes, risk appetite, competencies, and behavior that determine a company's commitment and style of risk management. To build a desired risk management culture within the organization and to inform management about specific risk management tools and processes, Risk Awareness Programs must be implemented consisting of training, workshops, and informational sessions.

Although the ERM program is embedded within a company's organization, it is generally administered and facilitated by an individual or a group, who are independent of line management responsibilities frequently reporting functionally to the Audit Committee of the Board of Directors. Ownership of the ERM function is normally housed in one of several departments such as Internal Audit, Legal, Finance, or a separate ERM group. To maintain effectiveness, it is important that the group reports to an administrative function rather than departments such as operations, sales, and so on; since these groups will also be responsible for managing activities to run the business on a day-to-day basis.

Risk Categories and Definitions

Risks are categorized based on the corporate objectives to which they relate. The following are the categories of company goals and objectives pursuant to the COSO ERM.[1] While this is from the older version of COSO framework, it still applies at the top level and aligns with the core functions and activities of nearly all companies.

---

[1] COSO. 2004. *Enterprise Risk Management—Integrated Framework*, (See: www .coso.org/documents/Framework%20Reference%20Secured.pdf (accessed January 11, 2022).

Strategic

Risks are categorized under strategic when they relate to *high-level goals, aligned with and supporting the Company's mission and business objectives*. Examples include: reduction in business vitality due to changing and disruptive technology, loss of intellectual property and trade secrets, competition for talent, and negative impact to brand reputation and loss of consumer confidence.

Operational

Risks are categorized as operational when *specific goals are operational in nature, driving effective and efficient use of the Company's resources*. Examples may include product supply disruption, cost of poor quality, physical assets and property damage, inefficient use of resources, increased product cost, and disruptions in data flows, systems, and communications.

Financial

Risks are categorized as financial when the *goals relate to providing reliable accurate reporting to investors and stakeholders*. Risks related to proper accounting, completeness, valuation, presentation, and disclosure of business transactions may include foreign currency exchange ("FX"), financial misrepresentation (including violation of the Sarbanes–Oxley Act), funding, cash flow, and credit conditions.

Legal and Compliance

Risks are categorized as Legal and Compliance for *goals that relate to compliance with applicable laws and regulations*. In a complex regulatory requirement environment, the business's ability to comply and maintain compliance may constitute a compliance risk. Examples may include: breach of governing environmental laws and regulation, employee health and safety ("EH&S"), personal data protection, product quality and safety, and local tax and statutory laws.

A company called the Corporate Executive Board (now Gartner) conducted an analysis of public information identifying the causes of Share Price Decline Drivers during 2004–2013 (see Figure 4.1). They captured

Share Price Decline Drivers (2004-2013)
Top 200 Companies by Market Capitalization in the Fortune 500

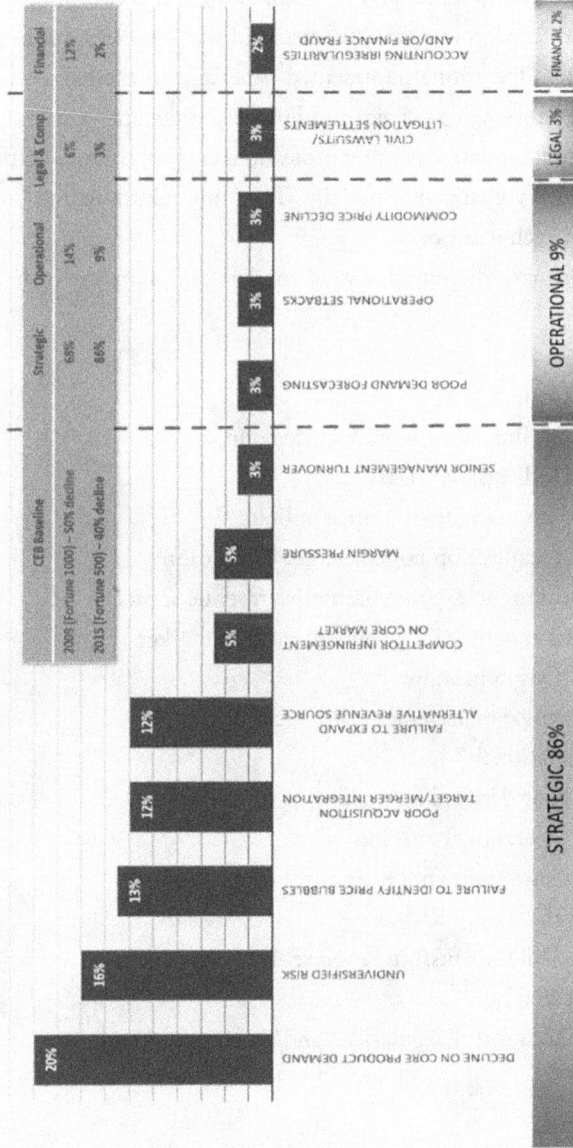

CEB Baseline	Strategic	Operational	Legal & Comp	Financial
2009 (Fortune 1000) – 50% decline	68%	14%	6%	12%
2015 (Fortune 500) – 40% decline	86%	9%	3%	2%

DECLINE ON CORE PRODUCT DEMAND — 20%
UNDIVERSIFIED RISK — 16%
FAILURE TO IDENTIFY PRICE BUBBLES — 13%
POOR ACQUISITION TARGET/MERGER INTEGRATION — 12%
FAILURE TO EXPAND ALTERNATIVE REVENUE SOURCE — 12%
COMPETITOR INFRINGEMENT ON CORE MARKET — 5%
MARGIN PRESSURE — 5%
SENIOR MANAGEMENT TURNOVER — 3%
POOR DEMAND FORECASTING — 3%
OPERATIONAL SETBACKS — 3%
COMMODITY PRICE DECLINE — 3%
CIVIL LAWSUITS/LITIGATION SETTLEMENTS — 3%
ACCOUNTING IRREGULARITIES AND/OR FINANCE FRAUD — 2%

STRATEGIC 86%   OPERATIONAL 9%   LEGAL 3%   FINANCIAL 2%

Source: CEB Audit Leadership Council

Figure 4.1 Share price decline drivers

and assessed the Top 200 companies by market capitalization in the Fortune 500. The company events that aligned with the decline in stock value were gathered and segregated into the four types of categories of risks (Strategic, Operational, Financial, and Legal and Compliance). The startling conclusion was that 86 percent of the events were risks classified as Strategic! Operational represented 9 percent of the risks, while Legal and Compliance was 3 percent and Financial only 2 percent. This analysis has since been updated by other professional organizations and the results have not really changed materially. The same takeaway and conclusion holds with each iteration.

The primary drivers of loss of market capitalization included such areas as:

- Strategic:
  - Decline on core product demand
  - Undiversified risks
  - Failure to identify price bubbles
- Poor acquisition target/merger integration
  - Failure to expand alternative revenue source
  - Competitor infringement on core market
  - Margin pressure
  - Senior management turnover
- Operational
  - Poor demand forecasting
  - Operational setbacks
  - Commodity price decline
- Legal
  - Civil lawsuits/Litigation settlements
- Financial
  - Accounting regularities and/or Finance fraud

CHAPTER 5

ERM Framework

To deliver value to customers, communities, and shareholders, a business must establish the ERM Framework that best supports its commitment to manage corporate risk and strengthen its corporate governance process across the entire organization. Fundamentally, a good risk management program together with sound internal controls are critical for the long-term success of a business.

Probability of a negative event in combination with the impact of its consequences represents a risk to business. Negative events are in general all incidents that can prevent value creation or erode existing business, investor, and shareholder value, customer loyalty and behavior, and so on. ERM is defined as a process, effected by an entity's Board of Directors, management, and other personnel, applied in a strategy setting across the enterprise, designed to identify potential events that may affect the entity, manage risk to be within its risk appetite, and to provide reasonable assurance regarding the achievement of entity objectives.[1]

The overall ERM process (see Figure 5.1) is very common and consistent for most companies. The variation or customization takes place based on the company size, geographic footprint, complexity, industry, and other pertinent factors.

The ERM team must first establish context around the current conditions in which the organization operates on an internal, external, and risk management perspective. The ERM Implementation Team reviews the current year's company risk factors, annual financial plan, industry and economic events relevant to a company business.

---

[1] COSO. 2004. *Enterprise Risk Management—Integrated Framework*, (See: www .coso.org/documents/Framework%20Reference%20Secured.pdf (accessed January 11, 2022).

Annual (Prior to AOP & PSP)	End of Quarter	Beginning of Next Quarter	Throughout the Quarter
Risk Identification	Risk Assessment	Risk Reporting	Risk Response

✓ Risk Assessment Meetings
  ▪ 1:1 with Frontline Leaders
  ▪ Risk Workshops (scenario analysis, risk interrelationship, postmortem)
✓ External Resources
  ▪ Distributor visit
  ▪ Customer feedback
  ▪ Competitor 10K Risk Factors
  ▪ Investor Analysis/Reports
  ▪ External Organization Risk Reports and Insights (Protiviti, NCSU, CEB/Gartner, PWC, Navex, KPMG, AON, NACD, Marsh, McKinsey)
	✓ Risk Category: Strategic, Operational, Financial, Legal
	✓ Risk Response: Reduce, Transfer, Avoid, Exploit, Accept
	✓ Quantify Risk Impact and Assess Likelihood
	✓ Assess Effectiveness of Risk Mitigation Plan
	✓ Assign Residual Risk Rating
	✓ Risk Heat Map Buy-Off from e-Staff
	✓ Risk Heat Map Buy-Off from CEO & CFO
		✓ Risk Heat Map
		✓ Risk Status and Trend
		✓ Input to:
		  ▪ Company Plan & Strategy
		  ▪ Corporate CSF
		  ▪ 10K/10Q Risk Factors
		  ▪ Quarterly Operations Reviews
		✓ Corporate Risk Trend
			✓ Assign Risk Ownership and Accountability
			✓ Develop Risk Treatment Plan:
			  ▪ Risk Condition
			  ▪ Root Cause
			  ▪ Risk Response (Avoid, Transfer, Mitigate, Accept, Exploit)
			  ▪ Accountability
			  ▪ Action Plan
			  ▪ Performance Metrics
			  ▪ Quantification/Severity
			  ▪ Embed Risk Monitoring in Normal Business Operations (e.g., CSF, Operations Reviews, BU Metrics)

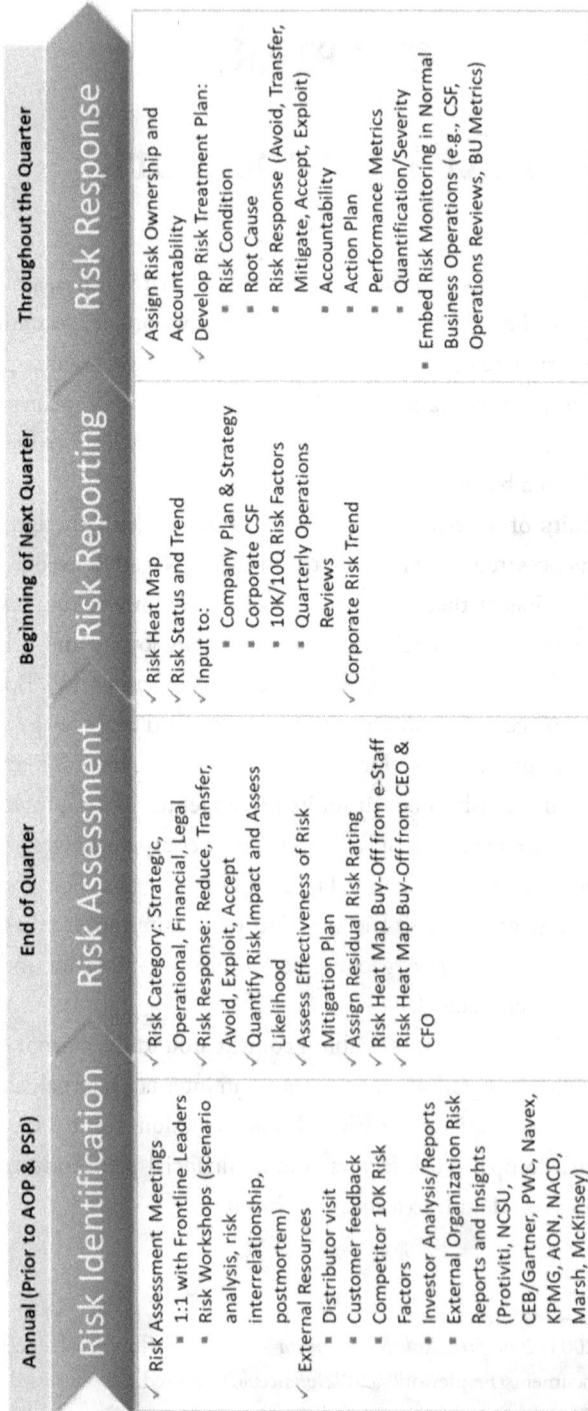

Figure 5.1 ERM process

The risk management framework process has two key programs: **Short-term risk management** and **long-term risk management**. Short-term risk management typically looks at the next 12-month risks while long-term risk management covers larger scope (typically up to a five-year outlook). The following discussions cover the process for both short- and long-term risk management.

Establishing Context

As part of the strategic planning process and day-to-day management of the business, functional leaders identify internal and external events that may affect the achievement of a company's objectives. Events that have positive effects (potential to enhance value) represent opportunities and those with negative effects represent risks (see Figure 5.2). ERM Administration Team conducts the Enterprise Risk Assessment where the team surveys a section of individuals across all company offices (selected Directors, VP level and up). Different approaches may be used for obtaining risk topics depending on the size of the company, geographic footprint, and preferences that work best in given cultures. Normally the options are questionnaire surveys or interviews (either in person or remotely via phone or video call), or a combination of both. Surveys will also have the option of being very specific by general topics or blank sheet approach with no topical guidance. Surveys can lend to efficiencies in accumulating risk points and reducing time in conducting interviews. Interviews in person generally allow for more flexibility interaction, giving the interviewee options to expand thoughts and ask questions on risk management perspective, and can more easily interject their departmental goals and objectives. It also allows the Risk Management Team to ask interpretative questions to better understand the risk and relevant timing and impact. Either approach requires an assessment of who and what level to interview, ensuring there is adequate cross-functional and geographical representation. To facilitate respondents thought process, it is also helpful to share common industry risks. This will allow the broader thinking of "what if" scenarios that may not be thought about otherwise. See the following example (Figure 5.2) for the semiconductor industry:

A sample guide for holding in-person interview assessments is shown in Figure 5.3, which provides a more open-ended approach.

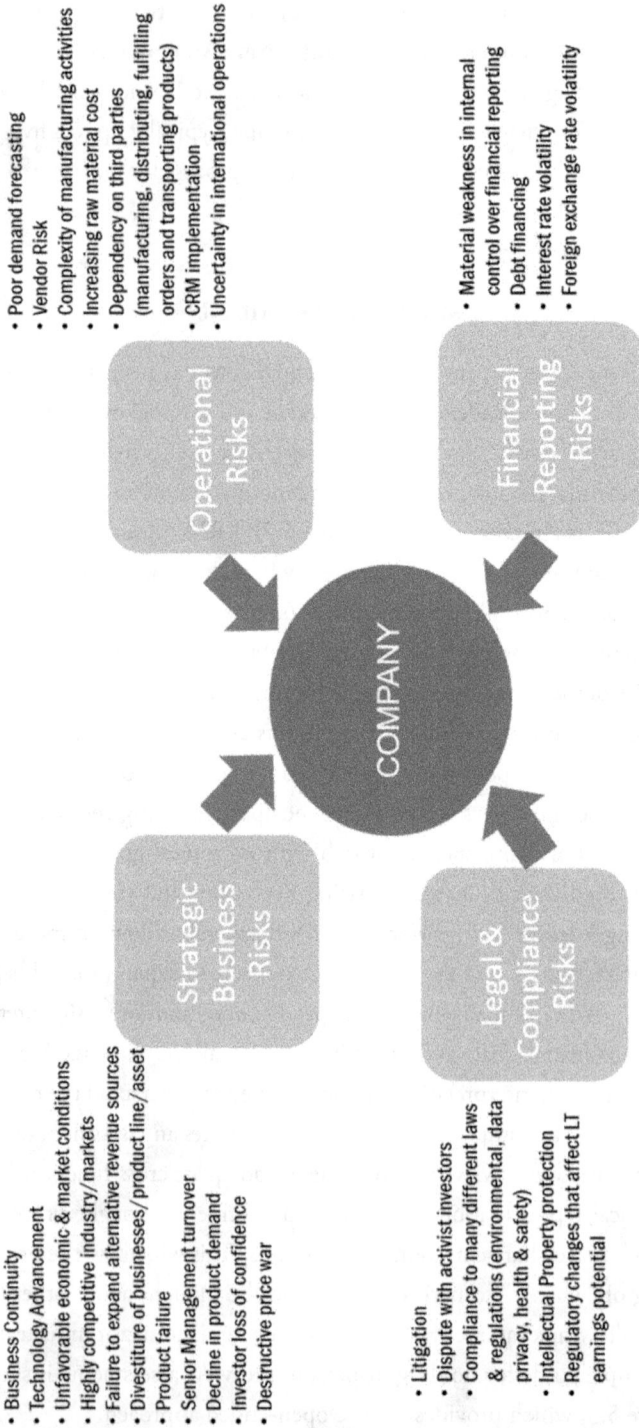

- Business Continuity
- Technology Advancement
- Unfavorable economic & market conditions
- Highly competitive industry/markets
- Failure to expand alternative revenue sources
- Divestiture of businesses/product line/asset
- Product failure
- Senior Management turnover
- Decline in product demand
- Investor loss of confidence
- Destructive price war

- Poor demand forecasting
- Vendor Risk
- Complexity of manufacturing activities
- Increasing raw material cost
- Dependency on third parties (manufacturing, distributing, fulfilling orders and transporting products)
- CRM implementation
- Uncertainty in international operations

- Litigation
- Dispute with activist investors
- Compliance to many different laws & regulations (environmental, data privacy, health & safety)
- Intellectual Property protection
- Regulatory changes that affect LT earnings potential

- Material weakness in internal control over financial reporting
- Debt financing
- Interest rate volatility
- Foreign exchange rate volatility

Operational Risks

Financial Reporting Risks

Strategic Business Risks

Legal & Compliance Risks

COMPANY

Figure 5.2 Common industry risks

What are your organization's objectives that support Cypress mission and objectives?

Are there current activities in your group that focus on identifying and managing risks?

What are the top 5 risks in achieving your organization's objectives?

Internal strategy and operations risks (budgetary changes, reorganization, infrastructure change)
External risks (political environment, market or industry trend, competitor climate, customer behavior)

•Do we have plans to implement a new strategy?
•What must go right for a new strategic initiative to be successful?
•What impact might this new strategy have on our existing business?

•Are you aware of any future changes that may affect your business?

•Are you aware of potential black swans or long-term (2-5 years) risks to Cypress?

•Do you see any potential opportunity for cost containment or additional revenue source in your area?

•Are you aware of ways to enhance leveraging of data, tools and supporting systems to improve operational effectiveness?

Where is the highest potential for fraud?

Customers

Leaders

External

ERM Risk Register

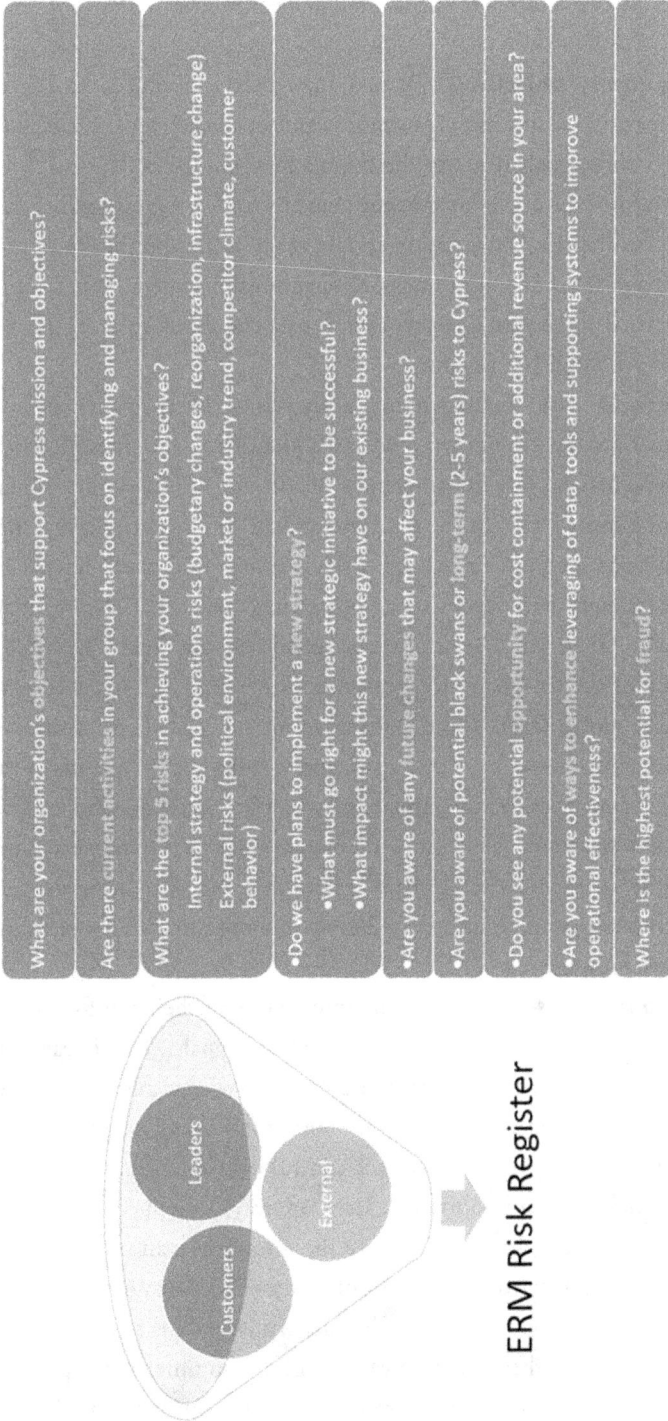

Figure 5.3 Interview risk assessment guide questions

The interview topics to include could be as follows:

1. **Company objectives**—Discuss the goals and objectives for the interviewee's specific organization and/or department. Understand how those goals relate to the overall company goals. It is helpful to also know how the interviewee tends to track progress against these goals. The risk conversation should really relate specifically to these particular goals and the risks of accomplishing them. What are the internal and external factors that impact the ability to accomplish or not accomplish the goals?

2. **Existing risk management activities**—Many departments or functions have their own process for identifying and managing risks. Some may be very informal but still add value to the ability of managing overall risks to the objectives. Other groups may have a more rigorous program to manage risks. Their program will have a different sensitivity level that addresses their particular level of materiality. There will be the obvious need to elevate their risk profile to that of the Company to determine which risks will make it to the more global level. The departmental or functional risk assessment programs should be encouraged, and it would be even better if they were able to utilize the same basic structure of the overall Company ERM program, using similar templates and terminology to more easily layer into the ultimate result. This will also allow the same terminology to be utilized reducing miscommunications or misunderstandings.

3. **Top five risks**—Inquire of the interviewee of their top five risks to meeting their departmental or functional goals. This is easier for them to speak to since they are very knowledgeable of their own operations. Ensure they focus on both internal and external risk factors. Whether they have direct control over risk statements makes no difference in importance. There are ways to reduce risks that are more external driven. Also, give the interviewee an opportunity to speak to perceived risks outside of their own department. They could be impacted by risks from other departments in the business cycle. Additionally, they may be aware of risks in an unrelated department that may not surface in the real risk owners' conversations. This dia-

logue gives a more complete opportunity to ensure all risks are identified.

4. **Future changes in business**—Engage the thought of future risks
   by discussing any upcoming known changes in business model or
   systems. Future risks need to be assessed as to the velocity and may
   need to be addressed prior to the change. The impact of upcoming
   changes could drive risks into other departments, which have not yet
   been considered by those other departments ... maybe they were not
   even aware of the upcoming changes. Other changes may include
   geographic implications such as doing business in a new world of
   regulations not well understood by the current company management team.

5. **Black Swan risks**—These risks are generally defined as an *unpredict-*
   able event that is beyond what is normally expected of a situation and
   has potentially severe consequences. Black Swan events are characterized
   by their extreme rarity, severe impact, and the widespread insistence
   they were obvious in hindsight. The term "Black Swan event" has
   been part of the risk management lexicon since its coinage in 2007
   by Nassim Taleb in his eponymous book titled *The Black Swan: The*
   Impact of the Highly Improbable. Mr. Taleb uses the metaphor of the
   Black Swan to describe extreme outlier events that come as a surprise
   to management, and in hindsight, the individuals rationalize that
   they should have predicted the event.

6. **Potential opportunities**—When one thinks of risks, they do not
   really consider them opportunities as well. Risks can be exploited
   to result in additional value-add to the organization through
   additional revenue, reduced operating costs, or positive reputational impacts. Opportunities can come in all sizes and should
   be tracked either within the ERM program or as a supplemental
   deliverable to the ERM program still offering value-add to the
   Company.

7. **Improvements in operating effectiveness**—Generally, this topic
   would relate to identifying new information sources as well as better
   utilization of systems to gather and analyze data into information.
   This would also include machine learning languages, artificial intelligence, and data mining.

8. **Fraud potential**—Fraud costs the business world billions of dollars annually. While fraud risk assessments are usually conducted by most companies on an annual basis, it deserves the conversation to ensure new fraud opportunities have not been created. Known fraud incidents are not always well communicated within the company, so not everyone of interest has heard about them (including the ERM team members).

Event Identification

Information gathered during the interview related to material risks/threats to the organization's achievement of its objectives are synthesized in common themes and documented in the risk register. This register also includes areas that the organization may exploit for competitive advantage (recommended audit areas, potential fraud, opportunities to reduce cost and other positive events, etc.).

Another option for risk identification is to hold group meetings or sessions. Key personnel from the same function are assembled while an ERM team member usually facilitates the session. A similar approach to individual interviews can be followed. The success really depends on the openness of the culture to discuss issues, which may be uncomfortable to discuss with peers in the same meeting room. See the process steps shown in Figure 5.4.

Selection of Respondents

The selection of respondents is an important step in the planning process. This audience will vary depending on the company industry, business model, size, geographic coverage, employee count, and other characteristics. Overall, it is important to obtain feedback from all functions and all geographies within the company footprint. Later you will see the importance of having the right representation of respondents in the population. Respondents should include the following categories at varying degrees or weighting preferences:

1. **Board members**—It is generally best to obtain input from all Board members, but at minimum ensure that all members of the Audit

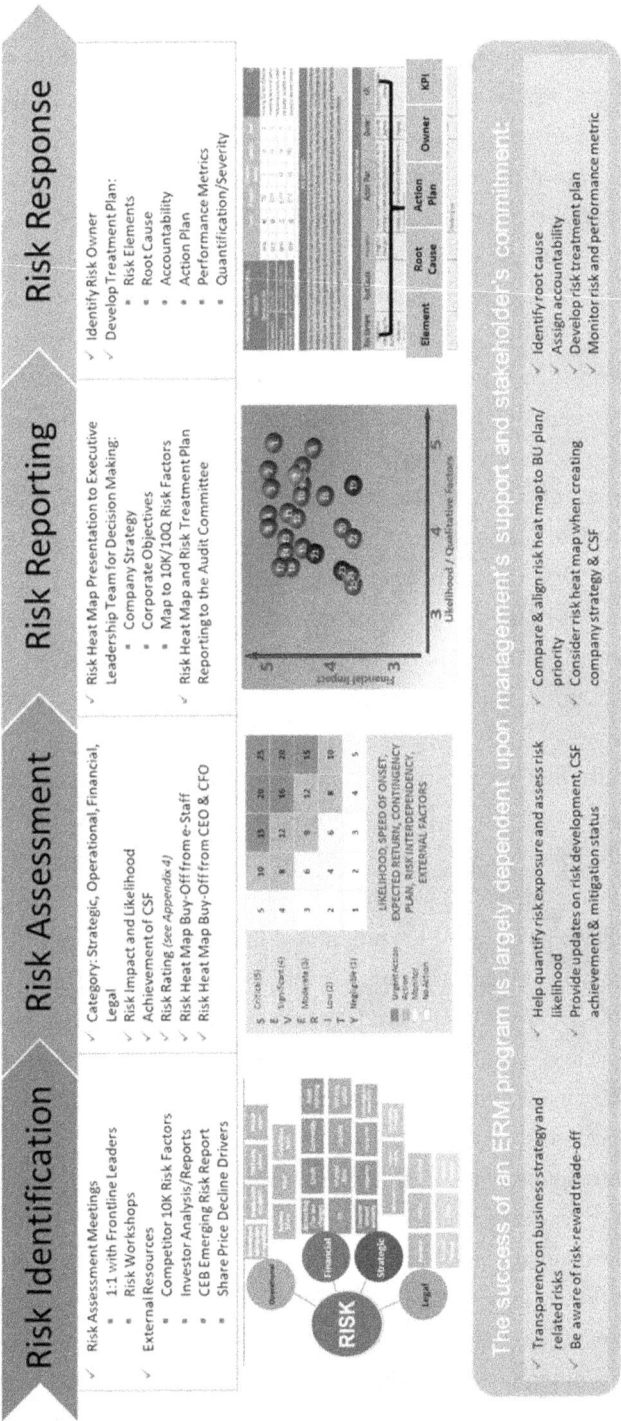

Figure 5.4 ERM process steps

Committee are selected. Risk management clearly falls within their duties and responsibilities to ensure a company has such programs that are effective and timely. Most, if not all, will be more than cooperative and welcome the opportunity to be involved.

2. **CEO and direct reports**—This group should be covered near 100 percent unless there are staff level fellows, which may not be able to provide this level of exposure. In general, this level will be the most helpful in sharing a company's goals and objectives and will view risks at a higher level. This ensures that all functions are represented. Additionally, they may be more vocal in sharing the risks of other departments, which affect the performance of their specific function. This group also tends to be more engaged with outside groups and organizations, which provide broader industry trends and risks.

3. **Extended leadership**—This group would generally consist of Senior Directors and above. The population of this group could be quite large and will therefore require some judgment to select the most pertinent members of management who will provide solid contribution, while minimizing extensive overlapping or duplicative coverage.

4. **Middle management**—This group would be generally defined as Director and below in most organizations. Obviously, this group would have a larger population, which requires a very prescriptive judgment on which positions or people to select. Consideration should be given to the job function with the expectation of including those who are regularly engaged in various security or risk management activities. Other considerations would be the depth of business knowledge possessed by the employees, tenure of employees with the company, and their role particularly if they are a "leader" over a smaller geography or location.

5. **External sources**—There are other sources that should be considered other than employees of a company. The external auditor firm of the company is an excellent source particularly for financial risks. Additionally, one source that is often overlooked is the Voice of the Customer or business partners. They usually have a notable volume of customer surveys tracked by the company. After all, Customer Service is normally one of the top missions or priorities of every

company. Other external partners might include distributors or contract manufacturers, which could also share some feedback over business complexity, efficiency, effectiveness, market, and so on.

After the selection, a draft or proposed list of respondents should be analyzed to ensure the list appropriately represents the company's full composition. By company composition, we mean that a financial services industry will have different attributes than a company that sells product, which it also manufactures. The latter would need to make sure there is a heavier mix of manufacturing or operations personnel than a company that sells products but does not have its own manufacturing or distribution functions. Figure 5.5 is an example of a pie chart representing to population mix of the respondents in the form of "By Functional Area," "By Geographical Region," and "By Job Level."

Risk Register

There are two levels of risk registers. One is a working file to maintain the respondent replies (either via survey or interviews) in draft form. It becomes a file of risk comments made with enough information to be able to track the risk assessment/identification process. The second one is a file of the synthesized risk statements taken from the various risk comments. It will house the main information that drives the risk heat map with prioritized risks. In this section, we will discuss the working file created during the identification process for the respondent replies.

The format can vary based on desire and preferences related to the company size and other factors, but below is a very simplified sample risk register. Keep in mind that it may be modified if this is your first time to conduct a risk identification or assessment. After the first cycle, it will be easier and more granular. Let's explore some specific comments for each of the columns noted in the example document. This example is more in line with having interviews/discussions with the respondents, but similar process would exist with a more automated survey approach.

1. **Respondent name**—name of the individual from which the responses are created. While we keep the name in the file, it is always

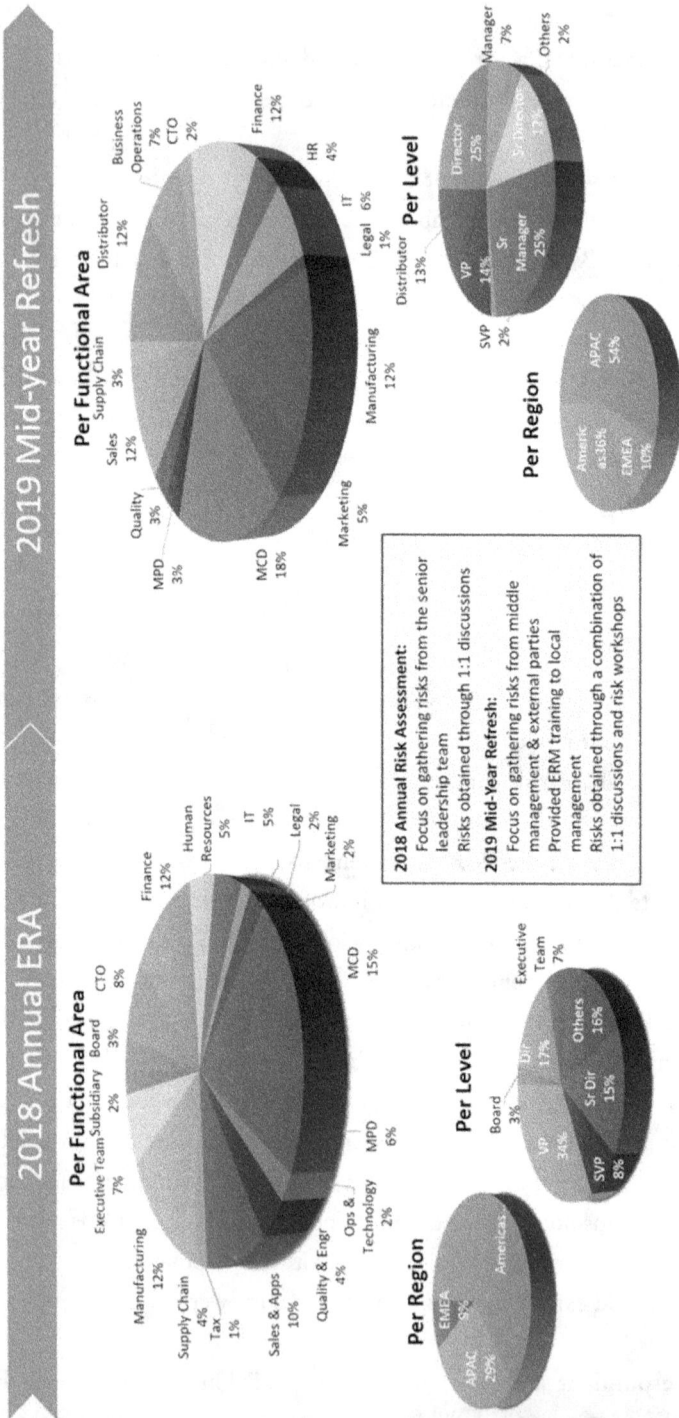

Figure 5.5 Actual risk assessment respondent profiles

a good idea to confidentially secure the name and events provided. Having these conversations and requests in confidence will generally yield more open commentary.

2. **Respondent title**—title of the individual from which the responses are created. The titles need to be documented in a way to be able to sort and filter by such. Maybe consider using categories as developed in the planning stage, such as Executive Leadership Team (ELT including the CEO and direct reports), Extended Leadership Team (XLT including Senior Director including all titles up to the ELT). This needs to be sortable for your reporting templates.

3. **Function/Organization**—the organization or function in which the respondent represents. Generally, most companies have 13–15 business cycles which can be considered as this level or categorization. However, another way would be to mirror the names of organizations of the CEO direct reports. The latter may help assign accountability to the various risk statements.

4. **Geographic location (region)**—the geographical location of the respondent. This is generally where they reside but can also be the region for which they are responsible even though they may physically reside elsewhere. There has been a stronger correlation to match the physical location of the person to the risk statements. The person is around peers in their physical location and could represent a more corporate view (if they reside at corporate) and would be useful to know.

5. **Risk description/comments**—the individual statements that the person states as risks. These can range from none to any amount but try to get at least two risk statements. More than five statements may be too granular from a materiality standpoint. Either way, note them in this column. It is not required to note all discussion comments, but rather just the salient points for the risk statements. Remember, you can always go back to the person for follow-up questions.

6. **Risk general topic**—the major topic of risk theme. If this is the second time around in conducting a risk assessment, you will have a much better sense of what these high-level topics will be. If it is your first time, then assign high level categories such as Cash Flow, New Product Introduction, Inventory, product margins, product quality,

employee retention, and so on. These topics can be fluid as you have your first interviews and gain a general perspective of topics.

7. **Risk subtopic**—the next level lower than the major topic or theme noted in the General Topic categories discussed above. These also become clearer as you move through this process for the first time. For example, a major topic could be cash, while the subtopic could be capital spend, operating spend, cash management, and so on.

8. **Risk category**—the four categories of the overall risk program specifically include Strategic, Operational, Financial, and Regulatory. This level of categorization is required for reporting purposes. It is also important to know how your company compares to the control group noted in the earlier chapter in the study of the risk elements conducted by other firms. The variation of percentage of risks among the four categories could present a different viewpoint of where the company stands in total risks.

9. **Previous risk assessment comments**—can be used as a refresher by the respondent if needed. It also gives you the ability to compare the direction of risks in this individual's function (see Figure 5.6).

Note that this section includes only the people-oriented sources. Later in this book, there will be discussions of other supplemental activities and sources such as use of technology including Artificial Intelligence, continuous monitoring, and data analytics. These sources are generally used more in assessing the elements and quantifications of the risk elements but may also be considered as a source.

Risk Assessment

This includes the synthetization of risks comments, calibration, and, if possible, creation of probability distributions of outcomes for each material risk. This step also includes the aggregation of all risk distributions, reflecting correlations and effects, and the formulation of the results in terms of impact on the organization's key performance metrics. At this stage, the risk statements are also mapped to the identified risks to the company risk factors (10K risk factors), Finance top issues and aligned with the significant risks or issues dealt with by the risk management subcommittees:

- Each individual risk narratives are documented in a raw risk register.
- A copy of the risk narratives are sent to the related respondent for confirmation.
- Each risk narrative is mapped to existing ERM risk topics.
  - New subtopics are incorporated into the risk assessment phase
  - New subtopics for a Top 25 risk topic are discussed with the related risk owner(s).
  - A deep dive of a specific risk topic is provided to management, as necessary.
  - Entirely new topics are added to the Risk Universe and reported to the Risk Committee and Audit Committee.

ENTERPRISE RISK MANAGEMENT
RAW RISK REGISTER
2019 RISK ASSESSMENT EXERCISES

Respondent Name	Job Level	Business Unit	Office	Region	Meeting Type	Risk Description	Category (Risk or Opportunity)	Sub Topic	Risk Topic	Mapping to Q1 ERM Risk Register
John Doe	Vice President	Sales	San Jose	North America	1:1	xxx	Risk	Competition Risk	Speed of MCD Margin & Growth	Speed of MCD Margin & Growth
Emma Watson	Director	Finance	Taiwan	EMEA	Workshop	xxx	Risk	Slow moving stock Inventory Build-Up	Continuous Pricing Pressure	NA
Arrow	Distributor	Distributor	Korea	APAC	Workshop	xxx	Opportunity	Phantom Rate	Continuous Pricing Pressure	Continuous Pricing Pressure

Figure 5.6 Risk assessment comments table

Executive Product and Safety Committee; Investment Committee; and the Information Security Risk Committee (see Figure 5.7). This part of the ERM process can be very time consuming as it requires digesting the risk comments, and heavy level of confirming interpretation and messages.

Synthesizing Risk Comments

Synthetizing is the process to digest and begin formalizing the risk content. The quality of the raw risk register compiled from the interviews/surveys will drive the efficiency and effectiveness of the synthetization process. The comments noted in the register should be refreshed and worded concisely, then given to the respondent to allow them the opportunity to edit as appropriate ensuring the message was accurately captured. While it seems to be a straightforward task, it could take some time depending on the availability of the many respondents. Once the raw risk register is completed and confirmed by all respondents, the next step is to start synthesizing the comments by topic and subtopic. This will ultimately give a holistic list of all risk statements of the company. Each respondent will probably provide an average of about five risk comments. Including about 100 people in your process could generate about 500 individual risk comments to pull together into precise statements. One would expect to see the number of synthesized risk topics in the range of 50–75 individual statements for the entire company. This could obviously vary but given the size of the company and related materiality it would make sense that the number of risks would be in that range.

Assessing/Prioritizing Risk Exposure/Perception

This includes the determination of the contribution of each risk factor to the aggregate risk profile, and the appropriate prioritization. The process for this stage can be fairly time intensive, but worth every minute to generate a high-quality result. The first time for this exercise will take longer than subsequent updates and assessments. It is important to be consistent in this step moving forward for comparability.

Once you have a draft risk list from the synthetization process noted in the previous section, take note of the volume and judgmentally rank them

Annual (Prior to AOP & PSP)	End of Quarter	Beginning of Next Quarter	Throughout the Quarter
Risk Identification	Risk Assessment	Risk Reporting	Risk Response

Risk Identification

✓ Risk Assessment Meetings
 - 1:1 with Frontline Leaders
 - Risk Workshops (scenario analysis, risk interrelationship, postmortem)

✓ External Resources
 - Distributor visit
 - Customer feedback
 - Competitor 10K Risk Factors
 - Investor Analysis/Reports
 - External Organization Risk Reports and Insights (Protiviti, NCSU, CEB/Gartner, PWC, Navex, KPMG, AON, NACD, Marsh, McKinsey)

Risk Assessment

✓ Risk Category: Strategic, Operational, Financial, Legal
✓ Risk Response: Reduce, Transfer, Avoid, Exploit, Accept
✓ Quantify Risk Impact and Assess Likelihood
✓ Assess Effectiveness of Risk Mitigation Plan
✓ Assign Residual Risk Rating
✓ Risk Heat Map Buy-Off from e-Staff
✓ Risk Heat Map Buy-Off from CEO & CFO

Risk Reporting

✓ Risk Heat Map
✓ Risk Status and Trend
✓ Input to:
 - Company Plan & Strategy
 - Corporate CSF
 - 10K/10Q Risk Factors
 - Quarterly Operations Reviews
✓ Corporate Risk Trend

Risk Response

✓ Assign Risk Ownership and Accountability
✓ Develop Risk Treatment Plan:
 - Risk Condition
 - Root Cause
 - Risk Response (Avoid, Transfer, Mitigate, Accept, Exploit)
 - Accountability
 - Action Plan
 - Performance Metrics
 - Quantification/Severity
 - Embed Risk Monitoring in Normal Business Operations (e.g., CSF, Operations Reviews, BU Metrics)

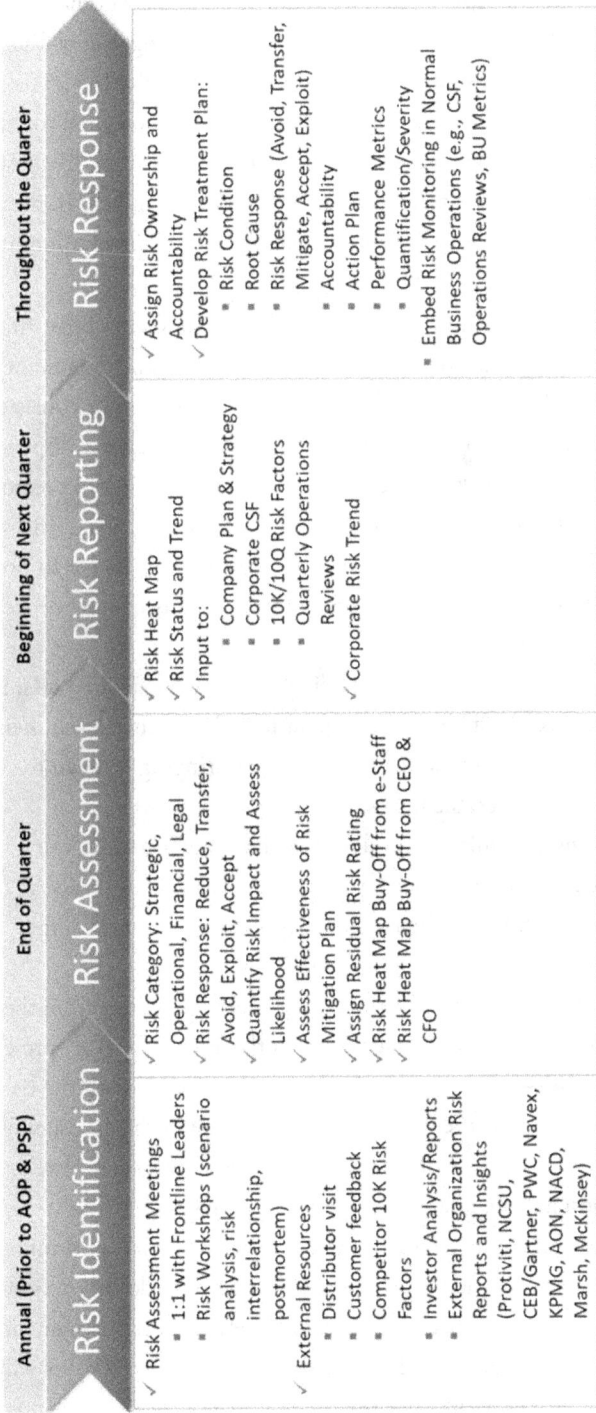

Figure 5.7 ERM process

from high to low just to get a starting point. The ranking will change dramatically, but this helps to position your mind in the ranking, and will allow you to focus on the higher—more obvious risks. Start with the Top 25 risks from the list. Generally, the list of all risks identified will be long and could range anywhere from 50 to 70 or so depending on the company. In this illustration exercise, we will assume there were 50 risk themes identified. In the master risk register of synthesized risks, start building out additional columns.

1. Start by assigning the original risk statement into the four categories—Strategic, Operational, Financial, and Regulatory. The initial assignment may not be completely accurate or consistent, so keep refreshing it. Keep in mind to note the general dispersion of the number of risks in each category and assess if it looks reasonable.

2. Next is to determine options for how to treat the risk. This will be confirmed later with the risk owner but take initiative to populate it with a logical option. There are five options of how to treat risk response including:

   • **Reduce**—act to reduce the likelihood or impact of a loss. If the risk is just above your appetite and tolerance level, then reduction is a reasonable strategy for bringing it down to within acceptable limits.

   • **Transfer**—this option does not eliminate or reduce the chances of it occurring, but instead delegates or *transfers* responsibility of the risk to a third-party, by purchasing insurance or warranties for example.

   • **Avoid**—eliminate the threat to protect the project from the impact of the risk. An example of this is canceling the project.

   • **Exploit**—eliminate the uncertainty associated with the risk to ensure the event happens. An example of this is assigning the best workers to a project to reduce time to complete or adding more resources to finish early. This could also increase the probability or the positive impacts of a risk/opportunity.

   • **Accept**—acknowledge the risk, but do not take any action unless the risk occurs. There will likely be other risks outside your tolerance where one of the other response options will not be a good fit since the probability and/or the impact is so low that it does not make sense to expend resources to avoid, transfer, or reduce the risk. An example of this is documenting the risk and putting aside funds in case the risk occurs.

Next is to quantify risk impact and likelihood. Prior to assessing these two elements, start with the understanding that the first assumption is to measure on an Inherent Risk level, then fine-tune to a Residual Risk level at a later stage. See the following Figure 5.8.

Inherent Risk is typically defined as the level of risk in place to achieve an entity's objectives and before actions are taken to alter the risk's impact or likelihood. Residual Risk is the remaining level of risk following the development and implementation of the entity's response. This step will drive the heat map positioning of each risk. To be effective with this approach, parameters must be documented and used consistently for all risks to compare them side by side. There are two major elements to this, which are most commonly referred to as Impact and Likelihood. The definitions of these two terms will vary widely as well, but again stay consistent in usage for proper prioritization. The basic definitions used in this book will be as follows:

- Impact is the financial impact of the risk should the event happen. The measure is monetary and quantitative.
- Likelihood is the expected chance that the risk will occur. The measure should include several qualitative elements.

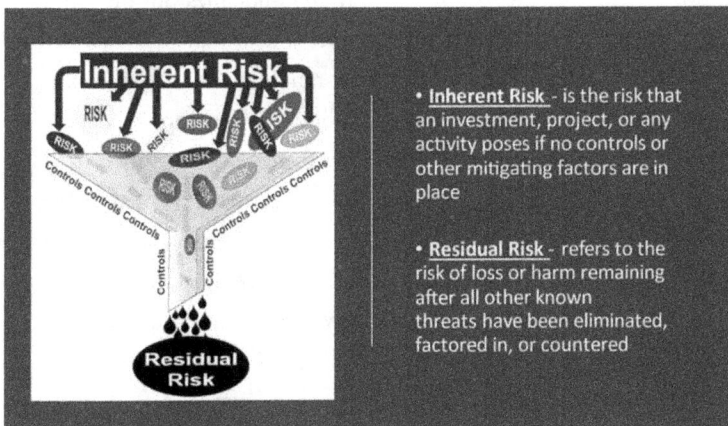

Figure 5.8 Inherent versus residual risks

Quantifying the risk financial impact should be positioned around a set of documented assumptions. As a matter of definition, financial risks are those risks quantified compared to the annual financial plan. Risks are not expected to happen at the maximum level of financial impact, and accordingly, are not incorporated in a company's business plan. In order of preference, try to measure risks in terms of operating margin, operating expense, cash flow, and lost revenue. For unusual risks, other options might include the reduction of Enterprise Value or lost project Return on Investment (ROI). In measuring financial impact, it is better to measure on a unit of measure that is comparable. For example, measuring some risks as revenue dollars against other risks at margin dollars, will artificially inflate the revenue risk higher than the operating margin risks and will be misleading. All revenue can be estimated at a margin level, so that is a better unit measure. There may be lost revenue associated with a risk. Again, convert to operating margin for that revenue.

If there is no revenue income statement impact, but more aligned with operating expense, use the operating expense unit of measure of raw dollars. If the measure is a balance sheet item, try to measure in terms of cash flow. If there are no direct impacts to the financial statements but more to reputation, then possibly try to measure based on enterprise value (market cap or other ways).

Risk Response and Control Activities

This includes the development of strategies for managing and exploiting the Top 25 risks. See the section "Heat Map Guidelines" for the guidelines employed to converge the risk register into a heat map. That section will discuss an approach to determine a draft ranking of all the risks based on the two components of Impact and Likelihood. A response is determined based on the overall risk exposure, which is considered as a function of likelihood, speed of onset, and impact of the occurrence. As noted earlier, risk responses may include avoidance, acceptance, mitigation, and/or transfer of the risk. Control activities are established to ensure that risk responses are carried out effectively and consistently throughout a company.

Information and Communication, and Monitoring

Information and communication channels are in place to make the organization aware of the risks that fall into their area of responsibility and the expected behavior and actions to mitigate negative outcomes. Management reviews and assessments are in place to ensure that risks are effectively identified, and appropriate responses and controls are in place to effectively mitigate the risk. This includes the continual measurement and monitoring of the risk environment and the performance of risk management strategies for the identified Top 25 risks.

Reporting will generally be at two levels:

○ Internal level with the Risk Committee and executive teams; and
○ External level with the Board of Directors or Audit Committee.

On a quarterly basis, the ERM Administration team will meet with risk owners to discuss the risk register and respective Risk Treatment Plans. It is also the venue where new risks are identified, discussed, and analyzed. Risks previously in the Top 25 that did not decrease in risk rating within the quarter, but were pushed down by other risks, are also revisited to ensure that they are adequately mitigated. Meetings are also held with risk co-owners (if any) to discuss the updates on quantification and treatment plans. Results of the quarterly update is presented to the Risk Committee for further discussion and conformance, then to the Audit Committee of the Board of Directors. The report contains, at minimum, statistics of the interviews/meetings performed (number of risks gathered, new risks identified, frequently identified risks, updated risk listing, distribution of interviewees—geography and function etc.), Top 25 risks, and audit plan proposal.

The CEO frequently requires an update during the Quarterly Operations Reviews for each of the Top 25 risks being monitored. A more in-depth discussion is held around the Treatment plans, status, key performance indicators (KPIs), progress, and issues.

Heat Map Guidelines

There must be a set of documented guidelines that serves as the basis for quantifying, assessing, measuring, prioritizing, and communicating all the risks to a refined Residual Risk Register. Templates should be created and remain similar in format and context to ensure consistency of the process and to set a recurring, familiar reporting to the executives and board members. This becomes a learned behavior with familiarity in the presentation from quarter to quarter. Understand the probability distributions for each risk topic based on available information from the risk identification phase. The overall process and objectives of this exercise are as follows:

- Assign a risk score for each risk topic using risk assessment methodology.
- Discuss and agree risk scores with assigned risk owner/s.
- Prioritize risk topics based on the residual blended risk score.
- Review and agree risk prioritization separately with the CFO and the CEO.
- Review and obtain approval of the risk prioritization with the Risk Committee.

Risk Quantification Assumptions

Risk to the financial plan in the event of risk occurrence (in order of preference) includes:

- Reduction in operating margin in dollars;
- Cash flow impact (increased cost, payment of penalty, reduction of cash inflows, project investment);
- Lost revenue;
- Reduction of enterprise value;
- Lost project ROI; and
- Assumed amount based on severity risk rating.

See example of a risk assessment matrix in Figure 5.9.

Each risk is positioned on the heat map based on the short-term and longer term severity of impact (see Figure 5.10), likelihood of occurrence, and speed of onset (see the example of the heat map in Figure 5.11).

Step 1: Calculate Short-term Impact

1.1 Rate the 12-Month financial repercussion from 1-5 for the **Quantitative Impact / Severity: (50% weight x Rating²)**

1.2 Rate the Qualitative factors from 1-5. **(50% weight x Rating):**

Likelihood After Control Maturity (20%)
Probability that the risk will happen.

Control Maturity (10%)
Completeness of coverage and current maturity level of internal control structure across significant processes

Detectability (5%)
Likelihood of discovering and correcting a hazard or failure prior to harm occurrence.

Recoverability (5%)
The ability for the Company to quickly recover if the risk happens and to resume to its normal operations.

Risk Interdependency (5%)
Level of interaction or damage caused to or received from other risks or risk elements.

External Factors (5%)
The level that uncontrollable external factors impact the risk likelihood and severity

1.3 Combine the 1-5 rating for the Short-term Quantitative and Qualitative scores.

Step 2: Assessment of Long-term Impact

2.1 Rate from 1-5 the **Long-term Quantitative Impact** which is overall benefit of taking the risk in the overall strategic direction of the Company: **Strategic Alignment: (50% weight x Rating)**

2.2 Rate from 1-5 the **Qualitative** factors **(50% weight x Rating):**

Contingency and Mitigation (30%)
Availability of contingency or crisis management plans in place.

Speed of Onset (20%)
The time that elapses between the initial signs of an event and the point at when the Company first feels the effects.

2.3 Combine the 1-5 ratings for the Long-term Quantitative and Qualitative scores.

Step 3: Evaluate Blended Risk Rating

3.1 Multiply the corresponding calculated ST and LT rating scores to the ST and LT weight using the table below:

LT Rating	ST Weight	LT Weight
≥ 4.2	20%	80%
≥ 3.2	40%	60%
≥ 2.2	70%	30%
≥ 1.2	90%	10%

3.2 Consolidate **Short-term and Long-term** scores to calculate the **Blended Risk Rating.**

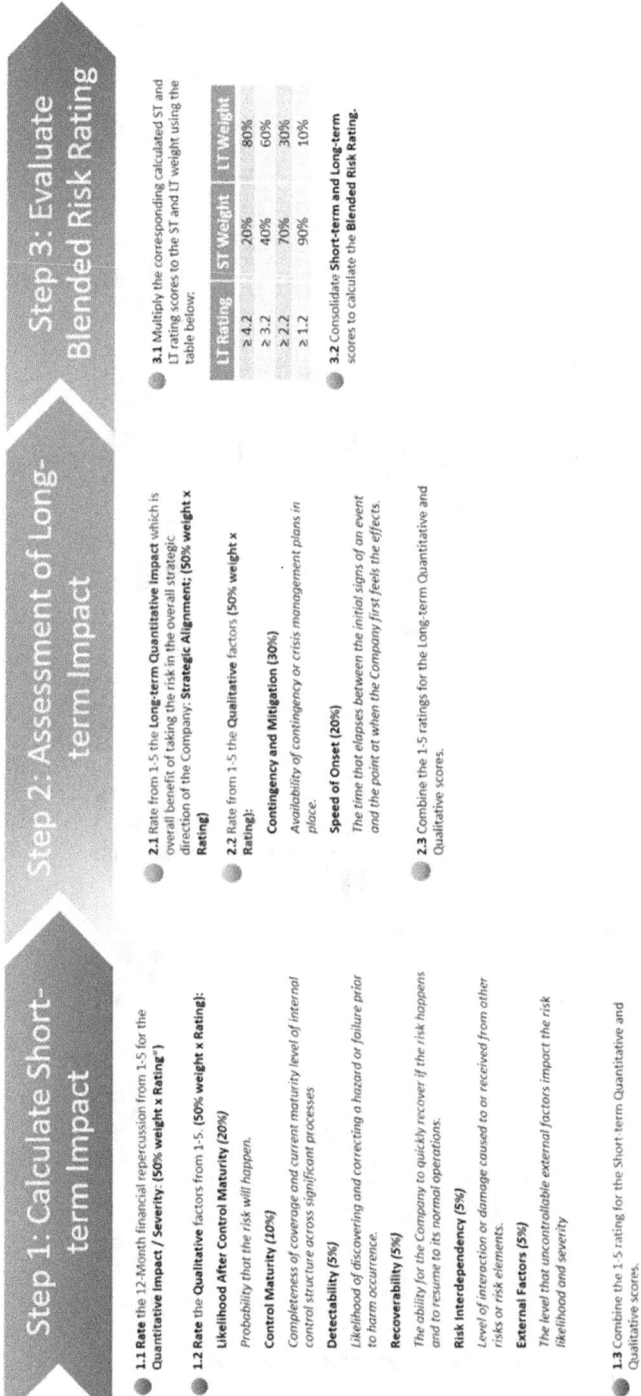

Figure 5.9 Risk assessment matrix

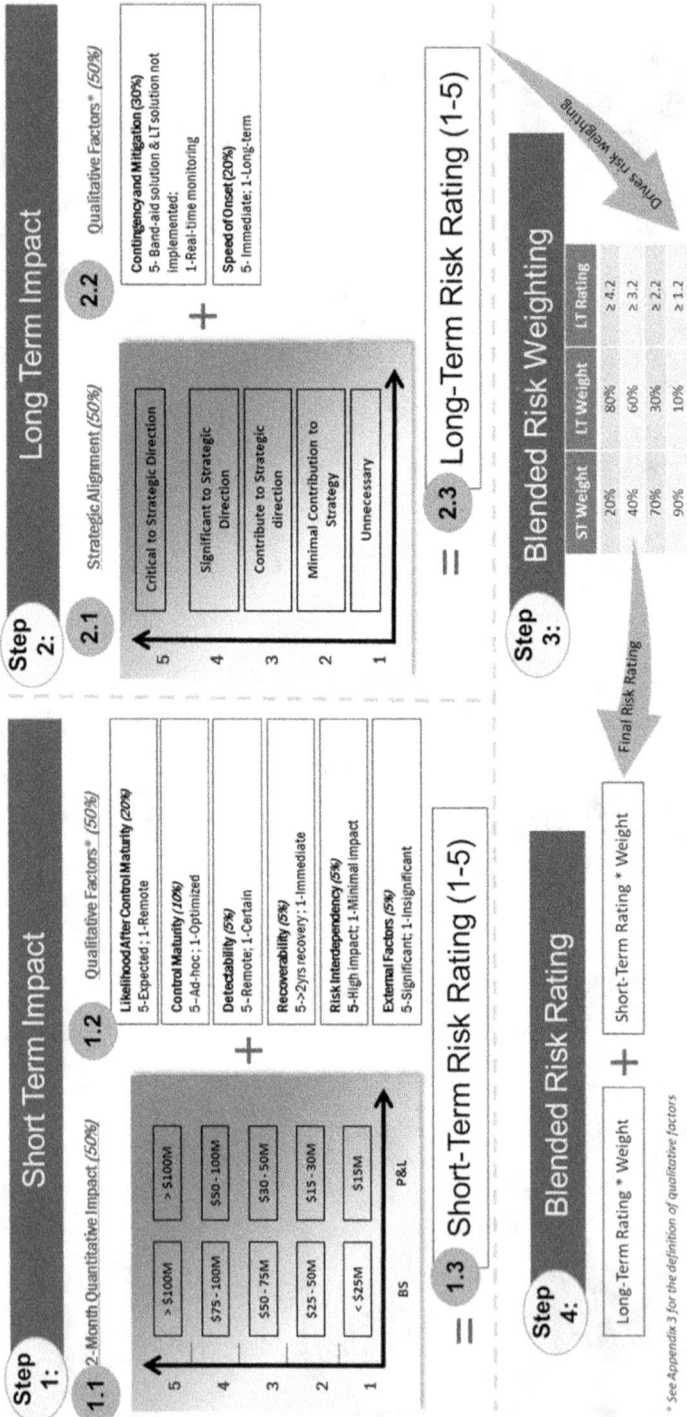

Figure 5.10 Calculation process for blended risk rating

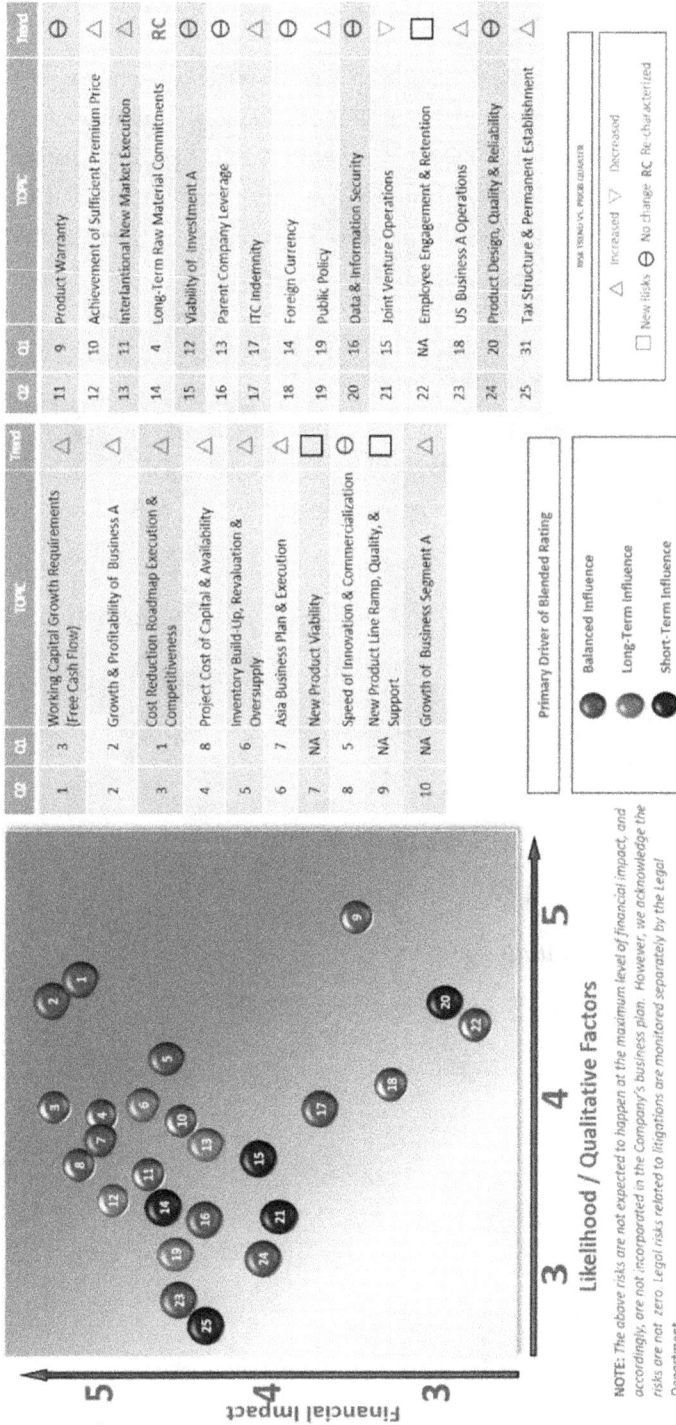

Q2	Q1	TOPIC	Trend
1	3	Working Capital Growth Requirements (Free Cash Flow)	△
2	2	Growth & Profitability of Business A	△
3	1	Cost Reduction Roadmap Execution & Competitiveness	△
4	8	Project Cost of Capital & Availability	△
5	6	Inventory Build-Up, Revaluation & Oversupply	△
6	7	Asia Business Plan & Execution	△
7	NA	New Product Viability	□
8	5	Speed of Innovation & Commercialization	⊕
9	NA	New Product Line Ramp, Quality, & Support	□
10	NA	Growth of Business Segment A	△

Q2	Q1	TOPIC	Trend
11	9	Product Warranty	⊕
12	10	Achievement of Sufficient Premium Price	△
13	11	International New Market Execution	△
14	4	Long-Term Raw Material Commitments	RC
15	12	Viability of Investment A	⊕
16	13	Parent Company Leverage	⊕
17	17	ITC Indemnity	△
18	14	Foreign Currency	⊕
19	19	Public Policy	△
20	16	Data & Information Security	⊕
21	15	Joint Venture Operations	▽
22	NA	Employee Engagement & Retention	□
23	18	US Business A Operations	△
24	20	Product Design, Quality & Reliability	⊕
25	31	Tax Structure & Permanent Establishment	△

RISK TREND VS. PRIOR QUARTER

△ Increased ▽ Decreased

□ New Risks ⊕ No change RC Re-characterized

Primary Driver of Blended Rating

Balanced Influence
Long-Term Influence
Short-Term Influence

Likelihood / Qualitative Factors

Financial Impact

NOTE: The above risks are not expected to happen at the maximum level of financial impact, and accordingly, are not incorporated in the Company's business plan. However, we acknowledge the risks are not zero. Legal risks related to litigations are monitored separately by the Legal Department.

Figure 5.11 Blended risk heat map

Financial Impact (Y-Axis of the Heat Map)

Financial repercussions of the risks may either relate to profit and loss or balance sheet. Should the risk impact profit and loss, its ultimate impact to gross margin and EBITDA (Earnings Before Interest, Tax, Depreciation, and Amortization) is quantified. Any impact to cash flow and so on is classified as balance sheet. The following example of materiality levels position the risk on the heat map (see Figures 5.12 and 5.13).

Twelve-Month Quantitative Impact

	Financial Impact (Millions)	
Severity	Profit and Loss	Balance Sheet
5	>$50	>$100
4	$37 - $50	$75 - $100
3	$25 - $37	$50 - $75
2	$12 - $25	$25 - $50
1	<$12	<$25

Figure 5.12 Twelve-Month impact

Five-Year Quantitative Impact

Severity	% of Multiyear Plan
5	20% and up
4	< 20%
3	< 15%
2	< 10%
1	< 5%

Figure 5.13 Five-year quantitative impact

Likelihood/Qualitative Factors (X-Axis of the Heat Map)

The following reference shows how the qualitative factors can be used. Some are used for short term and others for long term (see Figures 5.14, 5.15, and 5.16).

Short term:

- Likelihood
- Control maturity
- Detectability
- Recoverability
- Risk interdependency
- External factors

Long term:

- Strategic alignment
- Contingency and mitigation
- Speed of onset

Likelihood of Occurrence (12 Months)

Likelihood of risk occurrence is measured based on either the probability that the risk will happen or the frequency of happening. Figure 5.17 provides guidelines in measuring the likelihood of the risk.

Speed of Onset (Five Years)

Speed of onset refers to the time it takes for a risk event to manifest itself, or in other words, the time that elapses between the occurrence of an event and the point at which the company first feels its effects. See Figure 5.18.

Other Qualitative Assumptions (X-Axis of the Heat Map)

The risks are rated from 1 to 5, with 5 being the highest risk (least controlled) for each of the following assumptions:

Factor	5	4	3	2	1
Severity (SHORT-TERM)	**Critical** P&L (Operating Margin): > $100M Bal Sheet > $100M	**Major** P&L: $50M - $100M Bal Sheet $75M - $100M	**Moderate** P&L $30M - $50M Bal Sheet $50 - $75M	**Minor** P&L $15M - $30M Bal Sheet $25 - $50M	**Insignificant** P&L < $15M Balance Sheet $25M
Likelihood	**Expected** 90 - 100% probability; Occurred in the past 6months	**Highly Likely** 70 - 90% probability; Occurred in the past year	**Likely** 50 - 70% probability	**Less Likely** 10 - 50% likelihood	**Remote** less than 10% probability
Control Maturity	**Unreliable** (ad-hoc, informal)	**Standard** (Control exists, some reporting in place)	**Defined** (Policies defined, controls are repeatable, no formal monitoring)	**Managed & Monitored** (stable controls with formal performance indicators)	**Optimized** (Benchmark, highly automated, real time monitoring)
Detectability	**Remote** chance of discovery (< 10%)	**Low chance** of discovery (< 25%)	**Moderate chance** of discovery (< 50%)	**High chance** of discovery (< 80%)	Discovery is **almost certain** (> 80%)
Recoverability	> 2 years recovery	1 - 2 years recovery	6 months - 1 year recovery	1 - 6 months recovery	Immediate recovery
Risk Interdependency	High-level damage/impact on other risks		Moderate damage/impact on other risks		Minimal damage/impact on other risks
External Factors	Risk severity & occurrence is significantly influenced by external factors		Risk severity & occurrence is influenced by external factors		Risk severity & occurrence is entirely within the control of the Company
Strategic Alignment (LONG-TERM)	**Critical** to the strategic direction of the Company	**Significant** to the strategic direction of the Company	**Contributes** to the strategic direction of the Company	**Minimal contribution** to the strategic direction of the Company	**Unnecessary** to the achievement of strategy
Contingency & Mitigation	Band-aid solution & LT solution not implemented	Only band-aid solution is implemented	Both band-aid & LT solution in place without formal monitoring	Formal monitoring in place, but not available on real-time	Real-time monitoring of risk
Speed of Onset	**Immediate** Impacts the Company in < 12 months	**Mid-Term** Impacts the Company in < 2 years	**Mid-Term** Impacts the Company in < 2 years		**Long-Term** Impacts the Company in > 3 years

Figure 5.14 Risk assessment criteria

	Factor	Description
SHORT-TERM	Severity	Cash flow and/or operating margin impact within the year or next year AOP
	Likelihood	Probability that the risk will happen or the frequency of occurrence after considering controls in place
	Control Immaturity	Maturity level of mitigating controls in place that directly and indirectly address the identified risk. As the level of maturity increases, risk becomes more manageable
	Detectability	Likelihood of discovering and correcting a hazard or failure prior to inflicting harm to the Company
	Recoverability	The ability to recover from the impact of the risk (ability to resume to its normal operations)
	Risk Interdependency	Level of interaction or damage caused to or received from other risks
	External Factors	How significant external factors that are outside of the Company's control (e.g., public policy, economy, acts of God, competitors actions, consumer desires, etc.) impact the risk likelihood and severity
LONG-TERM	Strategic Alignment	Benefit of taking the risk in the overall strategic direction of the Company
	Contingency & Mitigation	Availability of contingency or crisis management plans in place Level of maturity of risk management activities and reporting of key performance indicators.
	Speed of Onset	The time that elapses between occurrence of an event and the point at which the company feels its effect

Risk ratings include quantitative impact and qualitative factors in the short-term (1 year) and the long-term (2-5 years) to find a balance between short-term business requirements and longer-term growth.

Figure 5.15 Risk assessment factors

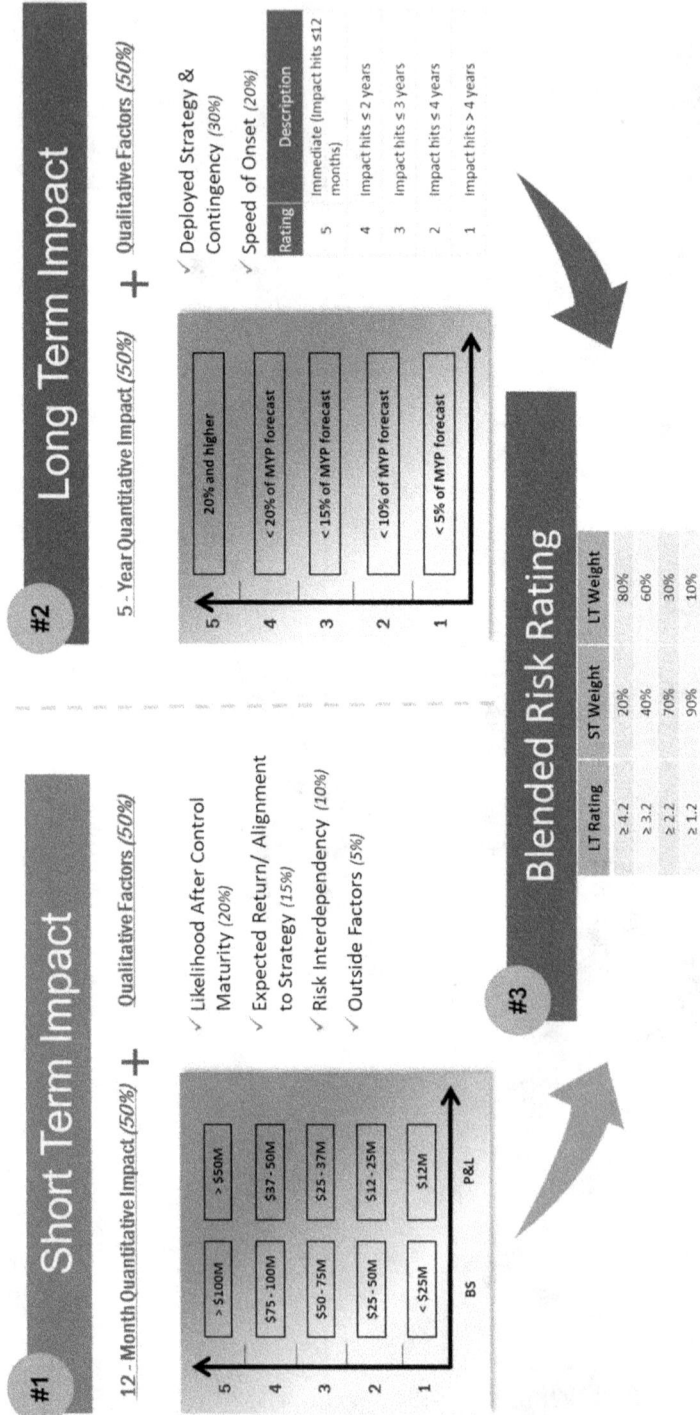

Figure 5.16 Risk assessment matrix

Score	Rating	Consideration	Description of Likelihood	
			Probability	Frequency
5	Expected	The risk event or circumstance is relatively certain to occur, or has occurred within the past 6 months	90-100%	Almost Yearly
4	Highly Likely	The risk event or circumstance is highly likely to occur	70 – 90%	Every 2 to 3 Years
3	Likely	The risk event or circumstance is more likely to occur than not	40 – 70%	Every 4 to 6 Years
2	Less Likely	The risk event or circumstance occurring is possible	10 - 40%	Every 7 to 9 Years
1	Slight	The risk event or circumstance is only remotely probable	<10%	Every 10 Years and Beyond

Figure 5.17 Likelihood of occurrence

Rating	Description
5	Immediate. Impact strokes the Company in less than 18 months
4	Impact strokes the company in less than 2 years
3	Impact strokes the company in less than 3 years
2	Impact strokes the company in less than 4 years
1	Impact strokes the company after 4 years

Figure 5.18 Speed of onset

Complexity (12-Months)

There are varying degrees of complexity within given processes, controls, or business models. Complexity can be driven by manual processes, level of judgment involved, complicated principles or rules, interdependency with other groups, and so on.

New Business Model (12-Months)

Management of the risk will require new organizations, processes, infra-structures, and systems or exposure to rules, policies, and guidelines in new locations or countries. This may also include risks that surfaced from charting new territories and emerging markets with unknown activities.

Strategic Alignment (12-Months)

Some conditions affect the strategic direction of the Company, while oth-ers impact execution within normal operational or compliance activities.

Control Immaturity (12-Months)

Mitigating controls in place directly and indirectly addressing the identi-fied risk are assessed based on a framework shown in Figure 5.19. As the level of maturity increases, risk becomes more manageable.

Rate	Continuum	Characteristic of Capability	Key Characteristics
1	Optimized	(Optimizing Feedback) Issue management is a source of competitive advantage	Issue resolution strategy
			Flexibility to easily exploit business opportunities
			Strategy drives business
			Real-time monitoring of dashboards
2	Proven	(Quantitative) Issue measured/managed quantitatively and aggregated enterprise-wide	Reliance on preventive controls
			Control self-assessments
			Key performance measurements
			Infrastructure stable and proven
			Governance = Strategic
3	Defined	(Maintain and Operate) Policies, process and procedures defined and institutionalized	Uniform process
			Gaps detected/remediated timely
			Defined control infrastructure
			Informal performance measuring
			Governance = Strategic/Tactical
4	Repeatable	(Compliance Ready) Processes repeatable, but dependent on individuals; high materiality	Repeatable activity
			New unproven controls
			Stabilized infrastructure/policies
			High reliance on tenured personnel
			Governance = tactical
5	Unreliable	(Evolving) Dependent on heroics; institutional capabilities lacking; not sustainable	Ad-hoc activity
			Relies on initiative
			Reliance on key persons
			Disparate systems
			Fragmented control structure
			High percent of manual controls

Figure 5.19 Maturity control fraud risk (12-Months)

The rate of susceptibility to fraud could be rated hand-in-hand with the control immaturity.

Reputational Risk (12-Months)

This factor relates to the negative publicity that the risk may cause, if and when, it happens.

External Risk Factors or Outside Drivers (12-Months)

Events or other factors that are outside of the Company's control, such as legislation, economy, acts of God, competitors' actions, consumer desires, and so on.

Deployed Strategy With Measurable KPIs (5-Years)

Level of maturity of risk management activities and reporting of KPIs.

Contingency Plan in Place (5-Years)

Availability of contingency or crisis management plans in place.

Risk Interaction and Interdependencies (5-Years)

Level of interaction or damage caused to other risks or risk elements.

Management Judgment

Management (Risk Committee) may perceive the risks differently because of the considerations of the assumptions. This factor gives more flexibility of the mathematical calculation of the risk rating.

Risk Treatment Plans

From the process standpoint, once all risks have been identified, synthesized, quantified, and ready to be entered into a complete risk register, the next step is to assign the Top 25 risks owners who will be responsible for mitigating those risks. This chapter will discuss developing the risk treatment plans moving forward.

- **Identifying the root cause**
  Logically, the first steps would be to identify the root causes for the individual risks. The root causes could be one or could be many. If there are several root causes, then as you develop the plan, try to identify the top 20 percent of the root causes that would address a large percentage of the risk. The other root causes that are smaller in nature are likely not worth the time and effort based on the payback to be received and will be insignificant.

  Following the identification of the various root causes, the next step would be to identify and create risk responses. Initially, address this early on at a very high level. The options are to accept, transfer, avoid, mitigate, or exploit the risks. For each of the risk statements that have been identified, the owners need to determine which of the five responses is appropriate, keeping in mind the financial benefits of remediating the risk as well as the timeliness involved and the speed of onset to which the risk is related.

Going a little bit deeper into the definitions of the risk responses, the first option is reduce/mitigate. Risk mitigation reduces the probability and/or impact of an adverse risk event to an acceptable threshold. Taking early action to reduce the probability and impact of a risk is often more effective than trying to repair the damage after the risk has occurred. Risk mitigation may require resources and time, and thus presents a trade-off between doing nothing versus the cost associated with mitigating the risk completely. The vast majority of the risk statements will fall in this category—reducing or mitigating the risk.

- **Transfer**

  Transferring risk involves finding another party who is willing to take responsibility for the risk management and will bear the liability of the risk, should it occur. The aim is to ensure that the risk is owned and managed by the party that is best equipped to deal with it effectively. Risk transfer usually involves payment of a premium and the cost effectiveness of this must be considered when deciding whether to adopt a transfer strategy.

- **Avoid**

  Risk cannot be avoided by simply removing the cause of the risk or executing the project in a different way while still aiming to achieve project objectives. Not all risks can be avoided or eliminated, and for others, this approach may be too expensive or time consuming. However, this strategy should be considered early in the process.

- **Accept the risk**

  This strategy is adopted when it is not possible or practical to respond to the risk by the other strategies or when the responses are not warranted by the importance of the risk. When the risk owners decide to accept the risk, they are agreeing to address the risk if and when it occurs. A contingency plan, work-around plan, and contingency reserves may be developed for that eventuality.

The above four risk response categories apply to threats. There are two other categories for risk opportunities.

- **Risk opportunities versus risk threats**

  First response strategy is to exploit. The aim of this strategy is to ensure that the upside is captured. This strategy seeks to eliminate the uncertainty associated with a particular upside risk by making the opportunity happen. Exploit is an aggressive response strategy best reserved for those golden opportunities with high probability and impacts.

Now, that we have refreshed our memory on the treatment responses, refer to the sample risk treatment plan in Figure 5.20:

Another sample of a risk treatment plan shown in Figure 5.21 can certainly be customized but should always have the four primary sections. The upper left section, which is really the risk topic that will reference the risk category, also identifies the executive champion. Usually, it is a direct report of the CEO in small-to-midsize companies. It also identifies the risk owners, who the people lower in the organization are and who are responsible for developing and executing the plan. It could be one person, or it could be several people. It typically would be a vice president or a business unit leader, someone relatively high in the organization with the understanding that his or her specific team would be responsible.

Next, identify the risk driver as to whether it is a predominantly short term, long term, or balanced between the two.

The next section is a rolling four-quarter risk rating trend. That is the numeric value, which was developed in the previous chapter on heat map preparation. In this section, you can also include some identifiers such as the short-term risk impact in terms of dollars, and the long-term risk impact as a means of percentages with the next item being the rank. The short-term impacts cash flow, revenue, gross margin, or profit is the dollarization. The long-term risk impact expressed as a percentage is the estimated impact to revenue growth percent of the five-year plan as a standard.

This gives a trending view of the direction of the overall risk rating. The upper right-hand corner section is the KPIs that measures both

[Risk Topic]
[Risk Category]

Risk Champion/s:	eStaff
Risk Owners:	VP / Business Unit Leader
Primary Risk Driver:	Balanced – Long Term and Short Term risk factors

4-Qtr History	Q1	Q2	Q3	Q4	Status
Risk Rating (Trend)	4.24	4.19	4.06		S
Risk Impact (ST)*	$M	$M	$M	$M	
Risk Impact (LT)*	%	%	%	%	
Rank	1	1	2	6	

*Risk Quantification Assumptions.
ST: impact to cash flows, revenue, GM or profit
LT: estimated impact to revenue growth (% of the 5-year plan)

KPI / CSF	Status
Short-Term CSF: • xx • xx Long-Term KPI • Xx Key Risk Indicator	

Risk Elements	Root Causes	Action Plans	Project Owner	Timeline	Status
Process		[Short Term / Band-Aid Solution] [Long Term]			
People		[Short Term / Band-Aid Solution] [Long Term]			
System		[Short Term / Band-Aid Solution] [Long Term]			
External		[Short Term / Band-Aid Solution] [Long Term]			
Relationship		[Short Term / Band-Aid Solution] [Long Term]			

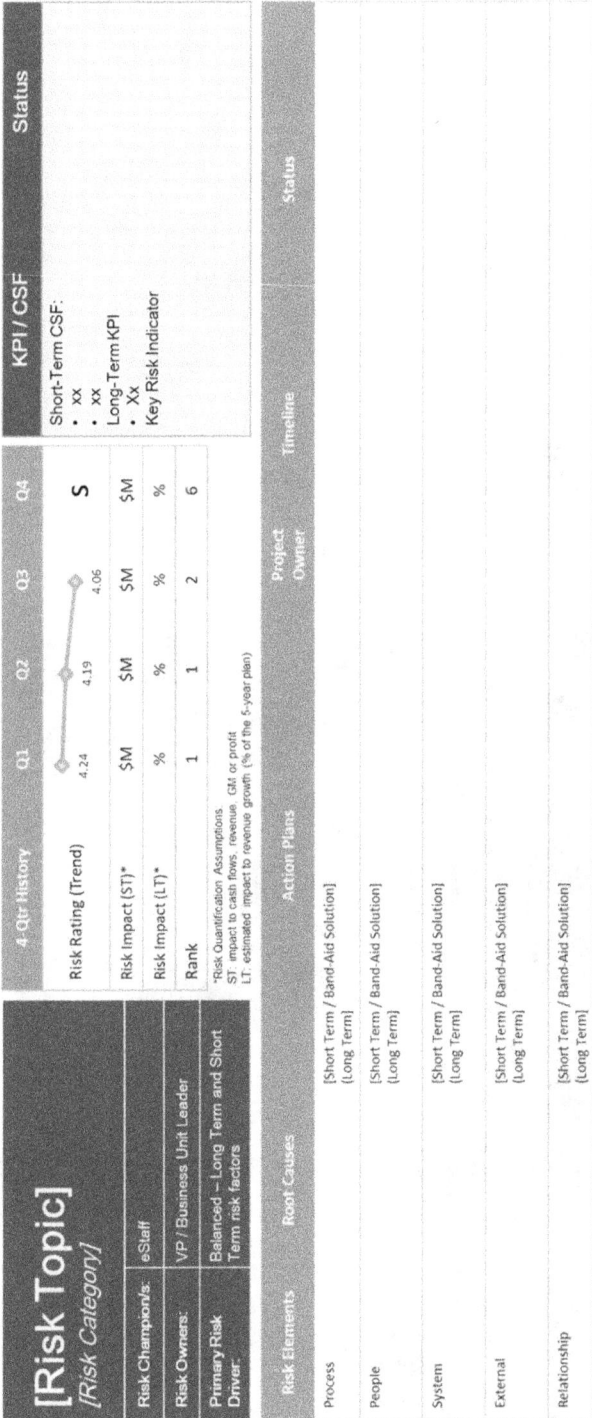

Figure 5.20 Risk treatment plan

[Risk Topic]	
Category:	[Strategic, Financial, Operational, Legal/Compliance]
Risk Champion/s:	[Accountable eStaff]
Risk Owners:	[Responsible Person]
SME:	[Subject Matter Expert]
Impact Window:	Short Term, Long Term, Balanced

Mitigation Success
KPI:

Risk Condition	Root Causes	Response	Action Plans	Owner	Timeline	Status
(Process)		Reduce Transfer Avoid Exploit Accept				Not Started Launched Completed On-Going Delayed
(People)						
(System)						
(External)						
(Relationship)						

Figure 5.21 Risk treatment plan template

short-term and long-term goals and objectives. These risk indicators can be either numeric (they generally are numeric) or they may relate to the completion of a project or other indicators. Once this KPI measurement is reached as a result of the remediation plans, it means the risk has been largely mitigated. Therefore, it is important to have KPIs for each risk topic in the register profile. However, even though the KPI may have been achieved in a given quarter, it normally does not drop until there has been three successive quarters with that same trend.

The Risk Treatment Plan template is a summary used for every risk profile that has been measured and addressed by management. The purpose of having a consistent template is to provide a familiarity in reporting and measuring all the risks for the Board of Directors and the executive team.

However, the detail supporting the summary level can be in any format the risk owners desire to use to track, identify, analyze, measure, and so on. The ERM Administrative group generally does not care about what is behind the detail, only that it is accurate and used consistently from quarter to quarter by all risk owners.

In the upper left-hand corner of the risk treatment plan is the risk topic and the category. Normally, it is a very short (one or two sentence) description. Also, the risk executive champion indicated is normally a direct report to the CEO and is at the highest level. In this case, the risk owners, who actually own the risk as well as the people who will be mitigating the risk and performing the action plans, are also identified. They are usually the business unit leader or a VP level.

This section also identifies the primary risk driver whether it is a long-term balanced risk, a short-term balanced risk, or a blended long-term/short-term balance risk, which we already discussed in the previous chapter.

The middle section of this template shows a rolling four-quarter history of the risk rating (usually between 1 and 5), to show a trend of performance. It also reflects the risk impact from a short-term perspective, particularly the impact to cash flows revenue, gross margin, or profit.

It also reflects the risk impact from a long-term perspective shown as a percentage. It is the estimated impact to revenue growth, shown as a percentage of the five-year strategic plan.

The last item in this section is **the ranking of the risk** in the risk profile register. Usually, the company would want to track the Top 25.

The third section in the upper right-hand corner shows the KPIs that are used to measure the success and the status of each of the risk topics. Typically, they are broken down into short-term and long-term risk indicators and are tied to performance goals and objectives of the employees in their compensation plan.

KPIs are generally numeric ratings that measure a given risk topic. Once that KPI has been achieved, it is an indication that the risk may have been mitigated to an acceptable level. The normal practice is for the KPI measurement to meet the KPI goal for at least three consecutive quarters thus developing a trend that provides some credibility that the risk has been effectively mitigated.

The bottom section is dedicated to the high-level root causes and related action plans. Typically, it is good to identify the risk element root causes by category in terms of process, people, system, external, and relationship. The owner would develop the action plans addressing the root causes, or at least the most important root causes, which yield the biggest impact. The identified project owner is responsible for the execution of the action plan and the timeline, specifically the date of expected completion of risk mitigation and the status against each action plan.

Once again supporting the details of this section can be a series of other supporting documents whether in Excel, or some project software format. The format is not important, as long as the documents roll up to the common treatment plan template used for all the risks. This ensures the executives are looking at the same information for all the risks and can develop their own opinion of how well the treatment plan is progressing.

Of course, this is much easier to understand with examples. We will provide an actual case study in a later chapter toward the end of this book. Although some of the information will be anonymized, it will be detailed enough to show how the above can be implemented.

The Top 25 risks will be closely monitored and managed by the owners. Treatment or mitigation plans are established and revisited every quarter to determine the effectiveness in managing the risks. Again, the treatment plan is owned and maintained by the risk owners, not the Risk Administration Team.

The following requirements will be present in establishing the mitigation plan:

Root Cause

Conduct a fishbone/3WIs analysis (8D or its equivalent) to uncover the root causes of the risks.

Risk Response

Risk Response (example shown in Figure 5.22). Management will decide on how they will react to the risk based on the root causes identified. Management's response is based on several assumptions such as threshold or tolerance and risk appetite. Risk appetite is defined as the amount of risk exposure, or potential adverse impact from an event, that the organization is willing to accept/retain. Once the risk appetite threshold has been breached, risk management treatments (accept, avoid, transfer, or mitigate) and business controls are implemented to bring the exposure level back within the accepted range.

Accept

Typically, management accepts the risk (no mitigation plan needed) when the risk level is within the risk appetite/tolerance. The action required is only to monitor the risk trend.

Avoid

Eliminate the risk by diversification if not totally getting out of the situation.

Transfer

Partner with a third party to manage the risk (e.g., insurance where risk of loss is transferred to the insurance agency when the risk occurs).

Mitigate

Implement measures to reduce or mitigate risks to an acceptable level.

For Threats	For Opportunities
Reduce/Mitigate. Risk mitigation reduces the probability and/or impact of an adverse risk event to an acceptable threshold. Taking early action to reduce the probability and/or impact of a risk is often more effective than trying to repair the damage after the risk has occurred. Risk mitigation may require resources or time and thus presents a trade-off between doing nothing versus the cost of mitigating the risk.	*Exploit.* The aim is to ensure that we capture the upside. This strategy seeks to eliminate the uncertainty associated with a particular upside risk by making the opportunity definitely happen. Exploit is an aggressive response strategy, best reserved for those "golden opportunities" having high probability and impacts.
Transfer. Transferring risk involves finding another party who is willing to take responsibility for its management, and who will bear the liability of the risk should it occur. The aim is to ensure that the risk is owned and managed by the party best able to deal with it effectively. Risk transfer usually involves payment of a premium, and the cost effectiveness of this must be considered when deciding whether to adopt a transfer strategy.	*Share.* Allocate risk ownership of an opportunity to another party who is best able to maximize its probability of occurrence and increase the potential benefits if it does occur. Transferring threats and sharing opportunities are similar in that a third party is used. Those to whom threats are transferred take on the liability and those to whom opportunities are allocated should be allowed to share in the potential benefits.
Avoid. Risk can be avoided by removing the cause of the risk or executing the project in a different way while still aiming to achieve project objectives. Not all risks can be avoided or eliminated, and for others, this approach may be too expensive or time consuming. However, this should be the first strategy considered.	
Accept. This strategy is adopted when it is not possible or practical to respond to the risk by the other strategies, or a response is not warranted by the importance of the risk. When the risk owners decide to accept a risk, they are agreeing to address the risk if and when it occurs. A contingency plan, workaround plan and/or contingency reserve may be developed for that eventuality.	

Figure 5.22 Risk response

Remediation Plan

Programs, projects, or controls instituted to manage the risk to an acceptable level.

Remediation Owner

Person/s, a team who is/are responsible in developing and executing the treatment plan.

Key Performance Indicator

Event, status, or metric that when met, the remediation plan in place is deemed to be effective and the risk is mitigated to an acceptable level. It is a manifestation that the risk was appropriately managed.

Risk Scorecard

The ERM Risk Committee requires that treatments plans be evaluated to provide assurance that Champions and Risk Owners are implementing necessary actions and measures in managing the risks identified, assigned to them. Each risk has its corresponding scorecard. This document is owned and controlled by the ERM Administration Team. It shows the trend of risk rating, KPI achievement, mitigation capability rating, and overall assessment (see the example of the scorecard template in Figure 5.23).

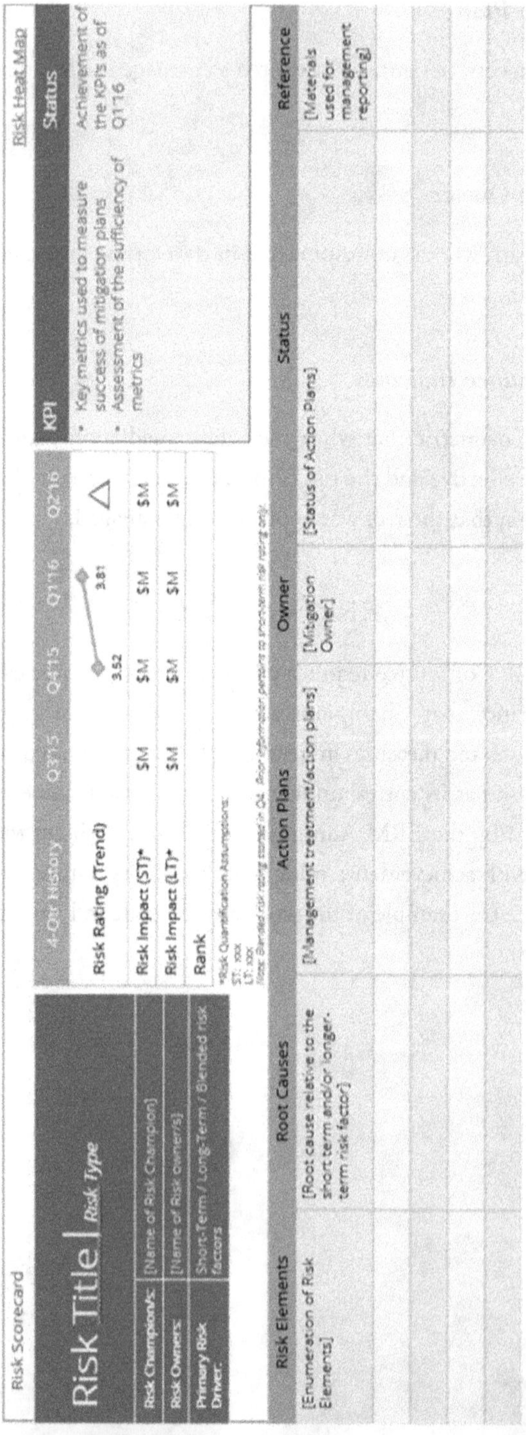

Figure 5.23 Risk score card

CHAPTER 6

Reporting ERM Results and Status

Once a robust ERM program is established and the infrastructure is in place including the risk owners being familiar with the ERM terminology and treatment plans created, it is now time to report the results.

The frequency of the results reporting depends a lot on desires of executive management, but in general the quarterly reporting frequency is the most effective. This provides a more real-time reporting of both new and existing risks (as opposed to semiannual or annual reporting).

It is also good to have one uniform deck prepared for executive management and one deck prepared for the audit committee of the board of directors. Those decks will be different, meaning the board will have probably less detail and may only discuss the top 10 risks, while the quarterly report to executive management will have more detail, including all the summary templates discussed thus far in the previous sections. The score card that consolidates all these will be discussed later in this book.

Quarterly Executive Management Reporting

The quarterly presentation to the executive management (Risk Committee) generally happens after the risk owners have updated their Treatment Plans in preparation of the Quarterly Operations Review (QOR). Depending on the company closing schedules, sometimes the Risk Committee meeting is held before the QORs allowing the risk owners more time to refine the actions moving forward during the current quarter.

The quarterly reporting will start at the risk owner level and include a review in detail of the results for this quarter's activity for the individual risk statements assigned to each of these risk owners. As the results are discussed, the updates to the summary treatment plan are required, which do not include all the details, but they do have the key elements discussed earlier. They show which action plans are open/closed and any kind of slippage in the due dates. Most important is to show the benefits of the actions taken throughout the past quarter and adjust the quantification for the remaining residual risk.

The core of the presentation for executive management would typically have the summary template for each of the Top 25 risks. Any details would typically not be included but would be available (should there be any questions from the executive team about the individual status and progress).

This takes place before the Risk Committee formal meeting is held and would be shortly after the quarter close, once the financial information has been obtained for the quarter to utilize in the quantification. The Risk Committee meeting would then be held after all the details have been reviewed with the action plan owners.

An example of content for the quarterly Risk Committee meetings could include the following:

Agenda—This will always change from quarter to quarter depending on changes to the program or time of the business year; however, there should always be certain content shown at every meeting to keep the consistency of messaging for executives. It will be easier for the executives to digest the format and information. The following sample agenda (see Figure 6.1) includes:

Agenda

- Corporate Risk Trend
- Q4'19 Revised Top 25 Risk Heat Map
- Residual Risk Performance
- Emerging Risk Report
- Risk Owner Presentation

Risk Owner	Rank	Risk Topic
Mark Keller	4	External Supplier Relationships & Dependency
Paul Sura	5	Business Continuity & Disaster Recovery

- ERM Next Steps

Figure 6.1 Quarterly meeting agenda

Corporate risk trend graph—Another level of reporting that executives may require is quantifying total risk at the corporate level for the Top 25 risks. An example is shown in Figure 6.2. The upper line (usually in red color) is the inherent risk score in the absence of mitigating actions. The lower line (usually in green color) is the residual risk score and the reduced impact after the effectiveness of mitigation actions.

The goal is to see the gap between those two lines widen, particularly the Residual Risk Score (green) bottom left hand side downward arrow—to approach closer to the bottom X-axis.

The trending is usually done for a rolling four quarters, and it is quantified on the left-hand side Y-axis of the graph.

This can be done one level deeper as shown in Figure 6.3 with a combination of the residual and inherent lines plus incorporated bar charts. It is also based on a rolling four-quarter average for each result for the two lines.

Once again, note that the spread between the inherent risk upper (red) line and the residual risk lower (green) line indicates management's effectiveness at managing the risks. The wider the spread between the two lines, the more successful remediation plans were implemented. The spread is also a net impact of new risks and mitigated risks to be able to keep it consistent. The four quarters of positive trend in the gap between inherent and residuals is significantly attributable to better-than-expected performance in particular areas, but conversely could go the other direction if risks keep escalating faster than remediation efforts. This chart can be maintained for the life of the ERM program. In this case it is a three-year plan, and it includes three years of a historical information. The graph bars have meaning as described next. The center light shade (yellow) bar indicates prior quarter's outstanding risk amount. The most upper darker gray (green) portion on the bar indicates new risk dollar amounts from newly identified risks. The bottom dark gray bar represents the managed risk from prior quarter, and the darker (blue) most bottom bar represents the managed risk during the current quarter. The light (above "0"—yellow) bar and the darker gray above bar (green) both represent the amount of risk from a top level, and the darker gray bar below "0" and dark gray bar on the most bottom (blue) both represent mitigation against those risks. Note that the lighter gray bar below "0", which is managed risks from prior quarters, gets continuously longer in

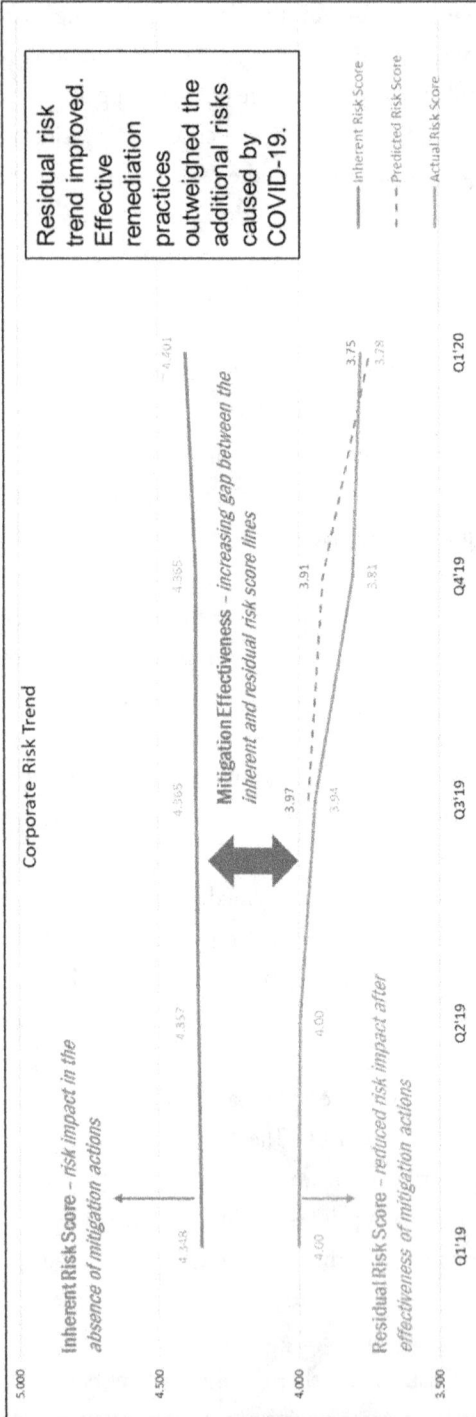

Figure 6.2 *Corporate risk trend (top 25 ERM risks)*

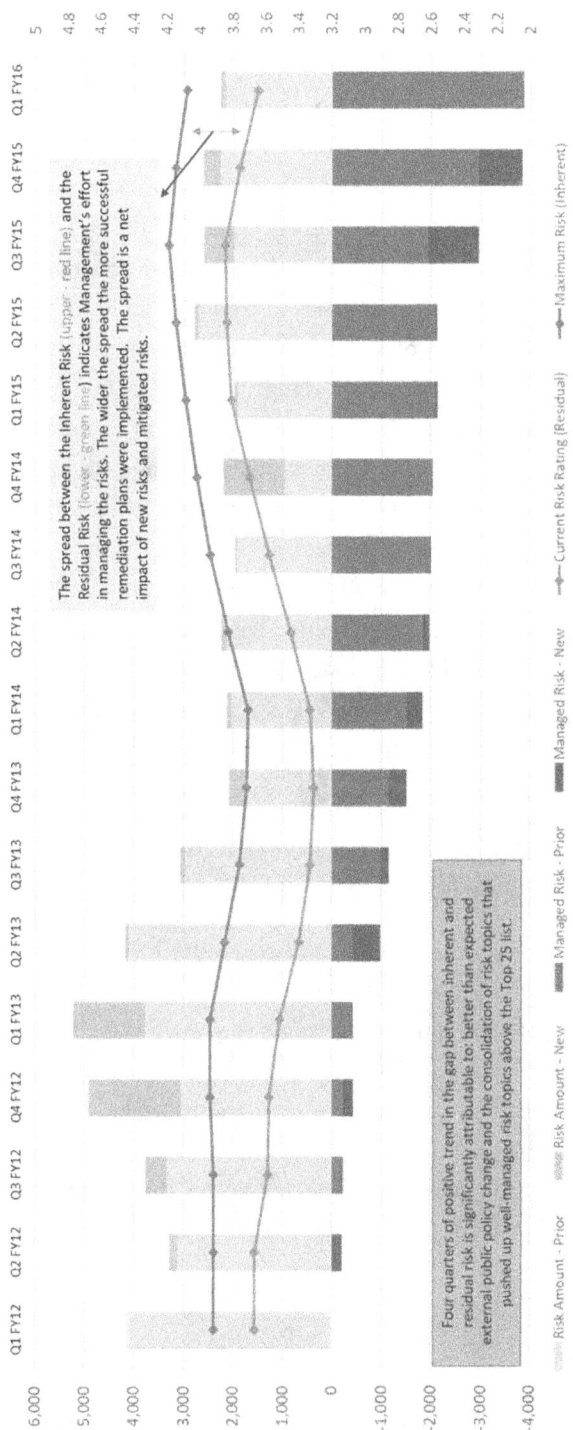

Figure 6.3 Corporate risk trend (four-quarter rolling average rating of top 25 short-term risks)

each quarter because it is a cumulative amount. That is the only bar that is cumulative. On the top side, the lighter gray above "0" (yellow) and the top gray (green) bars, which represent the unmanaged risk, are shorter, indicating that the level of remediation is higher than current unmanaged risks. This is the whole intent of the ERM program.

This was a difficult graph to initially explain to the audience but was effective once that was accomplished. Although the previous chart with just the two lines is somewhat easier to read and could be preferred by some teams, this more complex chart will continuously monitor and report more detail of historical efforts against the Top 25 risk profile.

Heat map—As previously discussed, the heat map includes the Top 25 risks and shows the trend in the current results, and how it compares to the previous quarter. It will have the balanced view of short-term and long-term implications. The 25 risks are categorized into three tiers to avoid major conversation of what is actually #1 versus #2, and so on. Tier 1 risks are the Top 5, which need immediate attention regardless of how they are physically ranked. Similarly, Tier 2 includes the next five risks with the next highest level of priority. Lastly, Category Tier 3 are the next 15 risks to round out the Top 25. The heat map typically is one of the front lead-in slides so the audience can see the big picture of the risk profile for the quarter.

Summary of Change

A summary of the change from the last quarter to the current quarter of the Top 25 risk profiles is better shared by inserting a chart showing a description of substantial key changes to reduce the reading required by the audience. Figure 6.5 shows an example of the change in ranking this quarter versus last quarter, and the narrative of key conditions that supported the increase or decrease in rating.

Of course, any new risks that are added that quarter would be mentioned here as well.

Web Graphs

There are different ways of reporting the status of the risk profile, but experience found that the web diagram is very useful, where all 25 risks can be

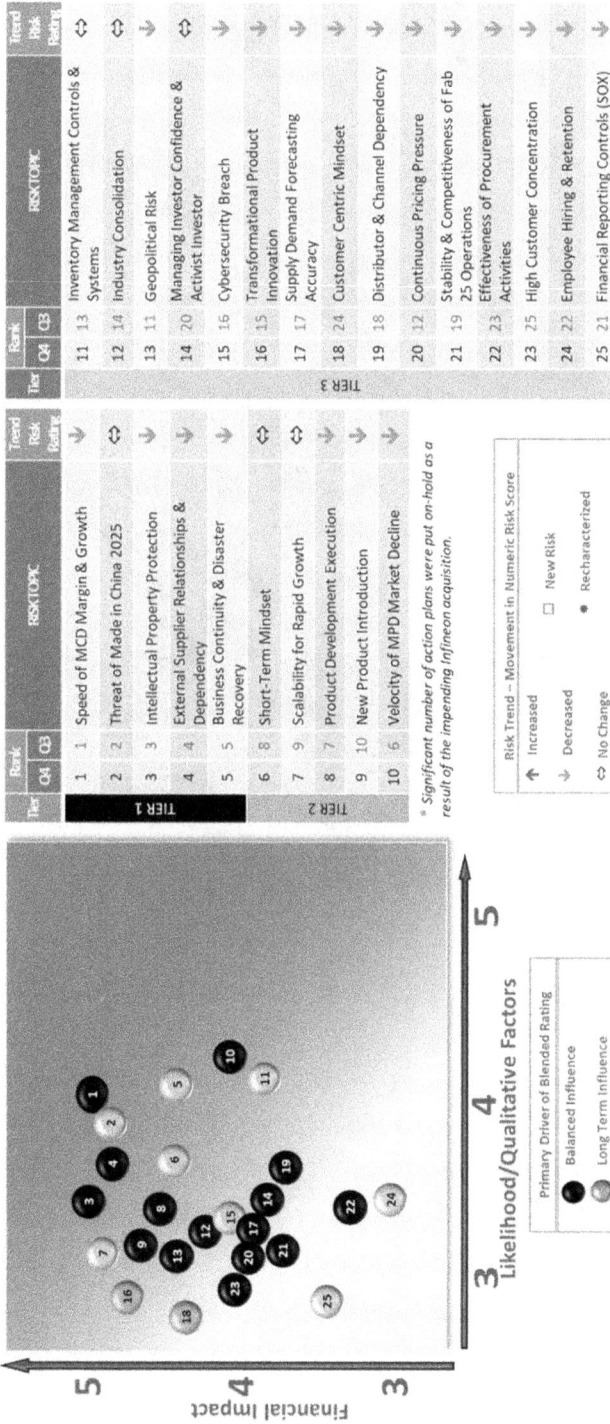

Tier	Rank Q4	CB	RISK TOPIC	Trend/Risk Rating
TIER 1	1	1	Speed of MCD Margin & Growth	→
	2	2	Threat of Made in China 2025	↔
	3	3	Intellectual Property Protection	→
	4	4	External Supplier Relationships & Dependency	→
	5	5	Business Continuity & Disaster Recovery	→
TIER 2	6	8	Short-Term Mindset	↔
	7	9	Scalability for Rapid Growth	↔
	8	7	Product Development Execution	→
	9	10	New Product Introduction	→
	10	6	Velocity of MPD Market Decline	→

Tier	Rank Q4	CB	RISK TOPIC	Trend/Risk Rating
TIER 3	11	13	Inventory Management Controls & Systems	↔
	12	14	Industry Consolidation	↔
	13	11	Geopolitical Risk	→
	14	20	Managing Investor Confidence & Activist Investor	↔
	15	16	Cybersecurity Breach	→
	16	15	Transformational Product Innovation	↔
	17	17	Supply Demand Forecasting Accuracy	↔
	18	24	Customer Centric Mindset	→
	19	18	Distributor & Channel Dependency	→
	20	12	Continuous Pricing Pressure	→
	21	19	Stability & Competitiveness of Fab 25 Operations	→
	22	23	Effectiveness of Procurement Activities	→
	23	25	High Customer Concentration	→
	24	22	Employee Hiring & Retention	→
	25	21	Financial Reporting Controls (SOX)	→

* Significant number of action plans were put on-hold as a result of the impending Infineon acquisition.

Risk Trend – Movement in Numeric Risk Score
← Increased   □ New Risk
→ Decreased   * Recharacterized
↔ No Change

Financial Impact

Likelihood/Qualitative Factors

Primary Driver of Blended Rating
Balanced Influence
Long Term Influence
Short Term Influence

Figure 6.4 Heat map

Q3	Q2	Risk Topic	Risk Updates
1	1	Speed of MXX Margin & Growth	Risk Trend: Decreased Company implemented quarterly monitoring of design wins and customer validation of product differentiation within the NPP process, which allowed better visibility on the margin funnel for MXX business. Margin improvement projects such as cost reduction initiatives, bundling and integration of multiple products, along with better marketing of the competitive assessment of products are ongoing. Company was able to increase its Q3 margin funnel by about $5M from XYZ China) due to increased pricing. New products and cost reduction efforts on Trab I, Wireless and CG7 products, are expected to yield margin results starting 2020. In addition, Trab II product introduction in Q2 was able to get a lot of traction and early design wins as samples were delivered within customer commit dates. The non compete term in the IoT contract of sale between Company and B-co expired in Q3. B-co went after company, and Company had to match price to keep the account. There is no indication that B-co is going after other accounts of Company.
2	9	Threat of Made in China 2025	Risk Trend: Increased Risk rating increased as Made in China program is pulled in earlier to 2022, just 2 years away from the timeline set by China for the program to be fully implemented. In addition, the prolonged and intensified trade conflict between the US and China may lead to enforcement of drastic measures to get a better position in the deal. Furthermore, a number of mitigation action plans expected to be initiated in Q3'19 were put on hold based on the direction by top management to reassess China strategy in light of the current geopolitical environment.

Figure 6.5 Top 10 risk updates

positioned around the web diagram. An example is shown in Figure 6.6. There can be additional charts as shown in Figures 6.7 and 6.8:

- The first graph (Figure 6.6) would typically show the actual for last quarter (Q3) versus current quarter (Q4) based on the numeric risk rating. The improvements will be reflected with a green (lighter gray) shade and conversely, red (darker gray) for the areas that are actually getting worse. Within certain parameters, highlights can be called out for any of the Top 25 on the chart to be able to get a high-level view causing the change.
- The second graph (Figure 6.7) can show predicted ratings. The CEO may desire to see a predicted risk rating for the next quarter's risk topic based on what the risk owners know at this point in the action plans, mitigation, and so on.
- The third graph (Figure 6.8) can then logically show a comparison of actuals for the quarter compared to what was predicted for that same quarter three months ago. Including this prediction gives a CEO and an executive management a feel for how close the risk owners are to the details and what type of progress has been made and is actively worked on, risk statement or not. They all expect some remediation to take place over a quarter. This would be a leading indicator if there's a concern that the risk might actually increase the next quarter and therefore it may get the adequate attention of the executives and may require them to be more proactive to try to determine what can be done to prevent this predicted higher risk rating from happening.

To better illustrate what the web graph looks like with both green-positive (lighter gray) changes and red-negative (darker gray) changes in a risk profile. Refer to Figure 6.9.

Comparative Heat Maps Side by Side

Another method of showing progress quarter over quarter is to have a heat map trend as illustrated in Figure 6.10. It shows, for example, the

Tier	Q4	TOPIC	Q3
TIER 1	1	Speed of MCD Margin & Growth	1
	2	Threat of Made in China 2025	2
	3	Intellectual Property Protection	3
	4	External Supplier Relationships & Dependency	4
	5	Business Continuity & Disaster Recovery	5
	6	Short-Term Mindset	8
	7	Scalability for Rapid Growth	9
	8	Product Development Execution	7
	9	New Product Introduction	10
	10	Velocity of MPD Market Decline	6
TIER 2	11	Inventory Management Controls & Systems	13
	12	Industry Consolidation	14
	13	Geopolitical Risk	11
TIER 3	14	Managing Investor Confidence & Activist Investor	20
	15	Cybersecurity Breach	16
	16	Transformational Product Innovation	15
	17	Supply Demand Forecasting Accuracy	17
	18	Customer Centric Mindset	24
	19	Distributor & Channel Dependency	18
	20	Continuous Pricing Pressure	12
	21	Stability & Competitiveness of Fab 25 Operations	19
	22	Effectiveness of Procurement Activities	23
	23	High Customer Concentration	25
	24	Employee Hiring & Retention	22
	25	Financial Reporting Controls (SOX)	21

LEGEND:

■ | Actual Q3

▨ | Actual Q4

Improvement in residual score in Q4.

Majority of the risks COMPANY actively managed showed a significant improvement in Q4'19.

Improvement is attributed to the maturing level of controls put in place to increase ability to timely detect and respond to risk events.

Actual Q3 vs. Actual Q4

Figure 6.6 ERM top 25 residual risk performance Q4 (vs actual for Q3)

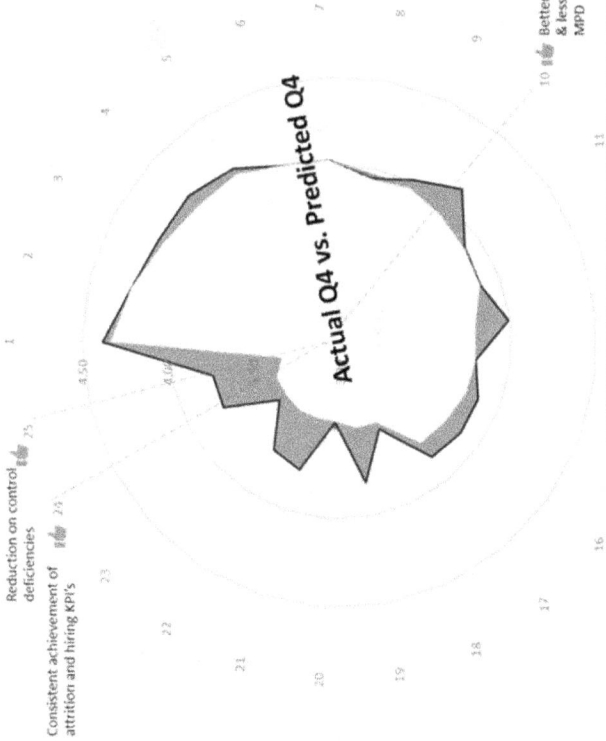

Tier	Q4	TOPIC	Q3
TIER 1	1	Speed of MCD Margin & Growth	3
	2	Threat of Made in China 2025	2
	3	Intellectual Property Protection	3
	4	External Supplier Relationships & Dependency	4
	5	Business Continuity & Disaster Recovery	5
	6	Short-Term Mindset	8
	7	Scalability for Rapid Growth	9
	8	Product Development Execution	7
	9	New Product Introduction	10
	10	Velocity of MPD Market Decline	6
TIER 2	11	Inventory Management Controls & Systems	13
	12	Industry Consolidation	14
	13	Geopolitical Risk	11
	14	Managing Investor Confidence & Activist Investor	20
	15	Cybersecurity Breach	16
	16	Transformational Product Innovation	15
	17	Supply Demand Forecasting Accuracy	17
	18	Customer Centric Mindset	24
TIER 3	19	Distributor & Channel Dependency	18
	20	Continuous Pricing Pressure	12
	21	Stability & Competitiveness of Fab 25 Operations	19
	22	Effectiveness of Procurement Activities	23
	23	High Customer Concentration (Apple, FitBit, Nintendo)	25
	24	Employee Hiring & Retention	22
	25	Financial Reporting Controls (SOX)	21

LEGEND:

Actual Q4

Predicted Q4

Performed better than expected

Did not perform as expected

Actual Q4 vs. Predicted Q4

Better market condition & lesser dependency on MPD

Most of the risks showed better than predicted trend as risk owners become more confident in the effectiveness of risk mitigation and monitoring plans.

Reduction on control deficiencies

Consistent achievement of attrition and hiring KPI's

Figure 6.7 ERM top 25 residual risk performance Q4 (versus predicted for Q4)

Tier	Q1	TOPIC	Q3
TIER 1	1	Speed of MCD Margin & Growth	1
	2	Threat of Made in China 2025	2
	3	Intellectual Property Protection	3
	4	External Supplier Relationships & Dependency	4
	5	Business Continuity & Disaster Recovery	5
	6	Short-Term Mindset	8
	7	Scalability for Rapid Growth	9
	8	Product Development Execution	7
	9	New Product Introduction	10
	10	Velocity of MPD Market Decline	6
TIER 2	11	Inventory Management Controls & Systems	13
	12	Industry Consolidation	14
	13	Geopolitical Risk	11
TIER 3	14	Managing Investor Confidence & Activist Investor	20
	15	Cybersecurity Breach	16
	16	Transformational Product Innovation	15
	17	Supply Demand Forecasting Accuracy	17
	18	Customer Centric Mindset	24
	19	Distributor & Channel Dependency	18
	20	Continuous Pricing Pressure	12
	21	Stability & Competitiveness of Fab 25 Operations	19
	22	Effectiveness of Procurement Activities	23
	23	High Customer Concentration (Apple, FitBit, Nintendo)	25
	24	Employee Hiring & Retention	22
	25	Financial Reporting Controls (SOX)	21

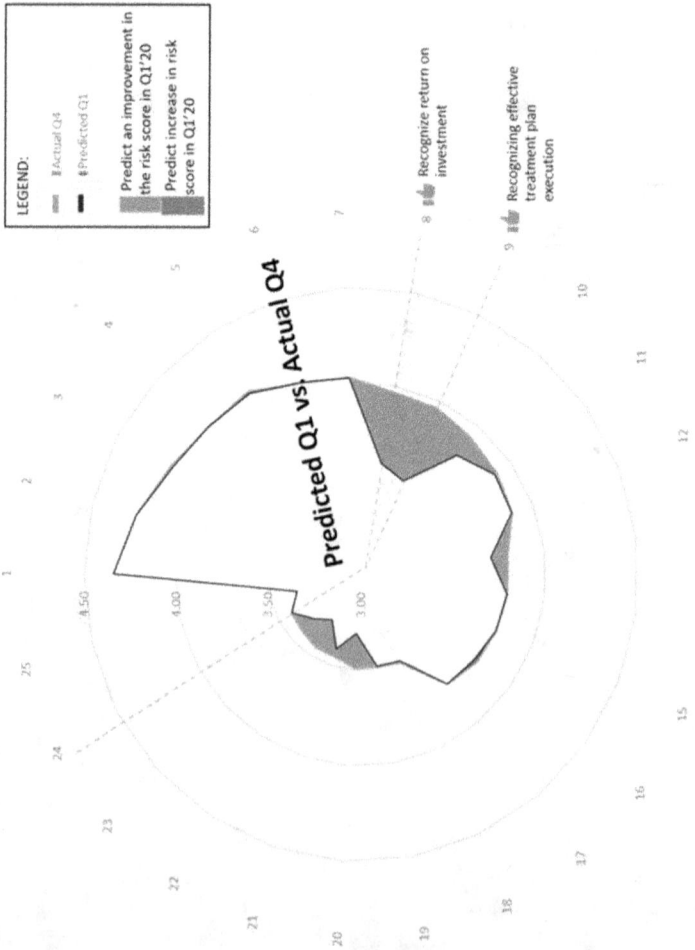

Figure 6.8 ERM top 25 residual risk performance Q4 (versus predicted in Q1)

Tier Q3	Q3	TOPIC	Q2
TIER 1	1	Speed of MCD Margin & Growth	1
	2	Threat of Made in China 2025	9
	3	Intellectual Property Protection	4
	4	External Supplier Relationships & Dependen	3
	5	Business Continuity & Disaster Recovery	5
	6	Velocity of MPD Market Decline	6
	7	Product Development Execution	2
TIER 2	8	Short-Term Mindset	12
	9	Scalability for Rapid Growth	14
	10	New Product Introduction	10
	11	Geopolitical Risk	7
TIER 3	12	Continuous Pricing Pressure	8
	13	Inventory Management Controls & Systems	16
	14	Industry Consolidation	19
	15	Transformational Product Innovation	13
	16	Cybersecurity Breach	17
	17	Supply Demand Forecasting Accura	15
	18	Distributor & Channel Dependen	20
	19	Stability & Competitiveness of Fab 25 Operations	23
	20	Managing Investor Confidence & Activist Investor	21
	21	Financial Reporting Controls (SOX)	22
	22	Employee Hiring & Retention	11
	23	Effectiveness of Procurement Activities	18
	24	Customer Centric Mindset	24
	25	High Customer Concentration (Apple, FitBit, Nintendo)	25

LEGEND:

- ▪▪▪ |Actual Q3
- — |Predicted Q3

Performed better than expected

Did not perform as expected

*See Appendix 2 for the methodology in assigning risk score to each risk topic.

Shows RED as well as GREEN

Predicted Q3 vs. Actual Q3

Measures effectiveness of risk mitigation during the quarter against expected performance.

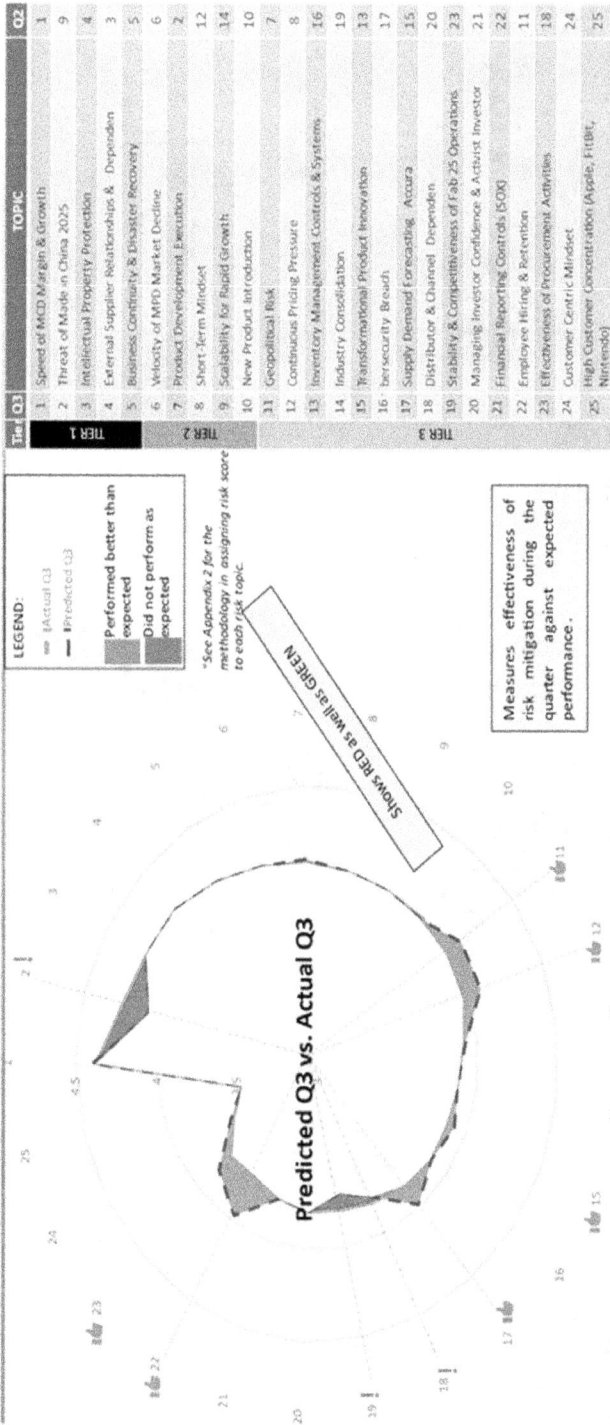

Figure 6.9 ERM top 25 residual risk performance Q3 (versus predicted Q3)

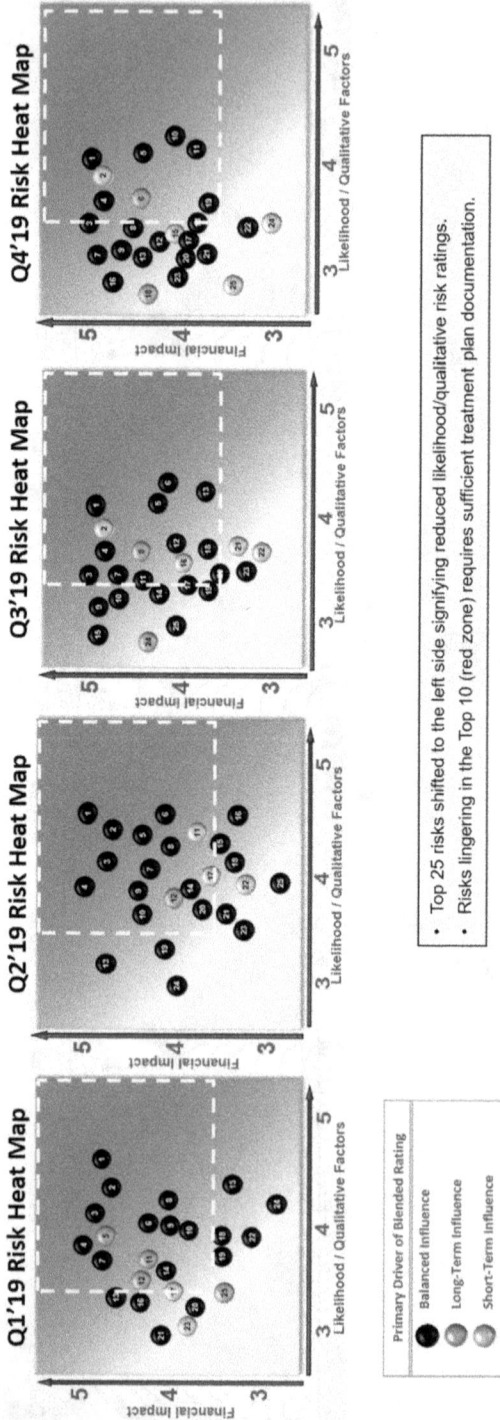

Figure 6.10 Risk heat map trend

last four risk heat maps side-by-side with short-term, long-term, and balanced risks. There is no indication or detail of the risk topics, but the purpose is to be able to visually see whether there continues to be a high concentration in the upper right-hand corner (the critical—red-darker gray—colored area), or are the associated risks gradually moving down and to the left, which indicates a good progress in mitigation of those risks. It is a good visual approach to track the overall Top 25 risk profiles. While this chart is extremely useful, it only has value shown once per the fiscal year. On a quarterly basis, the shifts may not be as obvious. Hence, showing this comparison heat map for the last four years really depends on the company requirements.

The quarterly reporting for the ERM program usually remains the same even for the annual reporting as well. Generally, there is not much difference other than being able to show longer trends and the direction of the overall effectiveness of the ERM program.

For every risk in the Top 25 profile, a company should have two templates. One is the summary risk treatment plan and the other shows the performance of the risk treatment plan.

Residual Risk Performance

The residual risk performance reporting process is illustrated in Figure 6.11.

This process is developed to set expectations of risk management performance for risk owners and to help the risk committee gauge the effectiveness of the overall ERM program. The Risk Performance Report is one level above the actual Treatment Plan and discusses the performance of the action plans.

The individual Risk Treatment Plan (template shown in Figure 6.12) that we discussed earlier centers around the accountability for key performance indicators (KPIs) for quantification, root causes, high-level plan timelines and owners.

The template for the individual Risk Performance Report is illustrated in Figure 6.13. The individual Risk Performance Report shows the trend against predicted scores, the achievement of the risk KPI for the last four quarters, a percentage of completion for the action plans that were due, and a description of the current quarter risk score trend.

ERM program objective is to identify risks and ensure risks are mitigated or exploited to increase shareholder value. The Residual Risk Performance is developed to set expectations of risk management performance for risk owners and help the Risk Committee gauge the effectiveness of the overall ERM program.

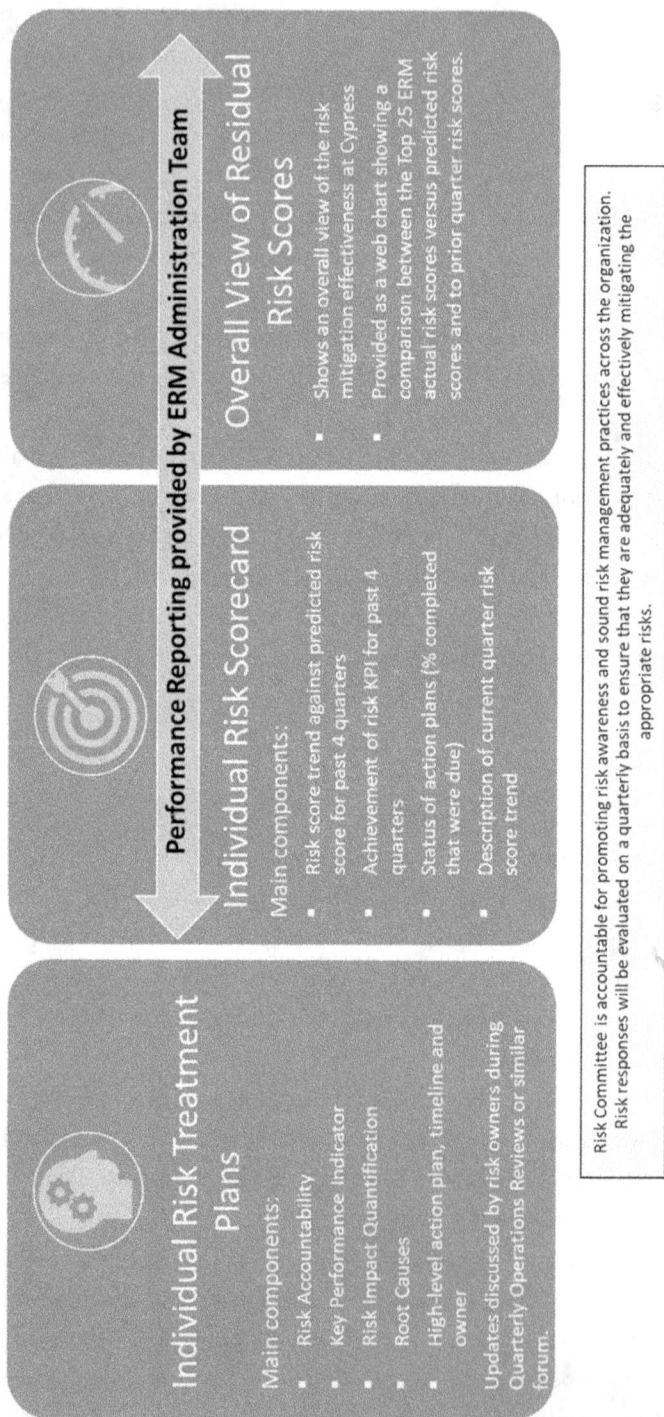

Performance Reporting provided by ERM Administration Team

Individual Risk Treatment Plans

Main components:

- Risk Accountability
- Key Performance Indicator
- Risk Impact Quantification
- Root Causes
- High-level action plan, timeline and owner

Updates discussed by risk owners during Quarterly Operations Reviews or similar forum.

Individual Risk Scorecard

Main components:

- Risk score trend against predicted risk score for past 4 quarters
- Achievement of risk KPI for past 4 quarters
- Status of action plans (% completed that were due)
- Description of current quarter risk score trend

Overall View of Residual Risk Scores

- Shows an overall view of the risk mitigation effectiveness at Cypress
- Provided as a web chart showing a comparison between the Top 25 ERM actual risk scores versus predicted risk scores and to prior quarter risk scores.

Risk Committee is accountable for promoting risk awareness and sound risk management practices across the organization. Risk responses will be evaluated on a quarterly basis to ensure that they are adequately and effectively mitigating the appropriate risks.

Figure 6.11 ERM residual risk performance

[Risk Topic]

Category:	[Strategic, Financial, Operational, Legal/Compliance]
Risk Champion/s:	[Accountable eStaff]
Risk Owners:	[Responsible Person]
SME:	[Subject Matter Expert]
Impact Window:	Short-Term, Long-Term, Balanced

Mitigation Success

KPI:

Risk Condition	Root Causes	Response	Action Plans	Owner	Timeline	Status
(Process)		Reduce Transfer Avoid Exploit Accept				Not Started Launched Completed On-Going Delayed
(People)						
(System)						
(External)						
(Relationship)						

Figure 6.12 Risk treatment template

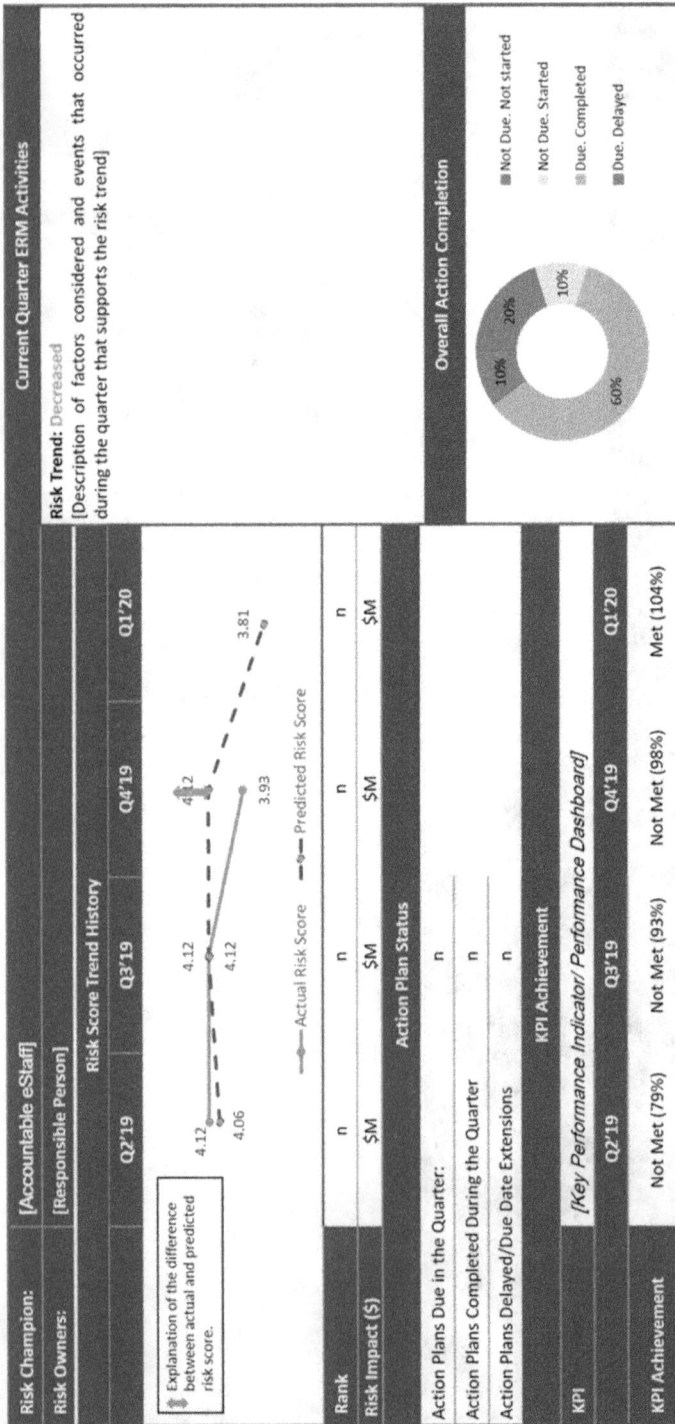

Figure 6.13 *Risk performance report template*

The Risk Performance Report template shows the last four quarters of activity based on actual risk score in the gray (blue) line against the predictive risk score in the dotted black line. It is the explanation of the difference between actual and predictive risk scores and will also show the ranking and the dollar impact moving from quarter to quarter. It has a section that discusses the action plan status. The risk treatment plan contained many action items assigned to different people with specific due dates. Those are summarized in the performance report. It will show the action plans due in the quarter, action plans completed during the quarter, and action plans delayed or with a due date extension during the quarter.

This next section of performance is called KPI achievement and as mentioned earlier, everyone must develop a statistic that is measurable. Once the actual performance reaches KPI statistic for that risk topic, there is a view that the risk is mitigated to an acceptable amount. However, that KPI must be met continuously for at least three quarters to ensure it is a trend and not just an anomaly or one-off situation.

Immediately below the KPI is the achievement and the related percentage as to whether it was met. The right-hand side at the bottom shows the overall actions completed. A pie chart was added to be able to visually see how many of the action plans (what percentage of the action plans) were due and how many were completed. In this case, it was 60 percent, which is a relatively good sign. Twenty percent of the action plans shown in dark gray was not due and not started. The light gray shows that 10 percent of the action were not due but were started. Lastly, the lightest gray (red) shows that 10 percent of the action plans were due but are delayed. So, hopefully the green (lighter gray) bar or the number of completions, shows a substantially higher percentage than the others.

Frequency of Risk Statements

As a result of the bottom-up risk assessment, there may be a large population of interviewees/respondents who report topics with a very high frequency. Although the risk may not be extremely high when it is actually quantified, the topic was brought forward by so many respondents that it is perceived to be a risk. Those must still be addressed to eliminate perceptions of a real risk, otherwise, the respondents might lose confidence level in the executive team and the ERM Administrative group if that just continues to be a frequently brought up subject.

It is good to show the Top 15–25 risks and compare the frequency of the risks to determine whether they improved or got worse versus previous year, as well as to be able to see how well the most frequent reported risks are trending. See Figure 6.14.

One of the main other items in the normal quarterly Risk Committee meeting is to show whether two or three risk elements tend to standout more than others. Having a larger positive change than expected or a change in the negative direction would automatically invite those risk owners to the risk committee meeting and present some detail around those elements in the Treatment Plan. This is beneficial because it will help risk owners understand the visibility of the ERM program and the type of questions committee members may ask. Additionally, it gives the Risk Committee members a chance to meet and converse with the typical risk owners.

After the Risk Committee meeting is held, and all updates, questions, and answers from the committee meeting are incorporated, a final deck will be developed for the Top 25 risks and all of the other supporting templates that would support the risk topics at the lower level. Those decks will then be archived as the formal results of the quarter for future reference.

This latest deck with the refinements must be turned around very quickly and given to the executive leadership team, who are typically the direct report of the CEO. They would in turn disseminate to their risk owners for the risk topics under their umbrella.

Risk owners will then incorporate refined information for presentation in the Quarterly Operations Reviews (QORs). The QORs are held with the CEO and executive management, and sometimes includes the extended leadership team. The QORs are normally used to discuss financial results, pipeline, operational issues and concerns, and also the Risk Treatment Plans for the applicable risk statements.

While the QORs are taking place, the ERM Administrative Team will begin preparing the deck for the board meeting. Decks for the board meetings will be much higher level. There could be six or eight

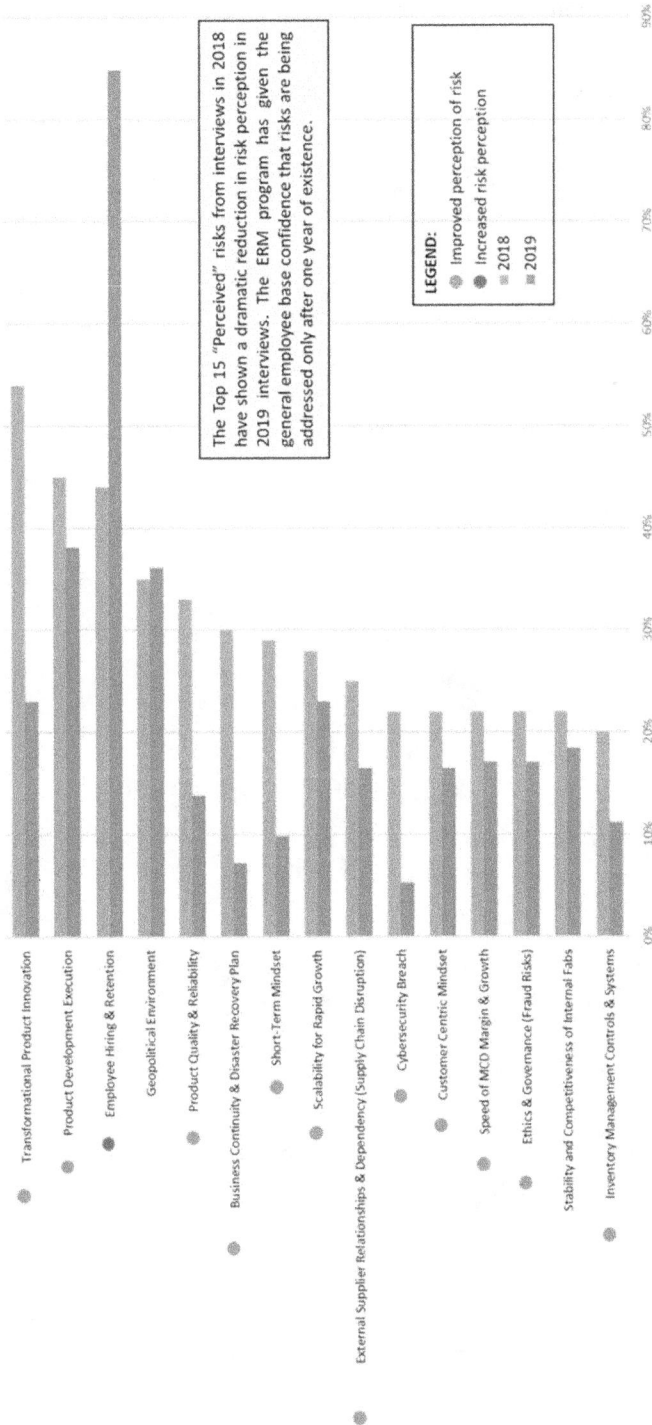

The Top 15 "Perceived" risks from interviews in 2018 have shown a dramatic reduction in risk perception in 2019 interviews. The ERM program has given the general employee base confidence that risks are being addressed only after one year of existence.

LEGEND:
- Improved perception of risk
- Increased risk perception
- 2018
- 2019

Risk categories:
- Transformational Product Innovation
- Product Development Execution
- Employee Hiring & Retention
- Geopolitical Environment
- Product Quality & Reliability
- Business Continuity & Disaster Recovery Plan
- Short-Term Mindset
- Scalability for Rapid Growth
- External Supplier Relationships & Dependency (Supply Chain Disruption)
- Cybersecurity Breach
- Customer Centric Mindset
- Speed of MCO Margin & Growth
- Ethics & Governance (Fraud Risks)
- Stability and Competitiveness of Internal Fabs
- Inventory Management Controls & Systems

Figure 6.14 Risk frequency comparison in subsequent years

key presentation slides with several slides in the appendix. Sometimes Treatment Plans or Performance Cards for selected risks might be in the appendix. But first and foremost, make sure the audit committee sees a similar type of reporting quarter-over-quarter to get used to the terminology and the slides for preview before the board meeting.

CHAPTER 7

Structure and Responsibilities

The reporting structure of ERM varies substantially by industry, company size, and business model. Figure 7.1 shows a summary of common practices of a risk committee created in 2017 by the Corporate Executive Board Company (CEB), acquired by Gartner from a survey for "state of the risk function." This survey connected with 158 companies.

Larger companies will frequently have a separate team that reports directly to the CEO or the Board of Directors and works in parallel with other functions such as internal audit and legal teams. The following survey results indicate that 23 percent of the companies had a board-level committee that focused on the risk management program. While there was no company size indicated, it is a fair assumption that these companies are generally over US$10 Billion in revenue. The more frequent arrangement within Fortune 1000 companies includes the responsibility of risk management vested with the audit committee of the board. About 60 percent of the surveyed companies reported this type of structure. Deeper within the organization there typically is an ERM function that is embedded into finance, legal, or internal audit functions and reports results to an executive-level (C-Suite) risk committee. About 53 percent of the surveyed companies reported this type of structure. Yet other companies have an executive-level risk committee that focuses on other compliance and risk activities, not just ERM. About 33 percent fall into this category. As one delves into the organization, 39 percent of the respondents stated that they have business-level committees that manage risks and report upward to executive levels and committees. This seems to be a fairly common practice when a traditional ERM function is in place and utilizes the results from the business-level committees. Fewer companies focus only on region-level or project-level committees for programs that most likely have a higher level of risks, whether it is geographical or companies whose revenue

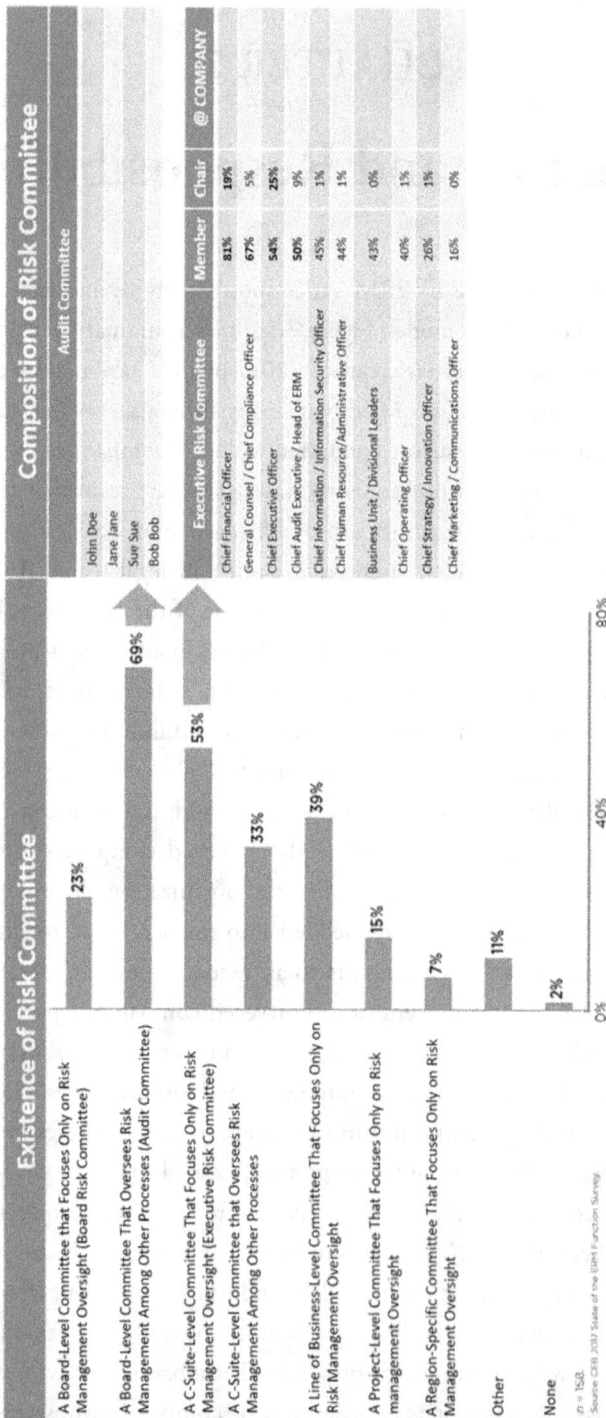

Figure 7.1 Common practices on risk committees

comes from very large projects. This book will discuss more of the transitional programs where an ERM program may exist and is facilitated by a function within the company (Finance, Legal, and Internal Audit) and reports results to the Audit Committee.

Overall Program Structure and Set Up

This book will illustrate the normal make up of a structure and then focus in more detail on the ERM Administrative Team and the Risk Committee members. Figure 7.2 shows the overall responsibilities of the Board of Directors, Risk Committee, Executive Leadership, Business Unit Management, and ERM Administrative Team.

The Board of Directors have continued to gain over time more and more responsibility for the company's risks. Company must look not only at internal management and executive management, but also the board members who have the strategy in mind and must ensure the company has appropriate risk planning to accommodate successes to avoid failures in strategic decisions. The reporting of risk updates was historically generally intended for the Audit Committee only, but more recently it is starting to include the full Board of Directors.

Before discussing the ERM Administrative Team and the Risk Committee member responsibilities in more detail, let us view a pyramid of a normal ERM Infrastructure that is generally adaptable to any type and size of an organization (see Figure 7.3). As one can see by looking at this pyramid, it is clear that the number of employees involved in ERM program can be quite large for the Top 25 risks. Experience has shown that the entire pyramid could include close to 100 employees who create and manage the Risk Treatment Plans. Despite that, the benefits far outweigh the resources and time commitment of the company.

ERM Administrative Team and Responsibilities

The Head of Internal Audit

The Head of Internal Audit is responsible for maintaining the ERM Framework. Annual review of this process documentation will be

Board of Directors	Executive Leadership	BU Management	Risk Committee	ERM Team
✓ Provide high-level expectation and oversight of Company corporate risk governance process ✓ Provide long-term vision and key priorities for ERM ✓ Review, challenge and concur with management on business strategies and the related risk appetite, and management risk response.	✓ Set and approve risk management policies and governance 　▪ frequency of reporting 　▪ risk assessment criteria 　▪ risk identification method ✓ Provide long-term goals, vision and key priorities for ERM ✓ Set clear expectations of risk management performance for business unit managers ✓ Set risk appetite ✓ Consider ERM results for strategic planning	✓ Hold overall responsibility for managing risks including: 　▪ Deploy ERM capabilities 　▪ Consider risk implication of business decisions/strategies ✓ Participate in semi-annual risk assessment ✓ Explain existing risk management activities ✓ Promote the importance of risk management among employees ✓ Establish clear expectations and accountability for risk management ✓ Develop risk mitigation action and measure performance indicators	✓ Oversight on risk governance structure 　▪ Provide overall leadership, vision, and direction 　▪ Review ERM Framework and procedures 　▪ Monitor ERM performance 　▪ Guide risk response to align with risk appetite 　▪ Implement change 　▪ Coordinate cross-functional risk management efforts 　▪ Review sufficiency of risk responses ✓ Review and discuss with management the Company's risk appetite and mitigation strategy relating to key risks ✓ Agree on top risks requiring Board attention	✓ Promote risk culture through employee training and awareness ✓ Assess risks through a standard methodology ✓ Facilitate Board discussion on key risks, emerging risk, risk reduction, changes to plans and deep dives ✓ Facilitate sharing of risk management best practices across the organization ✓ Monitor effectiveness of current mitigation plans, achievement of performance indicators and adherence to action plans ✓ Identify top risks including interdependencies ✓ Create gap analysis of risks identified and the risks disclosed in the Company's Annual and Quarterly Reports

Figure 7.2 Roles and responsibilities of key ERM

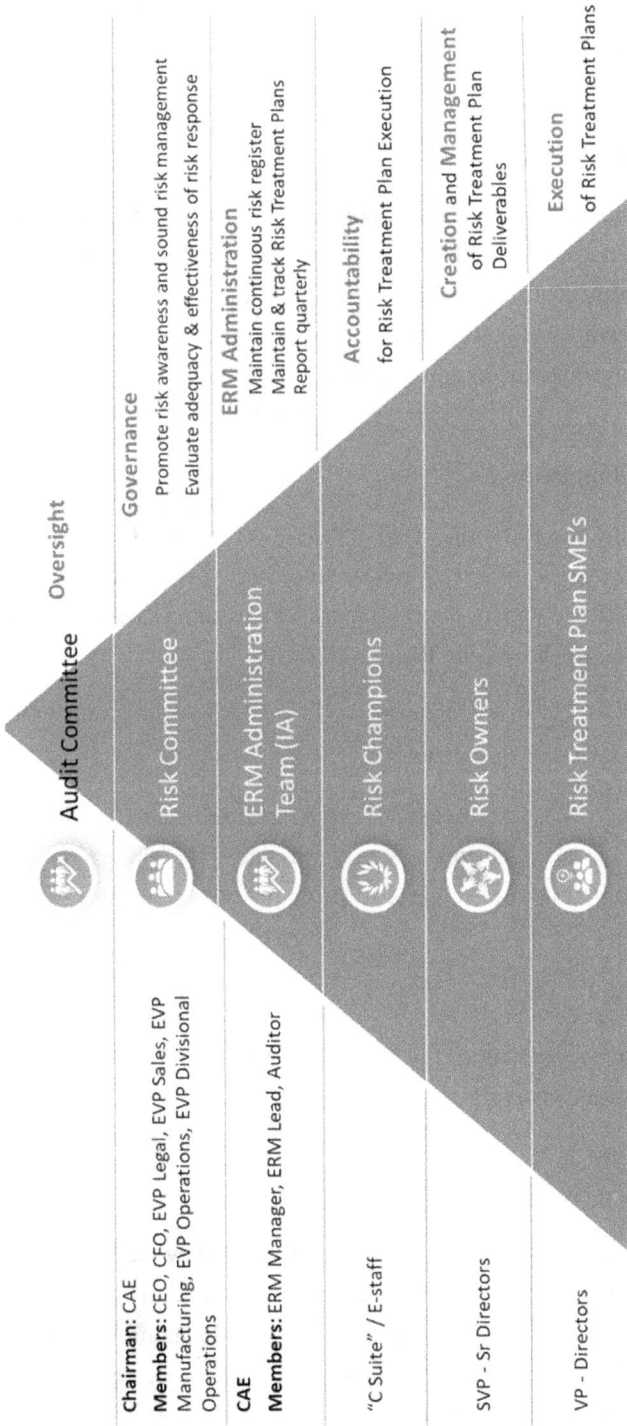

Figure 7.3 ERM infrastructure

Audit Committee — Oversight

Chairman: CAE
Members: CEO, CFO, EVP Legal, EVP Sales, EVP Manufacturing, EVP Operations, EVP Divisional Operations

Risk Committee

Governance
Promote risk awareness and sound risk management
Evaluate adequacy & effectiveness of risk response

ERM Administration Team (IA)

CAE
Members: ERM Manager, ERM Lead, Auditor

ERM Administration
Maintain continuous risk register
Maintain & track Risk Treatment Plans
Report quarterly

Risk Champions

"C Suite" / E-staff

Accountability
for Risk Treatment Plan Execution

Risk Owners

SVP - Sr Directors

Creation and Management
of Risk Treatment Plan
Deliverables

Risk Treatment Plan SME's

VP - Directors

Execution
of Risk Treatment Plans

performed. Any changes will be reviewed and approved by the Enterprise Risk Committee.

ERM Implementation Team

ERM Implementation Team—composed of the ERM Administrator, ERM Manager/s, and ERM program facilitator/s. This team is responsible for implementing the ERM program of the Company, ensuring that the framework is followed in the identification, mitigation, management, and monitoring of risks and opportunities.

ERM Administrator

ERM Administrator—the Head of Audit acts as the ERM administrator and Chairman of the risk committee meetings. The ERM Administrator facilitates the compliance to this program by working closely with the risk owners and the Enterprise Risk Committee.

Enterprise Risk Committee

Enterprise Risk Committee—reviews the quarterly update to the risk register and the treatment plans. The committee is the ultimate owner and has primary responsible in implementing the treatment plans.

Champion

Champion—Risk Committee members who are responsible for identifying, assessing, reporting, and managing risks.

Risk Owners

Risk Owners—also known as assignees, identified by the Enterprise Risk Committee members or Champions to monitor and manage the risks to resolution. Risk Owners assist the Champion in monitoring the trend of the risks, updating the risk exposure, and putting together treatment plans to mitigate the risks.

ERM Respondents

ERM Respondents—management individuals representing different areas and departments in the company who participate in the ERM exercise (bottom-up risk assessment).

ERM Committee

The ERM Committee Charter (the "Charter") codifies a company's approach to identifying, measuring, managing, reporting, and controlling risk. It documents sound practices to help ensure that risk is managed and measured in an effective and consistent manner across a company and describes the key elements of the Framework, including the main roles and responsibilities. The Charter also sets the basis of a company's risk culture.

The Executive Leadership Team (ELT) of a company must establish a corporate risk governance process to assist in the management of major risks that are inherent to a company providing reasonable assurance of achieving a company's key objectives.

The ERM Committee is formed by the ELT as the core committee in administering a company's ERM Framework (the "Framework"). The ERM Committee is responsible for establishing and maintaining a comprehensive Risk Management System for identifying, assessing, and managing risk with reasonable assurance of achieving objectives in a rapidly growing organization and changing competitive environment. The Committee serves as the umbrella for a company's various subcommittees supporting management in measuring and managing a company's aggregate risk profile and supporting a company's strategic plans in creating and protecting long-term shareholder value. These subcommittees are formed as part of its ERM Framework to ensure adequate risk measurement and management of a company's exposure to risk. These committees are jointly responsible for ensuring adequate risk measurement and management in their respective areas of authority. These committees may include: Executive Product and Safety Risk Committee, Investment Committee, and the Information Security Risk Committee.

Responsibilities of ERM Committee Members

The ERM Risk Committee is administered by the Head of Internal Audit executive (Chief Audit Executive, "CAE") and consists of various executive-level managers of the Company and meets quarterly. The CAE reports functionally to the Audit Committee and administratively to the CFO and provides overall leadership, vision, and direction for a company's ERM Framework. The CAE is responsible for the oversight of a company's risk governance processes to ensure alignment with leading practices.

The CEO and Board of Directors are responsible for oversight of a company's corporate risk governance process. The Board of Directors is actively involved in oversight of risks that could affect a company. This oversight is conducted primarily through committees of the Board, in particular the Audit Committee. Enterprise risk management is the primary responsibility of each function or service within a company.

The ERM Committee shall review, at least annually, the committee's charter and recommend any proposed changes.

Review at least quarterly the major risk exposures of a company and its business units, including strategic, operations, compliance, and financial reporting risks.

ERM is a part of every process and practice at every level. Risk owners are accountable to manage the risks. ELT should ensure that risk mitigation activities are successful in safeguarding assets, compliance and environmental standards are maintained, legal and regulatory obligations are met, as well as reinforcement of a company's mission, vision, and values.

Risk Owners are accountable to manage the risks.

The Committee's responsibility in this regard is one of oversight and review. Oversight function shall include:

Review of the ERM Framework and procedures for identifying, assessing, controlling, measuring, monitoring, and reporting risk exposure.

Discuss policy or process changes with respect to managing risks including, where appropriate, limits or guidelines reflecting the Company's risk appetite and tolerance in particular areas.

Discuss processes by which the Audit Committee is informed of matters reviewed and discussed by the Committee that also bear on the risks within the mandate of the Audit Committee, recognizing that the Audit Committee has primary responsibility for reviewing and discussing matters relating to the financial reporting and legal compliance components of compliance risk.

Risk Committee Charter

For an ERM program to be effective, the Risk Committee should be governed by a Charter, which codifies a company's approach to identifying, measuring, managing, reporting, and controlling risk. It documents sound practices to help ensure that risk is managed and measured in an effective and consistent manner across a company and describes the key elements of the framework, including the main roles and responsibilities. The Charter also sets the basis of a company's risk culture.

Membership of the Risk Committee

Members: The Committee shall be comprised of the following members of the executive management:

Chief Executive Officer
Chief Financial Officer
Chief Marketing Officer
Chief Operating Officer
General Counsel
President, Business Unit
Communications
VP, Corporate Strategy and Business Development
Senior Director Global Audit

Appointment and Removal: The members of the Committee are appointed and removed by the CEO.

Meetings

The Committee shall meet quarterly with the ERM facilitator (CAE) to discuss current status, results of any current assessments, the enterprisewide risk profile, and progress on risk mitigation and monitoring activities.

Quorum—at least half of the committee members must be present.

Reporting

Resolutions of the Committee will be reported as follows:

Executive Management quarterly (full version)
Audit Committee quarterly (condensed version)
Board of Directors quarterly (highly condensed version)

Processes and Controls

Risk Tolerance Guidance

It is the objective of a company not to incur any operational loss or damage to its reputation. For that purpose, a company must put policies, procedures, and systems in place to mitigate the impact and/or probability of occurrence of the risk inherent to its activities adopting a cost/benefit approach.

The risk appetite statement frames the risks the company should accept, the risks it should avoid, and the strategic, financial, compliance, and operating parameters within which the organization should operate, and seeks a balance between value creation and value protection.

Risk Management Framework

The Framework is a set of integrated processes, tools, and mitigation strategies that assist a company in managing and measuring risks consistent with COSO's Enterprise Risk Management—Integrated Framework.

The Framework supports a company's Senior Management in the alignment of business and risk management goals and provides a foundation, which enables a consistent approach to risk across the organization. Furthermore, the Framework aims at establishing a common understanding of risk and risk management, promoting consistent application of techniques, and capture of relevant data.

CHAPTER 8

Emerging and Unknown Risks

Emerging risk (in simple terms) are those that are new and foreseen that a company simply have not yet contemplated. These are risks that should be on a company's radar and management needs to be concerned about in the present day and over the next year. Emerging risks potential for harming a company or losses are not yet fully known. An effective ERM program requires a certain amount of attention to identifying these emerging risks. Most ERM programs historically just shuffled around the known "knowns," and then pushed them around on the heat map leaving the executives and committee directors asking: "Well, can you tell me something that I don't know?"

Emerging risks can be identified in multiple different ways. See Figure 8.1 that has been published by the World Economic Forum (WEF) after surveying approximately 350 senior risk analysts.

It tracks and discusses risks in five overall categories following an 18-month view of the post-COVID world. While some of these will be relevant within the next 12 months, others will only be relevant over the next three to five years. And others may not surface until 10 years from now, but they are certainly all on the horizon.

Let's explore the five categories as shown in Figure 8.1:

1. **Economic category** is hinged around a prolonged recession economic fallout due to job loss and reduced spending across the world, coupled with a supply chain shortage.
2. **Social category** is having the possibility of another COVID-19 outbreak or different variants from such, despite the global efforts to flatten the curve of infections with vaccinations and normal health protocol. Continued variants could become a new normal.

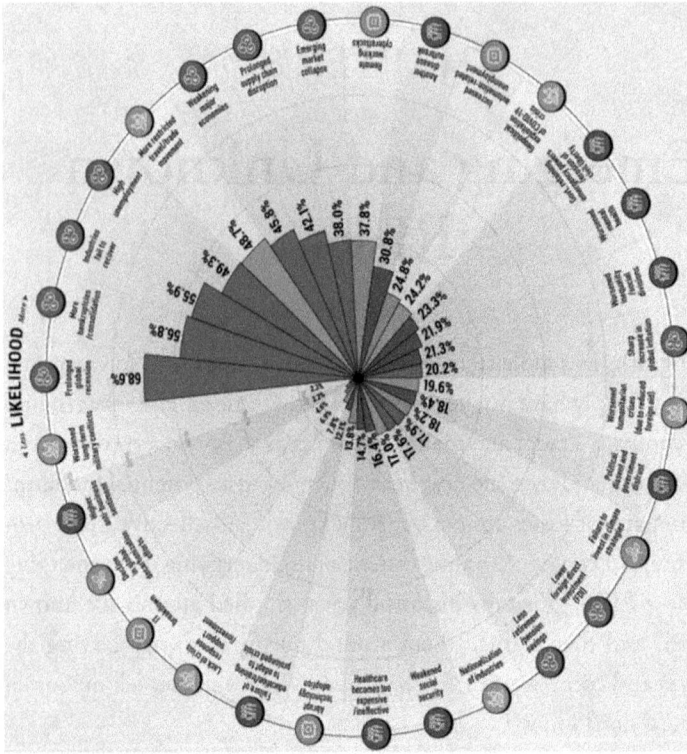

Figure 8.1 World Economic Forum: 18-month view of a post-COVID world

Source: The World Economic Forum (WEF) survey of 347 senior risk analysts.

Economic: A prolonged recession and economic fallout due to job loss and reduced spending across the world.

Social: Possibility of another COVID-19 outbreak, despite global efforts to flatten the curve of infections.

Geopolitical: Further restrictions on trade and travel movements.

Technological: Increased dependence on digital tools has enabled wide-scale remote working for business—but for many more without this option, the accelerated adoption of digital tools has hindered rather than helped.

Environmental: COVID-19 is potentially halting progress on climate action. Risk analysts also estimate a severe bounce-back effect on the environment as economies reboot.

3. **Geopolitical category** impacts our world today with further restrictions on trade as well as travel movements throughout the world. Those restrictions are unpredictable and are already changing regularly and are inconsistent through various regions of the world.

4. **Technological category** indicates an increased dependence on digital tools, which has enabled a wide-scale remote working for business. But for many more without this option, the accelerated adoption of digital tools stays hindered rather than helped.

5. **Environmental category** discusses how COVID-19 has potentially halted progress on climate actions. Risk analyst also estimate a severe bounce-back effort on the environment could happen as economies reboot. The publication has extensive detail of which risks are expected to happen sooner than later, although all of them need to be on every ERM programs list of considerations.

   When do the respondents' forecast risks that will become a critical threat to the world? Some extracted information directly from this publication can clearly be utilized in the foreseeable future and probably well into the future.

Short-term risks (0–2 years)—(see Figure 8.2) are referred to as Clear and Present Danger and are the risks a company must address immediately or prepare instantly.

About 58 percent of the WEF survey respondents obviously view infectious diseases as a livelihood crisis—which is not surprising in the context of COVID-19 pandemic. The top two risks identified by the most respondents are societal-oriented in general.

The other risk identified in the excess of 50 percent relates to extreme weather events, which seem to be happening more frequently in the last decade.

The next risk topics range from 35 to 40 percent and include cyber security, digital inequality, prolonged stagnation, terrorist attacks, youth disillusionment, social cohesion erosion, and human environmental damage.

Medium-term risks (3–5 years) are referred to as Knock-on Effects, meaning medium-term risks described as having a potential impact in three to five years—as shown in Figure 8.3.

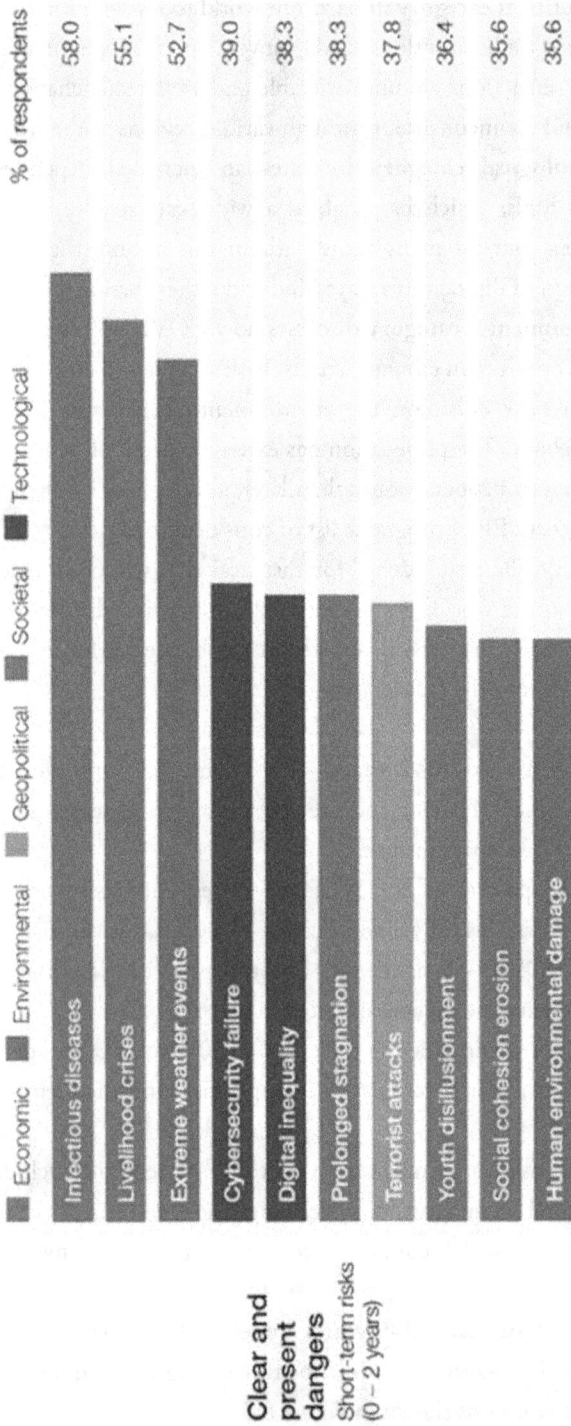

Clear and present dangers

Short-term risks (0 – 2 years)

Legend: ■ Economic ■ Environmental ■ Geopolitical ■ Societal ■ Technological

% of respondents

Risk	%
Infectious diseases	58.0
Livelihood crises	55.1
Extreme weather events	52.7
Cybersecurity failure	39.0
Digital inequality	38.3
Prolonged stagnation	38.3
Terrorist attacks	37.8
Youth disillusionment	36.4
Social cohesion erosion	35.6
Human environmental damage	35.6

Figure 8.2 WEF clear and present dangers

Knock-on effects

Medium-term risks (3 – 5 years)

Risk	Value
Asset bubble burst	53.3
IT infrastructure breakdown	53.3
Price instability	52.9
Commodity shocks	52.7
Debt crises	52.3
Interstate relations fracture	50.7
Interstate conflict	49.5
Cybersecurity failure	49.0
Tech governance failure	48.1
Resource geopolitization	47.9

Figure 8.3 WEF medium-term risks

Most relate to technology and are unpredictable with respect to the time when they will occur, but some are already being experienced. The remaining risks include interstate-relations fracture, interstate conflict, and resource geopoliticalization. There was not much visibility and attention given to these categories until the pandemic in 2019. The pandemic has created such a global impact much of which will remain around forever. Hence, the question is—"What is the speed of onset for this category?" One may think that looking at three-to-five years may be too far out for some of these topics; however, it is the perfect time to integrate emerging risk mindset within the ERM management teams.

Longer term risks from 5 to 10 years: The third category is referred to as Existential Threats shown in Figure 8.4.

The geopolitical risks rank the highest, with large concerns about weapons of mass destruction, state collapse, and multilateralism collapse.

These risks are followed by environmental concerns, such as biodiversity loss, natural resource crisis, and climate change action failure. It also includes an economic topic or risk they call industry collapse. These last three are in the 5-to-10-year range, and they all build upon each other.

In summary, in the zero-to-two-year timeframe there are more societal type of risks especially due to COVID-19 and lifestyle changes around the pandemic. It creates an economic issue, and ultimately, it should revert more to some of the geopolitical and environmental-type risks.

Considering the WEF study and the forecast, emerging risks are more important to consider now than the short-term risks or even medium-term risks. They will affect every strategy of every company in the world. This continues to add pressure to the board of directors and to the audit committee members. Any company should be expecting the board of directors to start asking questions around these inherent risks, such as:

Is there anything that's not on the list that management is truly concerned about yet not really brought forward, even as a long shot or a black swan? And how do these possibly impact the interrelationships among the relevant risks?

Another question to ask and the board will certainly want to know if they are being advised timely of any changes in the company risk profile,

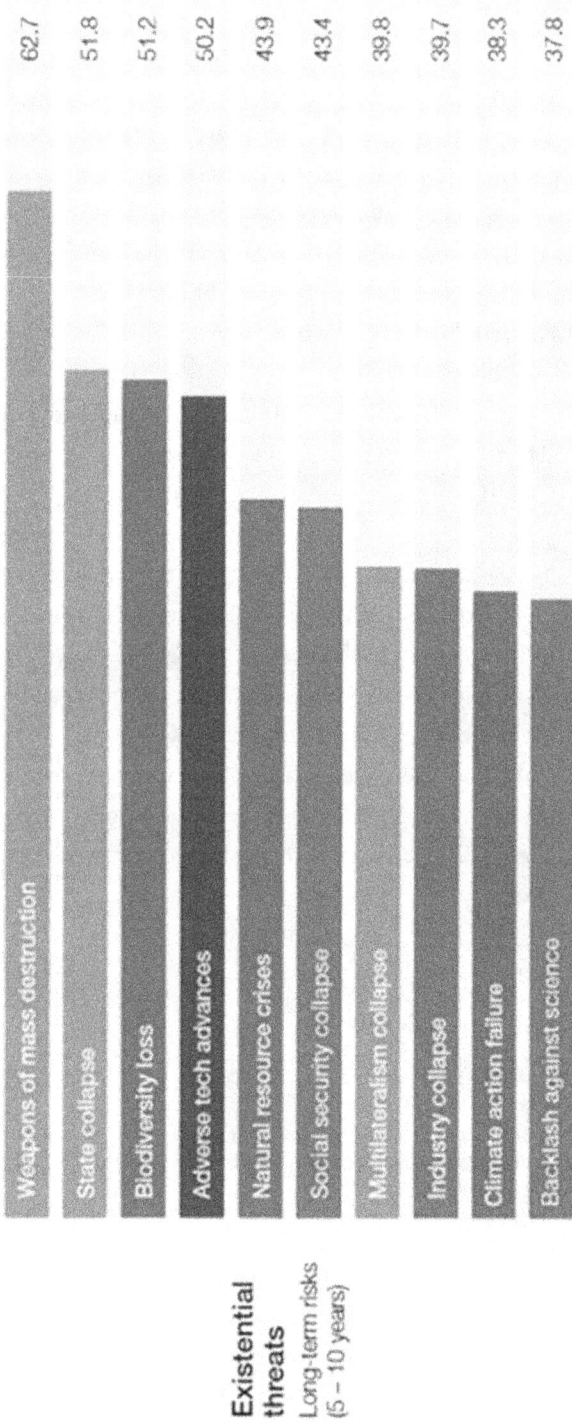

Existential threats

Long-term risks
(5 – 10 years)

Threat	Value
Weapons of mass destruction	62.7
State collapse	51.8
Biodiversity loss	51.2
Adverse tech advances	50.2
Natural resource crises	43.9
Social security collapse	43.4
Multilateralism collapse	39.8
Industry collapse	39.7
Climate action failure	38.3
Backlash against science	37.8

Figure 8.4 WEF existential threats

is "*What is the process that we have in place to identify emerging risks? How much attention is management putting on response plans or treatment plans for these emerging risks?*"

The last question to be asked by the board: "*Is the board adequately looking at the changes in the business environment and ensuring that these assumptions and impacts are being built into the corporate strategy?*"

These are the items that the ERM team should have in front and center of each of the core reporting to the board of directors.

The WEF certainly is not the only source. There are many other sources that are shown in Figure 8.5.

It is helpful to convert all these information sources to something more applicable to a company's specific industry. An example is in Figure 8.6—COVID-19 Potential Industry Impact.

Another good source of reviewing and thinking about emerging risks comes from North Carolina State University. They have listed a six-step process in trying to identify the unknowns and emerging risks, as shown in Figure 8.7—Identifying the Unknowns.

First step—identify what concerns others by leveraging surveys and studies. Possible sources were stated previously.

Second step—proactively address and reduce internal biases, the process is designed to ensure the efforts are viewed throughout a company, versus just in isolated pockets, which could prevent even considering some of the risks.

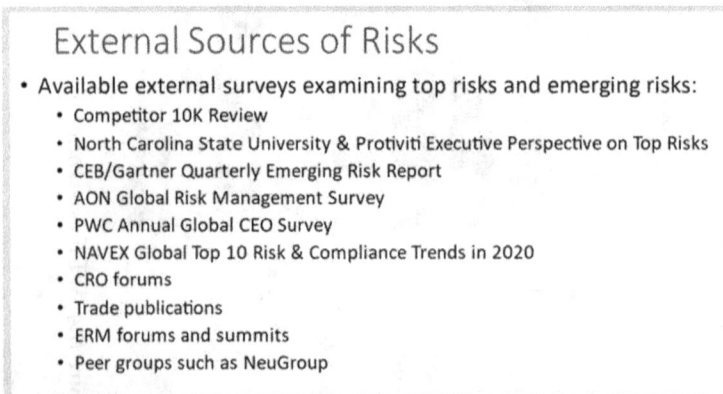

External Sources of Risks

- Available external surveys examining top risks and emerging risks:
    - Competitor 10K Review
    - North Carolina State University & Protiviti Executive Perspective on Top Risks
    - CEB/Gartner Quarterly Emerging Risk Report
    - AON Global Risk Management Survey
    - PWC Annual Global CEO Survey
    - NAVEX Global Top 10 Risk & Compliance Trends in 2020
    - CRO forums
    - Trade publications
    - ERM forums and summits
    - Peer groups such as NeuGroup

Figure 8.5 External sources of risk

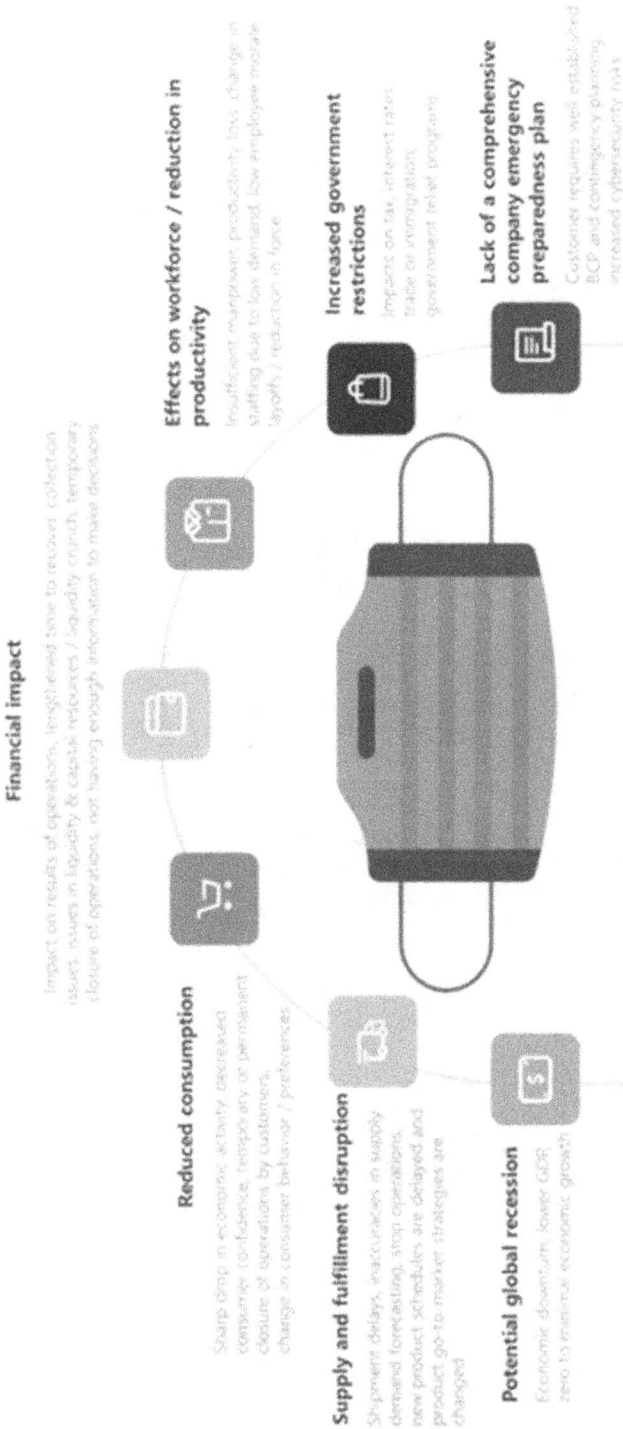

Financial impact

Impact on results of operations, lengthened time to recover collection issues, issues in liquidity & captive resources / liquidity crunch, temporary closure of operations, not having enough information to make decisions

Effects on workforce / reduction in productivity

Insufficient manpower, productivity loss, change in staffing due to low demand, low employee morale, layoffs / reduction in force

Increased government restrictions

Imports on tax, internet rates, trade or immigration, government relief programs

Lack of a comprehensive company emergency preparedness plan

Customers require a well-established BCP and contingency planning, increased cybersecurity risks

Reduced consumption

Sharp drop in economic activity, decreased consumer confidence, temporary or permanent closure of operations by customers, change in consumer behavior / preferences

Supply and fulfillment disruption

Shipment delays, inaccuracies in supply demand forecasting, stop operations, new product schedules are delayed and product go-to-market strategies are changed

Potential global recession

Economic slowdown, lower GDP, zero to minimal economic growth

Sources: KPMG, March 2020 COVID -19 Economic Impact;
McKinsey & Company, April 2020 Coronavirus Implications for the Semiconductor Industry;
PWC April 2020 COVID-19 CFO Pulse Survey [US]

Figure 8.6 COVID-19 potential industry impact

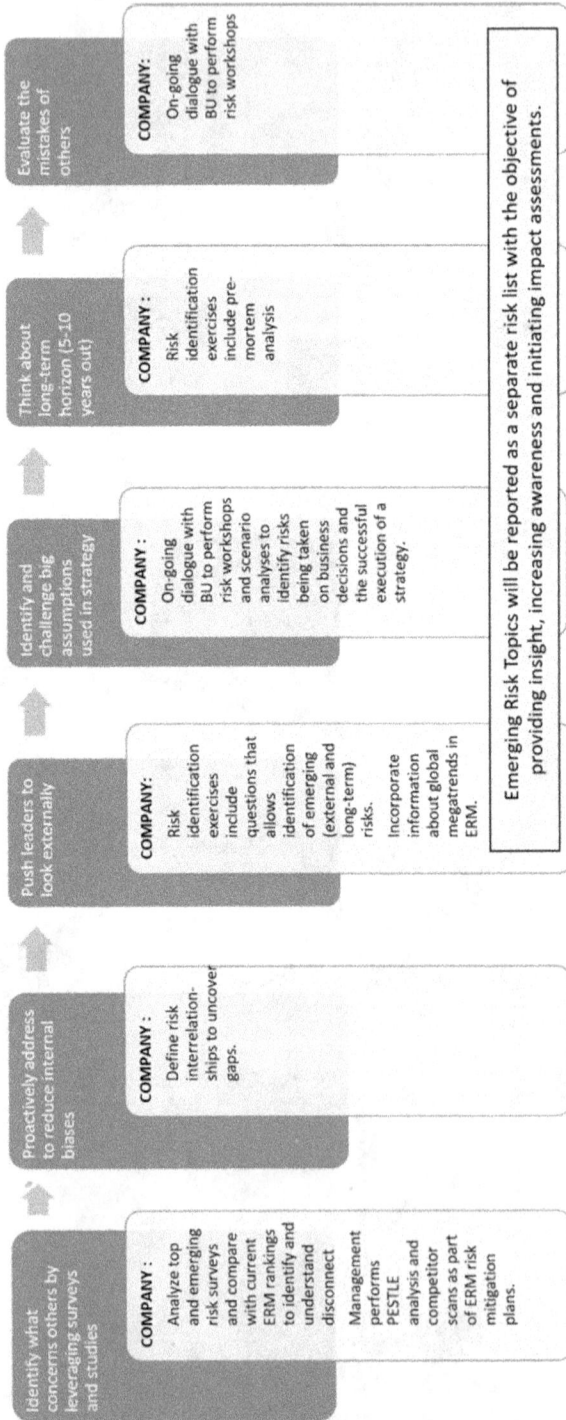

Identify what concerns others by leveraging surveys and studies	Proactively address to reduce internal biases	Push leaders to look externally	Identify and challenge big assumptions used in strategy	Think about long-term horizon (5-10 years out)	Evaluate the mistakes of others
COMPANY : Analyze top and emerging risk surveys and compare with current ERM rankings to identify and understand disconnect Management performs PESTLE analysis and competitor scans as part of ERM risk mitigation plans.	**COMPANY :** Define risk interrelationships to uncover gaps.	**COMPANY:** Risk identification exercises include questions that allows identification of emerging (external and long-term) risks. Incorporate information about global megatrends in ERM.	**COMPANY :** On-going dialogue with BU to perform risk workshops and scenario analyses to identify risks being taken on business decisions and the successful execution of a strategy.	**COMPANY :** Risk identification exercises include pre-mortem analysis	**COMPANY:** On-going dialogue with BU to perform risk workshops

Emerging Risk Topics will be reported as a separate risk list with the objective of providing insight, increasing awareness and initiating impact assessments.

North Carolina State University - Recommended Emerging Risk Process

Figure 8.7 Identifying unknowns

Third step—push the leaders to look externally. Sometimes leaders are confined by a "siloed vision" and only look within their company, processes, or their customers and don't pay attention to the changes that could take place affecting others. "The others" are not only within their company but look at what happens to the rest of the world and other companies.

Fourth step—identify and challenge big assumptions used in strategy setting. There are usually many different assumptions used when developing a company's strategy. Most strategies are generally longer term but also require short-term elements. To review and assess the various scenarios that are made when setting the strategy, a company needs to look for those anomalies that are underlying unusual points/events that must happen.

Fifth step—help everyone in the company think about long-term horizon, the 5–10 years span. This was just discussed in the WEF's emerging risks in the zero to two years; three to five years; and 5–10-year categories. It is important to get executives to take all these into a consideration and look at the other trends and predictions such as mega trends from MIT Sloan shown in Figure 8.8.

Sixth and last step—evaluate the mistakes of others. This is always a favorite approach in looking at the news and watching competitors. It does not even have to be in your same industry to see what is happening to them that has dramatically altered their strategic direction or their reputation. Many of these risks touch every company across almost every industry.

The mega trends in Figure 8.8 and noted in Step 5 are shown as follows. Megatrends are macroeconomic and geostrategic forces that are shaping the world. They are factual and often backed by verifiable data. By definition, they are big and include some of society's biggest challenges—and opportunities.

Consider building these mega trend concepts into your ERM terminology and focus specifically on the emerging risks. In some cases, it might be helpful to have a separate risk list for emerging risks. That really depends on the culture, the organization and the executive leadership team. Preferably, these should be built into the mainstream ERM program, knowing likelihood may be small, but repercussions could be extremely high.

Figure 8.9 shows an example of an update provided to ELT on a quarterly basis.

MIT Sloan Megatrends to watch:

- Demographics
- Urbanization
- Transparency
- Climate Crisis
- Resource Pressures/Constraints
- Clean Tech
- Technology Shifts *(IoT)*
- Global Policy
- Rise of populism *(nationalism and radicalism)*

Figure 8.8 Megatrends to watch

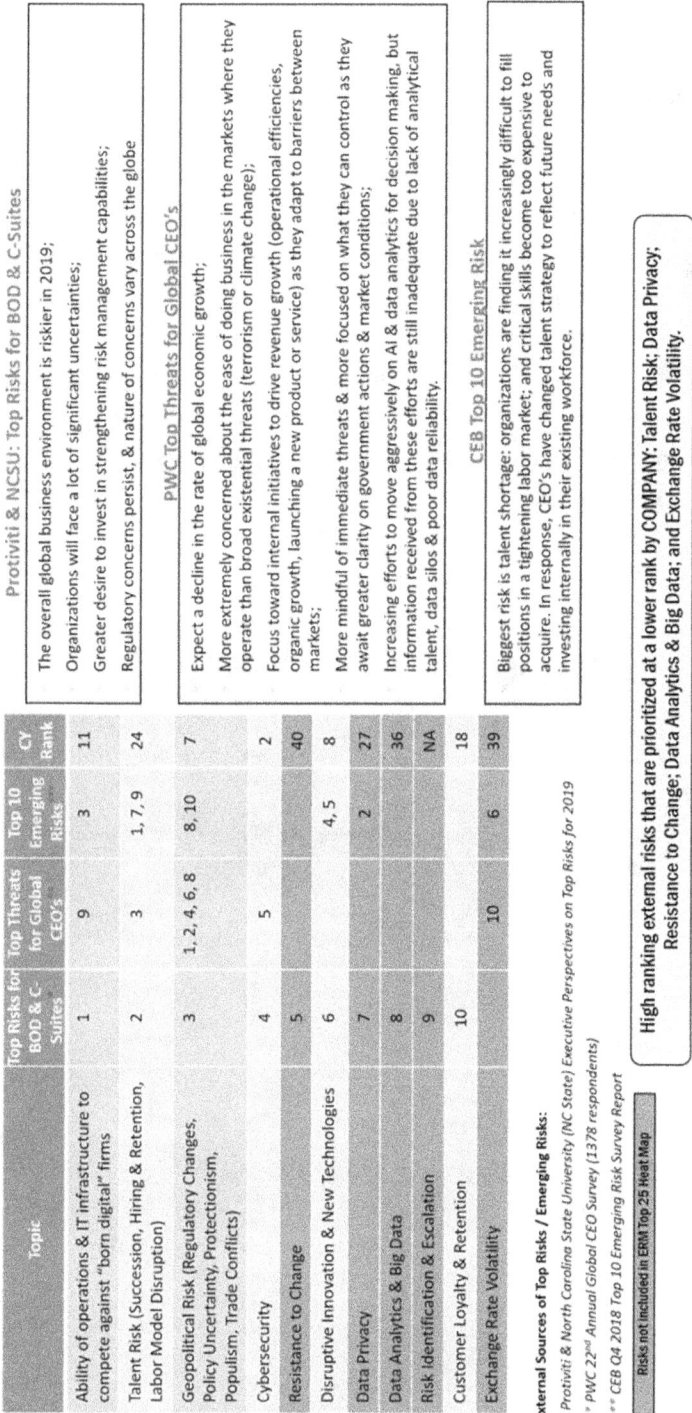

Protiviti & NCSU: Top Risks for BOD & C-Suites

- The overall global business environment is riskier in 2019;
- Organizations will face a lot of significant uncertainties;
- Greater desire to invest in strengthening risk management capabilities;
- Regulatory concerns persist, & nature of concerns vary across the globe

PWC Top Threats for Global CEO's

- Expect a decline in the rate of global economic growth;
- More extremely concerned about the ease of doing business in the markets where they operate than broad existential threats (terrorism or climate change);
- Focus toward internal initiatives to drive revenue growth (operational efficiencies, organic growth, launching a new product or service) as they adapt to barriers between markets;
- More mindful of immediate threats & more focused on what they can control as they await greater clarity on government actions & market conditions;
- Increasing efforts to move aggressively on AI & data analytics for decision making, but information received from these efforts are still inadequate due to lack of analytical talent, data silos & poor data reliability.

CEB Top 10 Emerging Risk

- Biggest risk is talent shortage: organizations are finding it increasingly difficult to fill positions in a tightening labor market; and critical skills become too expensive to acquire. In response, CEO's have changed talent strategy to reflect future needs and investing internally in their existing workforce.

Topic	Top Risks for BOD & C-Suites	Top Threats for Global CEO's	Top 10 Emerging Risks	CY Rank
Ability of operations & IT infrastructure to compete against "born digital" firms	1	9	3	11
Talent Risk (Succession, Hiring & Retention, Labor Model Disruption)	2	3	1, 7, 9	24
Geopolitical Risk (Regulatory Changes, Policy Uncertainty, Protectionism, Populism, Trade Conflicts)	3	1, 2, 4, 6, 8	8, 10	7
Cybersecurity	4	5		2
Resistance to Change	5			40
Disruptive Innovation & New Technologies	6		4, 5	8
Data Privacy	7		2	27
Data Analytics & Big Data	8			36
Risk Identification & Escalation	9			NA
Customer Loyalty & Retention	10			18
Exchange Rate Volatility		10	6	39

External Sources of Top Risks / Emerging Risks:

* Protiviti & North Carolina State University (NC State) Executive Perspectives on Top Risks for 2019
** PWC 22nd Annual Global CEO Survey (1378 respondents)
*** CEB Q4 2018 Top 10 Emerging Risk Survey Report

Risks not included in ERM Top 25 Heat Map

High ranking external risks that are prioritized at a lower rank by COMPANY: Talent Risk; Data Privacy; Resistance to Change; Data Analytics & Big Data; and Exchange Rate Volatility.

Figure 8.9 External/Emerging risk updates

Just a few other sources can be used to find external surveys for emerging risks are to look at competitors' 10K filings. Just to name some of the available resources—North Carolina State University, Protiviti executive perspectives, Corporate Executive Board (now known as Gartner) Core Emerging Risk Report, AON Global Risk Management Survey, PwC Annual Globe CEO Survey, and NAVEX Global Top Ten Risk and Compliance Trends. There are many, many more but these are the sources that were well connected with companies we worked with in the past. We have used all of them to monitor and assess report focused on change that could affect the way business operates considering emerging risk, microeconomic risks in megatrends. They provide an external perspective of risks that can be used to assess completeness of a risk universe.

CHAPTER 9

Competitor and Industry Public Information

It is a good practice to review the 10K reports for your competitors at least annually to see what risk factors they are considering. These are very useful even though they may be vague or just of an emerging nature.

The robustness of each company's ERM program varies, and some may be more helpful than others. However, publishing risk factors in a financial reporting requirement should be included and comprehensive. Figure 9.1 shows an example of the annual review for the semiconductor industry.

Usually, an analysis was performed of the risk factors for at least 10 competitors of various sized and geographical footprint. It was noted that there was a total of 67 different risk topics just among the 10 competitors. The risk factors were captured from all the competitors in an Excel worksheet as shown in Figure 9.2, including the column headings across the top for all the competitors as well as our company. Just to point out that most of this information is publicly available and accessible and needs to be considered.

As the 10K risk factors are compared, there will, of course, be some differences. ERM team just needs to highlight in red those where the competitors have a stronger dialogue, especially if such risk is not in a company risk register. Conversely, where we found a risk topic that is in a company's risk register and not in those of other companies it may represent an opportunity to exploit a risk to our company benefit.

Different types of analysis can be performed of the competitors' 10K risk factors when compared to a company. There is also the benefit of reading and digesting the competitors risk topics to see if a company ERM team could or should further modify the risk statements.

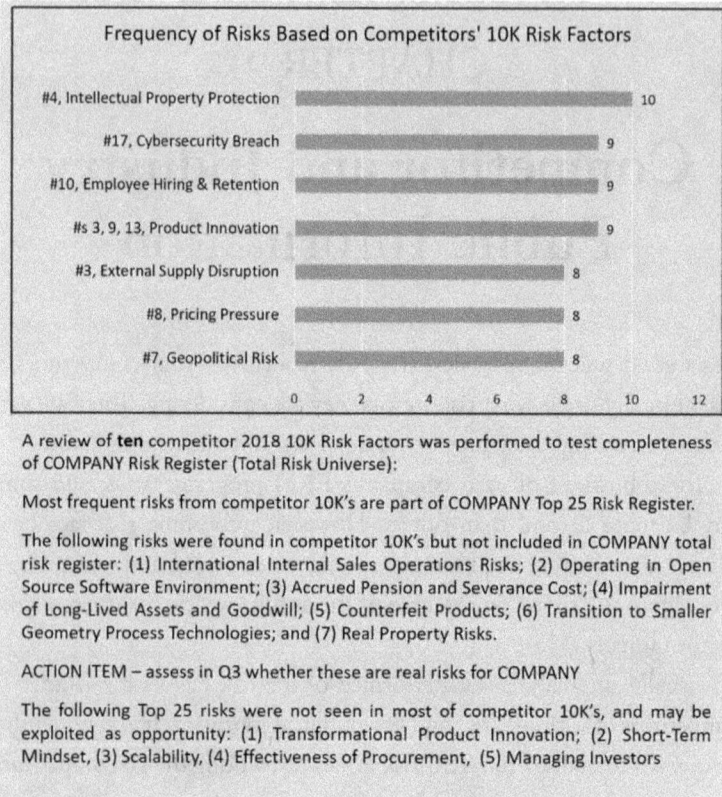

Frequency of Risks Based on Competitors' 10K Risk Factors

Risk	Value
#4, Intellectual Property Protection	10
#17, Cybersecurity Breach	9
#10, Employee Hiring & Retention	9
#s 3, 9, 13, Product Innovation	9
#3, External Supply Disruption	8
#8, Pricing Pressure	8
#7, Geopolitical Risk	8

A review of **ten** competitor 2018 10K Risk Factors was performed to test completeness of COMPANY Risk Register (Total Risk Universe):

Most frequent risks from competitor 10K's are part of COMPANY Top 25 Risk Register.

The following risks were found in competitor 10K's but not included in COMPANY total risk register: (1) International Internal Sales Operations Risks; (2) Operating in Open Source Software Environment; (3) Accrued Pension and Severance Cost; (4) Impairment of Long-Lived Assets and Goodwill; (5) Counterfeit Products; (6) Transition to Smaller Geometry Process Technologies; and (7) Real Property Risks.

ACTION ITEM – assess in Q3 whether these are real risks for COMPANY

The following Top 25 risks were not seen in most of competitor 10K's, and may be exploited as opportunity: (1) Transformational Product Innovation; (2) Short-Term Mindset, (3) Scalability, (4) Effectiveness of Procurement, (5) Managing Investors

Figure 9.1 Risk comparison against competitor 10K risk factors

Rank	Risk Topic	Risk Description	FUJITSU	MARVELL
4	Intellectual Property Protection	Intellectual Property protection is critical for the semiconductor industry as Company's design and manufacturing depends on a strong and balanced patent system and strong protection over	Risks associated with the manufacture and sale of similar products developed by third parties using the Group's own intellectual property Risks of infringing on other companies............................	We may be unable to protect our intellectual property, which would negatively affect our ability to compete. We have been named as a party to several legal proceedings and may be named..................

Figure 9.2 Sample register of competitor 10K risk factor comparison

Rank	Risk Topic	Risk Description	MICRON
1	International Internal Sales Operations Risks:		. Our international sales and operations are subject to a variety of risks, including: •export and import duties, changes to import and export regulations, customs regulations and processes, and restrictions on the transfer of funds; •compliance with U.S. and international laws involving international operations, including the Foreign Corrupt Practices Act of 1977, as amended, export and import laws, and similar rules and regulations;..

Above is an example of a risk in a competitors 10K, but not in the Company's risk profile, requiring further research to ensure that the Company's risk profile was complete in this area.

Rank	Risk Topic	Risk Description	FUJITSU	MARVELL
10	Short-Term Mindset	Some management leaders are concerned that Company may be too focused on short-term profits. The Company may not be adequately investing in its employees, in research, or in technology....................		

Above is an example of a risk in the Company's risk profile, but not in a competitors 10K risk factors. This could suggest an opportunity exploit our risk to the Company's advantage.

Figure 9.3 Competitor 10K risk factor comparison

CHAPTER 10

Monitoring Risk Events to Stock Price Changes

Correlation, Not Cause

Another analysis that can help show the effectiveness of the ERM program is by documenting major share price changes in relation to events occurred around the same time (as shown in Figure 10.1). This is not to say that these events caused the price to change but could potentially show some correlation to the subject matter. The events that are recorded are not just events that are related only to a company, but rather impacting the overall market or industry, or events that relate to competitors such as mergers and acquisitions or bankruptcies. Some of the events that happen during the same time of stock price changes and should be recorded in risk profile register are major marketing and sales campaigns and as noted—all joint ventures and acquisitions. Again, this is not suggesting that this type of analysis is going to explain the movement in stock price, but it does give executive leadership team some insights how the current events and topics that may potentially impact the company financials. Clearly, some core acquisitions will likely impact a company strategy and such analysis is of particular interest to the Investor Relations team.

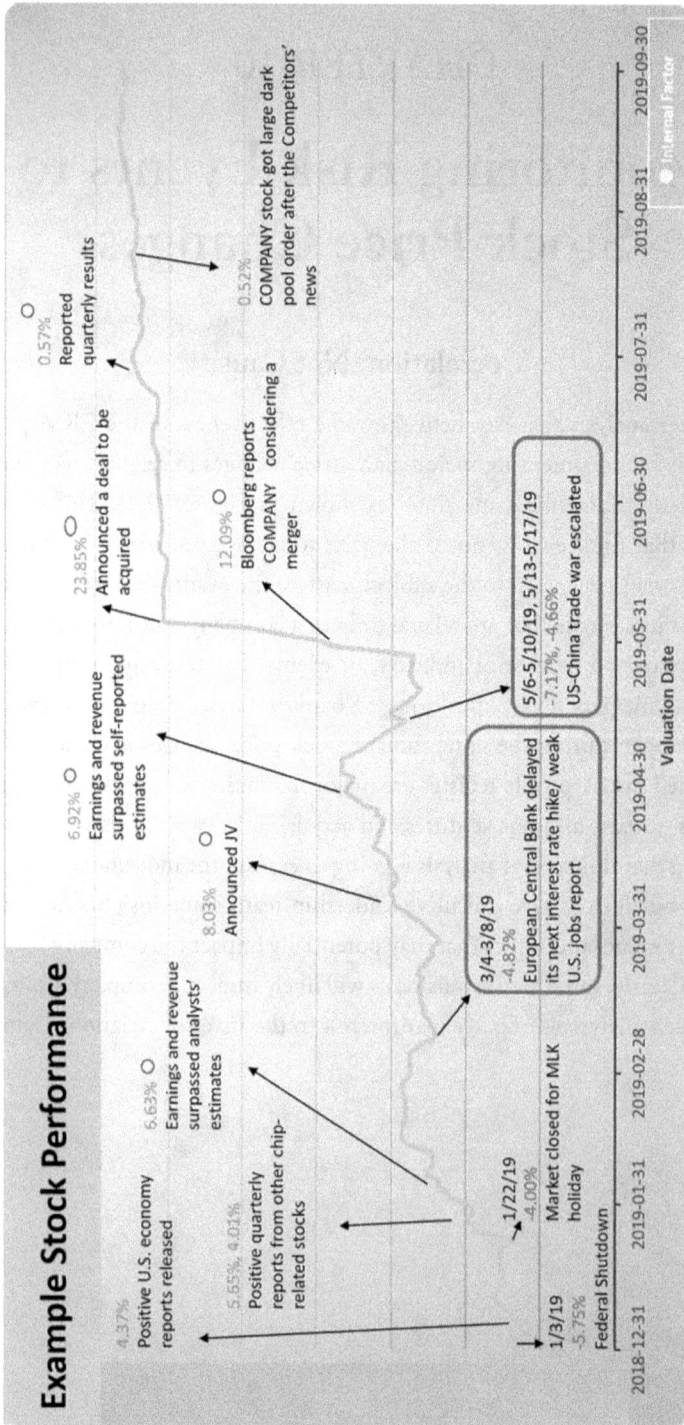

Figure 10.1 Example stock price analysis

CHAPTER 11

PESTLE Analysis Method

Some risks are extremely difficult to assess, especially if they are external to a company, or if there are "macro" type influences on your company (such as environmental, economic, geopolitical, societal, etc.). One way to help define these risks is to consider using the PESTLE analysis method. The PESTLE analysis has many uses and helps a company to determine its strategy. It considers all various influential (and often local) factors that can affect a company's products—regulatory, child labor, acts of nature, and other unique types, which certainly are not within the control of a company and its leadership. It is broadly used by many companies such as those shown in Figure 11.1.

There are six categories of the PESTLE process (see Figure 11.2):

1. Political risks,
2. Economic risks,
3. Social Cultural risks,
4. Technological risks,
5. Legal risks, and
6. Environmental risks.

As you continue to perform your risk assessment process, just think back about two years and remember the impact of certain risks that happened (such as COVID-19 pandemic or conflict in Ukraine) and presented companies with unexpected issues. All supply chain activities were hit hard, which subsequently rippled into sales. It became clear that most current supply chains were not "built" to adjust to such events. The dependency of companies on other countries became even more obvious, especially when it comes to logistics, materials/components, and production—such as China (rare earth minerals, manufacturing), Taiwan

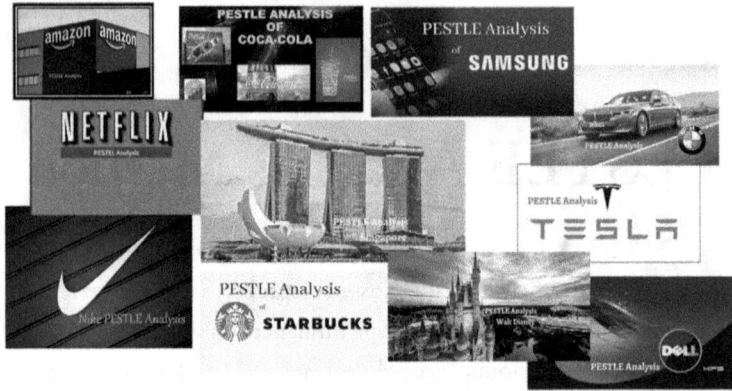

Figure 11.1 PESTLE analysis—across the globe

Figure 11.2 PESTLE analysis model

(components), Ukraine (neon, wheat), just to name few examples. Most companies scrambled to alter their supply chain model in order to survive.

We will go through each one of the PESTLE risk categories in more detail as follows:

Political risks: One can certainly understand how supply chain and third-party risks became a major factor for a company. There are many geopolitical factors surrounding these previously mentioned examples, which suggest that the global political landscape is extremely volatile in both countries with emerging economy as well as in countries with more established economies. There have been many examples of this, such as Brexit. The economic nationalism in the United States and the rise of populism throughout Europe have contributed to a dramatic political risk. As a result, the geopolitical factors by definition of the current day events create exposed risks to a company.

The globalization of markets and companies has ramped up the need to ensure there is a seamless and cost-efficient relationship with supply chain vendors. Most global companies have a footprint that covers most of the world, whether it is sales or supply chain to support the sales. There are many factors related to political risks, such as the instability of the political environment, where the change of leadership can shift the direction of a country's future and relationships with other countries. In many countries, there are also many levels of corruption in bureaucracy. And of course, the freedom of speech and press and the rule of law dramatically differs across the globe, which means that companies have to understand the local regulations and what drives the political behavior of a country and adjust the strategy accordingly.

Also, within the political area is the vast regulation and deregulation over many industries that are constantly changing. As a result of some of the changes, the impact on international trade, tariffs, and taxes (that impact not only the cost of a company's product but also their ability or inability to meet on-time deliveries) can be significant. The amount of legislation that has been developed over the last decade or so—to protect the environment, workers, and consumers—has increased 10-fold and requires companies to adapt.

In conclusion, all of these factors require a company to be proactive in the risk management process. This does not apply only to current products and relationships, but also to those that are strategic for the company's future. These are the key areas in both short term and particularly long term for a company to be able to achieve their growth and profit targets. The PESTLE analysis can facilitate such proactive work and assist in making strategic decisions in the best interest of a company.

Economic risks: There are many economic factors such as working capital flow needed to develop the business capabilities, and also the consumption and production that is required for business success, both current as well as future to ensure a profitability in the long term.

There are several ways governments can influence the countries' economic factors, and come primarily through taxation and tax laws, as well as managing interest rates. Interest rates, foreign exchange rates, taxes, and even inflation and recession, as well as the changes in demand can create substantial risk to companies. Interest rates, for example, particularly have a relevance for companies that have interest-bearing assets and the risks really arrive from that as interest rates fluctuate. Most companies must establish lines of credit and basic loans to be able to meet the cash flow needs of their business strategy.

Exchange rates also have a direct impact on what a company must pay its international vendors. Most exchange rates are very volatile and can be volatile even over a very short period of time, which can change all the rules related to importing and exporting goods and services.

Social risks: Societal risks not only affect present day but also impact future business, especially for companies intending to expand into new markets. Within this category, there are several demographic factors that need to be taken into consideration from the diversity of the people (including income and education base, as well as their gender and background), and the frequency for which they depend on immigration. The population growth and patterns of births and deaths are also important factors, as well as the age distribution reduces the population of workers to contribute to countries' economies and ultimately provide workforce for a company.

Societal risks also include personal beliefs such as religion. There are many followers of major religions who are driven by a tremendous influence of their religious leaders. There are also other types of beliefs such as local mythologies that influence behavior. These are potential risks that one just does not normally think about until they actually start doing a PESTLE analysis. While they seem to be a little bit benign in severity, they can become very significant very quickly.

Technology risks: Every company needs to anticipate changes especially when it comes to future technologies, as they will affect a company from both an operational standpoint as well as from a product development standpoint. Some of the most important technological factors gaining rapid attention today include cyberattacks, data theft and fraud, personally identifiable information fraud, and so on. On a positive note, some technologies such as artificial intelligence, machine learning, and natural language processing create a new era of more efficient information gathering and processing to influence business decisions. Risks then become relative to accuracy and timeliness of information and the decisions.

Many of the technology risks can be very disruptive. For example, the changes in technology had changed the music and entertainment industry dramatically, from the types of media the music was distributed on to online streaming today. Service organizations had to adapt their business models. For example, a group of service providers replaced the taxis in many cities. These changes happened fairly rapidly and offered more efficiency. Many taxi companies did not anticipate this shift and found themselves to be in a very dismal financial situation.

Some changes have longer acceptance period before such innovations are beginning to be accepted. For example, blockchain and cryptocurrency have been around for several years, but it was not until some of the major companies, such as Google and Tesla, started to buy cryptocurrencies and in the process boosted the technology behind the blockchain.

Other examples include self-driving and electric cars. When you think about those innovations, there is a certain number of legal risks that can amount exponentially. Supplying batteries for hybrid or electric cars or supplying batteries for solar power backups have indeed changed many companies' or country's technology focus, but they all represent certain level of financial risk that will ultimately impact a company's strategic risks.

Environmental risks: These types of risks are becoming even more important, especially in the context of global warming and climate change. With the numbers of wildfires, tsunamis, earthquakes, volcanic eruptions, and so on, there is likely to be another dramatic impact on supply chain efficiency. While natural disasters are becoming more frequent and are undeniably a result of climate change, the climate change alone is often underestimated because of the perception of "long time" required for the climate to change. However, when these events happen, they have a major catastrophic impact on all facets of business. The impact of floods in Thailand on hard drive industry in 2011 was historical. The pandemic over the last two years affected freight transport, customs at the import harbors, and so on, and continue to breed a layer of risk at all levels and all steps of a company's business model.

The good news is that since there are now more environmental concerns than before, regulations to protect the environment are becoming much stronger though in many cases they also create legal liabilities. While companies may take advantage of the few areas where the regulations are still relaxed, but ultimately doing so presents high reputational risk to a company.

Another topic within this category is the renewable materials, whether there is excess supply or restricted supply, and supply versus demand. Oil shortage has also created a great range of financial risks for organizations. The cost of transport has gone up dramatically to the extent that companies are required to absorb some of the higher freight cost and cannot always push all those additional cost onto consumers. Even if they are able to do so, the price increases generally lag the risks that are currently happening and could lag for two or more years before they are able to increase the prices to offset some of these more environmental or economical type of risks. Surcharges are becoming a common practice for many companies to counteract the cost increase in the short term. For some companies, it may be too late.

Legal risks: The PESTLE approach can be used very effectively especially in assessing those risks that relate to external influence and actions that are not within the control of a company and touch heavily on the geopolitical risks as well. This type of analysis is used by many Fortune 1000 companies, not only to assess the risks but also to help them understand new markets that they intend to start servicing. All the local laws and regulations, and economic conditions, can be very expensive if not recognized and anticipated in the very early expansion planning stage and incorporated into the business model.

CHAPTER 12

Porter's Five Force Analysis

When you think of an ERM program, one of the primary factors is to ensure that the risk profile related to the strategic elements of an organization/company are specifically assessed. As discussed earlier, the primary cause of business failures is typically the failure to identify and remediate strategic-oriented risks. Failures related to strategic elements were the root cause in around 86 percent of the companies whose capitalization reduced more than 50 percent during tested time period. The other elements were much lesser factor for a company's demise and generally related to compliance, financial reporting, and operational activities. Let us therefore focus on the strategic elements critical for a company to succeed.

Some of the key strategic elements include decline in core product demand, undiversified risk, and failure to identify price bubbles, poor acquisition target or merger integration, failure to expand alternative revenue sources, competitor infringement on core market, margin pressure, and senior management turnover. Those were the key strategic elements identified in publicly available information that drove the demise of leading 200 companies where the market cap fell by more than 50 percent. Therefore, since these strategic failures are the most frequent decline drivers, an ERM program must focus heavily on strategic elements in addition to the operational compliance and financial elements.

Most companies will have 5-to-10-year strategic plans that they are working toward. This plan gets updated every year to include the changes in many elements, either external or within the company. Resources within the company, which include people, systems, infrastructure, capital assets, manufacturing equipment, and so on, are major components of the strategic direction. While they are all integral parts of the strategic direction, they must meld into the strategic direction of a company's business model, the product line, the product mix, the target market, or the customers and the geographic area that a company wishes to serve and may also include other types of activities.

How does a company develop strategic direction over a 5-to-10-year period? There are many sources that help companies to develop it. However, the most helpful from an ERM perspective (when the ERM Administrative Team looks at strategic versus other types of elements in the risk profile) are:

1. **PESTLE** analysis (already mentioned in the previous chapter), which is used by many companies.
2. **Porter's Five Forces** analysis—an analytical tool, which has been utilized in many companies as it is a little bit easier to adapt to an ERM assessment. It is a very well-acknowledged model. See the following Figure 12.1.

The primary publication that introduced this style of analysis was written by Michael Porter in the book *Competitive Strategy: Techniques for Analyzing Industries and Competitors*. The first edition of this book was published in 1980. This analysis model has also been widely used in particular to analyze industry structure of a company, as well as its corporate strategy.

This analysis helps to explain why various industries can generate different levels of profitability and under which types of conditions. The book identifies five specific forces that play a major part (with some

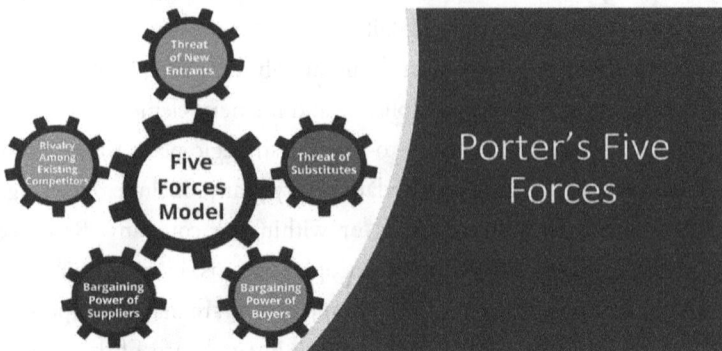

Figure 12.1 Porter's five forces

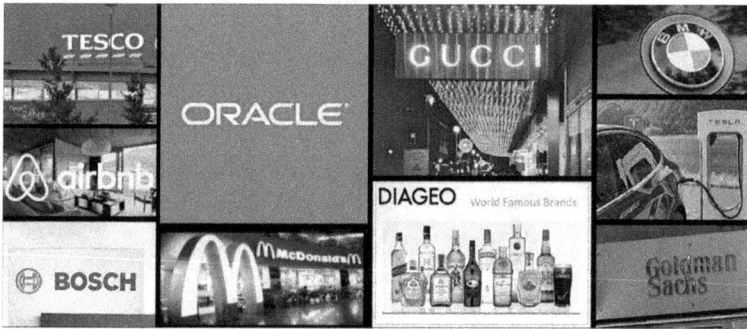

Figure 12.2 Porter's five forces analysis—across all industries

caveats of course) about shaping the industry and the market on a global basis. The five forces are generally used to measure the intensity of the competition, the profitability of the industry or market, as well as a general overall attractiveness in that market.

While both Porter's Five Forces and PESTLE analysis models can be used to improve competitive positions, Porter's Five Forces helps to digest and understand where the balance of power lies related to your competition, while PESTLE talks more about the various macro environmental factors that affect not only the entire industry and your competitors but also your organization/company. Both are similar in nature but provide slightly different angles. There are many companies that have successfully used Porter's Five Forces, some of which are shown in the Figure 12.2.

The Porter's Five Forces include **Threat of New Entrants, Power of Buyers, Threat of Substitute, Power of Suppliers**, and **Competitive Rivalry** as shown in Figure 12.3, and will be discussed in more detail.

Threat of New Entrants: Assessing the risks of a company is going to need to address threats related to new entrants. They must have a thorough understanding of the competitors' primary purpose (such as gaining market share, etc.). Most of the time, gaining market share is the primary focus. The success in entering any particular market depends on the barriers of entry present in that market. The larger or higher the barriers of entry for new entrants, the smaller the risk is for the "established" companies. Conversely, when the barriers of entry are low, the risk of new entrants is much higher for the incumbents.

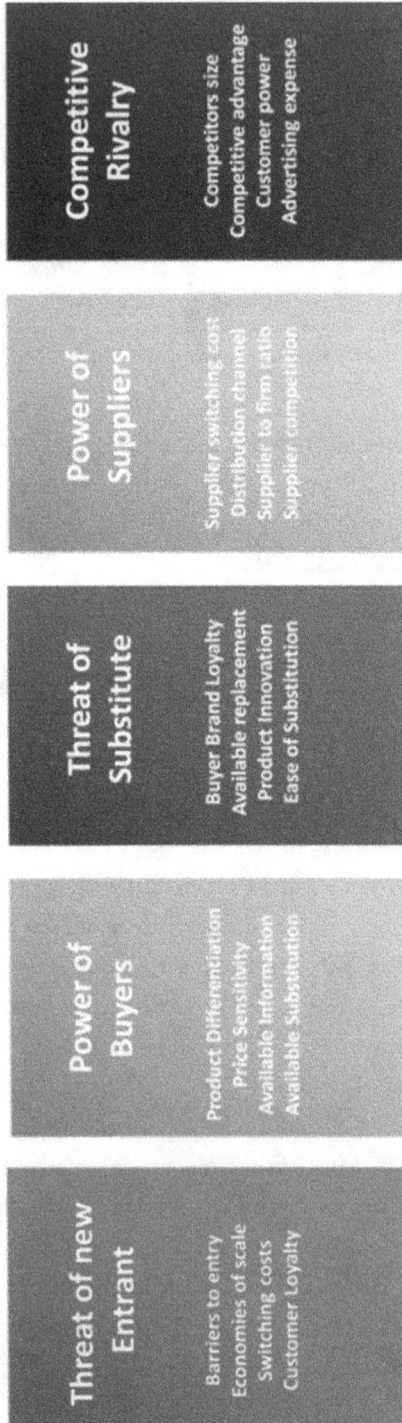

Porter's Five Forces

Threat of new Entrant
Barriers to entry
Economies of scale
Switching costs
Customer Loyalty

Power of Buyers
Product Differentiation
Price Sensitivity
Available Information
Available Substitution

Threat of Substitute
Buyer Brand Loyalty
Available replacement
Product Innovation
Ease of Substitution

Power of Suppliers
Supplier switching cost
Distribution channel
Supplier to firm ratio
Supplier competition

Competitive Rivalry
Competitors size
Competitive advantage
Customer power
Advertising expense

Figure 12.3 Porter's five forces

When we think about the level of difficulty to enter a market, there are several categories used to describe the barriers of entry. One is **economies of scale**; two is high **customer loyalty** or **brand loyalty**; three is the **size of capital requirements**; four, the need for **cumulative experience**; five would be **government policies and regulations**; and six would be the **distribution channel access**. All of these play a very important role in entering a new market. There are other barriers of entry that apply or would apply to a specific industry and a company (e.g., freedom to operate related to applicable technology and patent coverage, and others).

The threat of new entrants is not only just a short-term risk but it also applies more to the middle-term or longer term type of risks. While a company cannot predict when new competitors will enter a market, it usually takes a formidable competitor and a substantial amount of time to enter a market. Therefore, to assess the risks related to the threat of new entrants, one must assess the likelihood of such events to happen. Industry changes such as mergers and acquisitions, as well as divestitures and bankruptcies can trigger such events. An organization/company must be able to react relatively quickly to new entrants to the market. Whether an organization/company has that capability is another question, and further amplifies the risk of new entrants.

Bargaining Power of Suppliers: To assess how much strength and balance of power suppliers have over an organization/company, the supply chain must be analyzed. Do they have the high potential of raising prices without a notice? Do they have the ability to reduce or increase their supply? Do they have the ability to manipulate or manage their product availability?

The COVID-19 pandemic has shown a prime example of the bargaining power of suppliers as well as the bargaining power of companies. The bargaining power of suppliers stemmed from knowing they have a product that your company needs, knowing whether a comparable quality product may be readily available elsewhere, or if a product is not available anywhere. They played their upper hand in the cases where they are the sole source supplier of products and parts that a company needs. Note, we did not say single source—we said sole source. Single source means that a company has several suppliers to choose from and decides to select a single supplier to gain more purchasing power based on quantity. A sole source means there is virtually no other option and a company must purchase from that supplier, and because the supplier knows it, they can manipulate the price, quantity, and availability.

Bargaining Power of Buyers: This power is established at two levels. A manufacturer must buy raw materials or components from its suppliers to build products, therefore a manufacturer is the buyer. A customer is buying the final product from a manufacturer, and therefore the customer is the buyer. The basic philosophy works the same regardless of the position a company is in—either a manufacturer or a customer. In both scenarios, buyers can put pressure on the suppliers. The buyers have a lot of power if there are few of them in total and when there are many alternative suppliers from whom to buy. This is particularly true when it is easy for the buyers to switch from one supplier to another. But the buying power is very low when the buyers buy in small dollar amounts and particularly when the supplier's product is quite different from that of other competitive suppliers.

Therefore, when assessing the bargaining power of both suppliers and buyers, analyze the risk of having applicable types of dependencies, or balance of power, or lack of power, whether from your supply chain or from your customers. This will help in determining whether the company can absorb these types of situations and if its margins can absorb the negative impacts.

Threat of Substitute Products: Customers have the option of deciding how they want to purchase their products. Most competitive products are generally available from multiple suppliers and with relatively small differentiation in quality or functionality. This gives customers the ability to consider alternatives beyond their established suppliers. Products may serve a similar purpose and may just have different branding, different components, or even multiple uses. Being able to assess the risk of your company related to substitute products means one must understand the type of products, and whether each of the products are considered a commodity. It all makes a world of difference on the inherent risks as well as residual risks for your company.

Rivalry Among Existing Competitors: The next step is to assess your competitors' landscape including the number and strengths of your competitors. A company needs to identify how many competitors would be considered its rivals, and if the quality of their products and services is comparable to a company's products and services.

Where the competition is most intense, the competing companies will typically attempt to attract customers by launching high-impact marketing campaigns and may also aggressively cut down prices. However, in doing so they can make it easy for suppliers and buyers to go elsewhere if they feel that they are being pressured or squeezed for a margin or are not receiving a competitive deal from these competing companies. Conversely, where competition is low, and not many companies offer what a company does, then a company is likely to have more power as well as stronger margins.

In summary, it is important to remember the difference between the elements being reviewed using the PESTLE model and the Porter's Five Forces model. The PESTLE model will generally deal with factors that are more temporary in nature, such as industry growth rates, government interventions, and technological innovations. The Porter's Five Forces are more permanent parts of an industry's structure. However, both these forms of modeling are effective when trying to assess enterprise risks.

CHAPTER 13

The Three Lines of Defense (3LoD)

Most companies have multiple types of audit activities that take place throughout the organization. Examples could include quality control, supplier audits, distributor audits, process improvement functions, environmental testing, security audits, systems intrusion testing, and many others. All of these are generally performed by independent groups primarily to:

- comply with contractual terms and conditions;
- create more reliable products;
- comply with regulatory requirements;
- create more efficient and effective processes; and
- address other risk elements.

Typically, these groups are not cross-functional in nature, nor are there any synergies gained from their efforts. The primary common characteristic is that they are addressing risks of an organization. Does it make sense to have all these separate functions working relentlessly in silos to improve the company's performance without realizing or recognizing any synergies? This question brings us to our next topic—Three Lines of Defense (3LoD) model. The 3LoD model has been around for many years and was initially created by the military and later adapted in sporting events. After years of its existence in different "applications," the 3LoD was formalized for business purpose as the 3LoD model developed in 2008–2010 by the Federation of European Risk Management Associations (FERMA) and the European Confederation of Institutes of Internal Auditing (ECIIA) as a guidance for the 8th EU Directive stating in Section 41, 2b: "[...] the audit committee shall, inter alia: monitor the effectiveness of the company's internal control, internal audit where applicable, and risk management systems [...]."

While this definition is relatively vague, it has been a basis from which organizations and companies have structured their governance model. See the 3LoD model shown in Figure 13.1.

It seems only logical that the 3LoD activities should also be deeply engaged into the risk management function at all levels.

After the initial introduction of 3LoD, it is now time to share why we brought up the 3LoD topic in the first place. Let's consider a situation where a company CFO and CEO needed to respond to the organizations within their company that were experiencing audit fatigue. This fatigue was ostensibly being caused by the Internal Audit Department conducting an excessive number of audits in a very uncoordinated manner. These organizations claimed that there were overlapping audits, duplicative audits, surprise audits, audits lacking follow up, and so on. From a company's Chief Audit Executive point of view, it became obvious that the main reason for this was a wide misconception as to "who" the auditors were conducting all of these audits, because the company audit plan had only four audits spread out over the year.

The next mission then was to dig deeper to understand the sources of these allegations against the company's Chief Audit Executive function. After just a few conversations, it became abundantly clear that the sources of these audits were both internal and external to the company, and the vast majority were not from the Global Internal Audit function. After the reasons for the allegations were clarified, the company created the 3LoD model, as seen in Figure 13.2. This illustration was used to introduce the concept to the company's CFO and CEO, prior to requesting cooperation from other company's organizations to embark on the formal 3LoD program roll out.

A summary of the 3LoD elements is discussed as follows.

First Line of Defense includes the frontline activities that are conducted by the day-to-day operations, such as the direct labor (for example) in a manufacturing company. This level is really about the people and culture built into the primary functions of a company.

Second Line of Defense includes the group that monitors activities and mitigates risks related to real-time functions. Examples could include

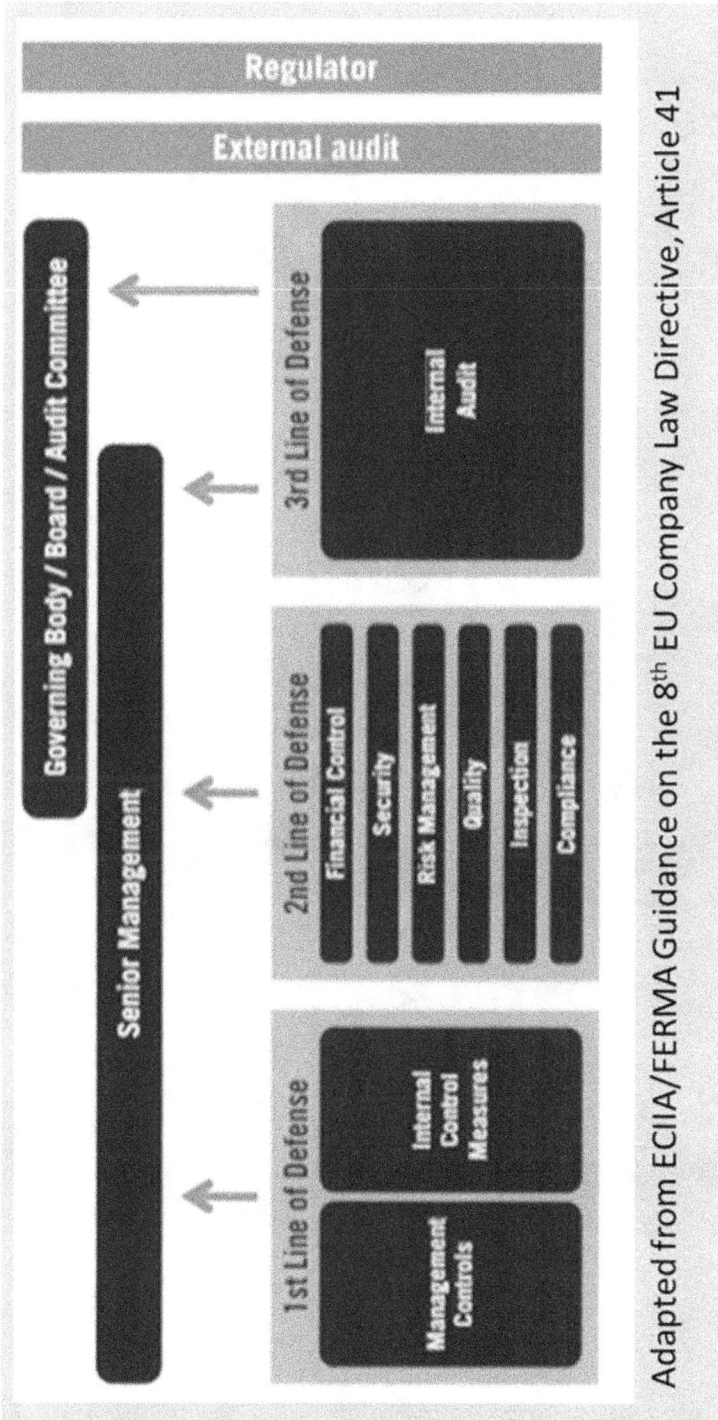

Figure 13.1 The three lines of defense model

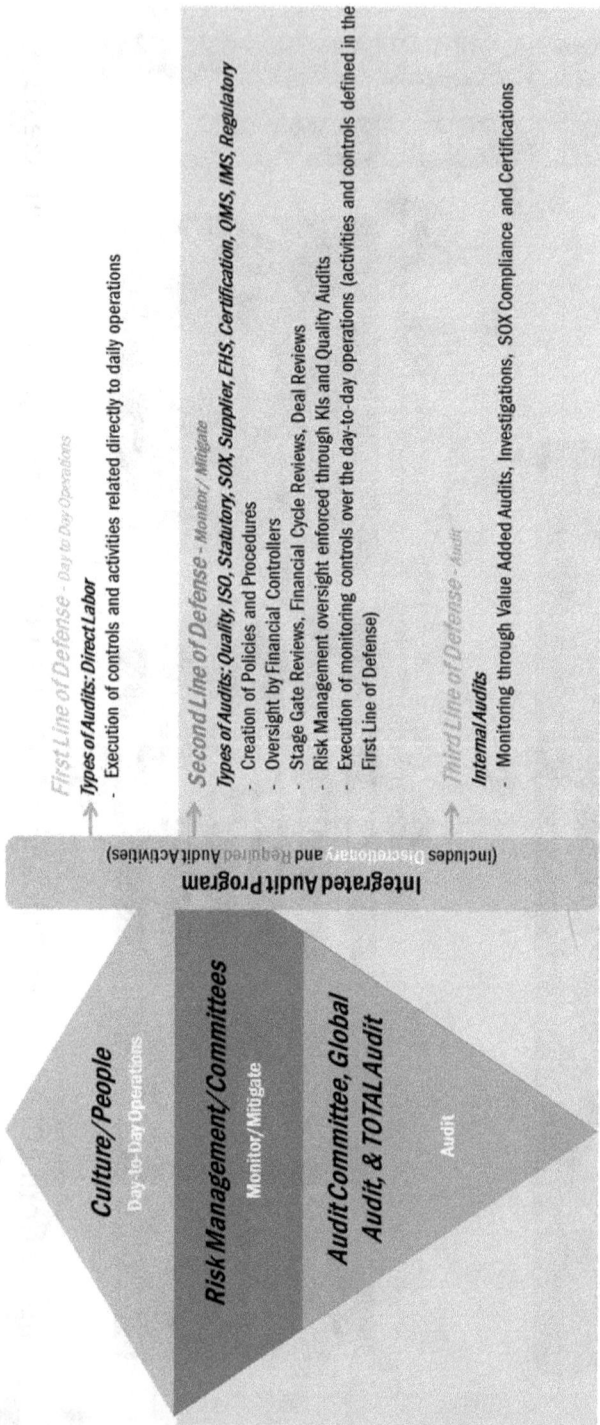

Figure 13.2 *Three lines of defense applied to an actual company*

committees assigned to particular job functions resulting in the end product, or risk monitoring activities performed on periodic and ongoing intervals. Other forms of this line of defense are shown as follows:

- Creation of Policies and Procedures;
- Oversight by Financial Controllers;
- Stage Gate Reviews;
- Financial Cycle Reviews;
- Deal Reviews;
- Risk Management oversight enforced through Key Performance Indicators and quality defined in the First Line of Defense.

Third Line of Defense includes the highest level of monitoring and reporting of risks and performance. This level of coverage is best illustrated by the efforts of a company's Internal Audit team, with oversight from the Audit Committee of the Board. Some views also include as a Line of Defense the external auditors of public companies. However, they along with external regulators may be better described as the fourth line of defense. But for the purposes of this book, we will only discuss those lines of defense that are "internal" to a company.

The next step is to refresh the problem statement to the broader executive team and present the purpose and benefits of the project. Some preparatory work must be done to assess the breadth of the audit activities for the recent 12-month period. As a primer, the following diagram (Figure 13.3) can be tailored to relate specifically to a company business model including the volume of hours by audit activity.

Prior to discussing the details of the company's specific project, here is an overview of the 3LoD structure and the general description of the departments for this specific project.

The First Line of Defense

There were two areas within the first line of defense, which monitored the ongoing quality in real time and generally consisted of about 3,000 man-hours. The two groups were mostly production-line driven and shown

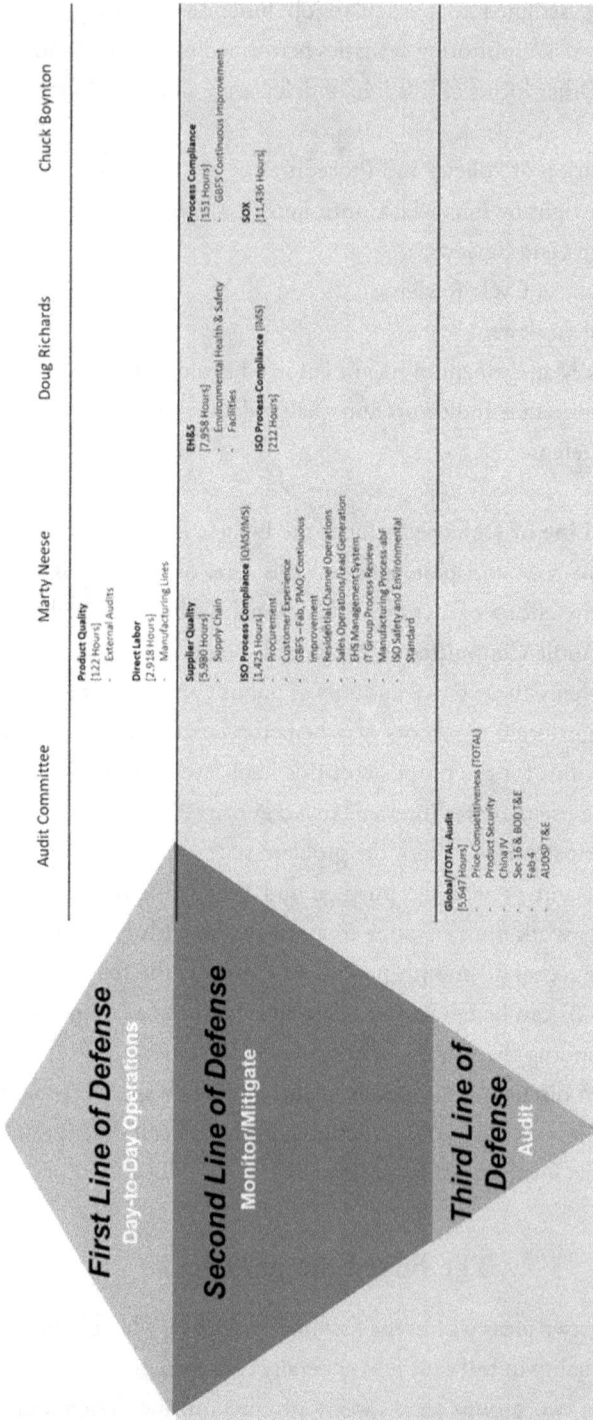

Figure 13.3 *Details of the three lines of defense activities*

as quality and direct labor. Neither of these groups performed an actual manufacturing process but were involved in testing to ensure there were no major deviations on the production line at key points of the process.

The Second Line of Defense

The second line of defense consisted primarily of four focus areas. **Supplier audits**, which were performed by the Supply Chain Department, were around 6,000 man-hours per year. The **ISO process compliance** organization devoted about 1,400 hours of audit activity. The **Environmental Health and Safety** or EH&S devoted about 8,000 audit hours and as well, they also had some ISO process compliance a little over 200 hours. The **Finance** Department had its internal staff that devoted about 150 hours to conducting continuous improvement. And lastly, the second line of defense was about 11,500 hours for **Sarbanes–Oxley (SOX) compliance.**

The Third Line of Defense

This section included audits conducted by the company's Internal Audit Department as well as a parent Company Internal Audit Department (in this example project, a company belongs to a group of companies with a parent company representative in a company's Board of Director). The audits that were conducted during this period accumulated to about 6,000 hours.

Overall, of the total 36,150 audit hours reported, the first line of defense included 3,000 plus hours; second line of defense contributed a little over 27,000 hours; and third line of defense around 6,000 hours. This gives a relative feel for the audit hours dedicated to these 3LoD and the respective hours in this particular company. This relative portion spread among the 3LoDs may or may not be representative to other companies and should not be used as a benchmark. Some functions, such as Operations, were included both first line and second line of defense audit hours but were reported separately for this purpose.

The key takeaways from the overall project are shown in Figure 13.4. This provides a glimpse of the end results and will help to understand the relations while reading the remaining sections of this chapter.

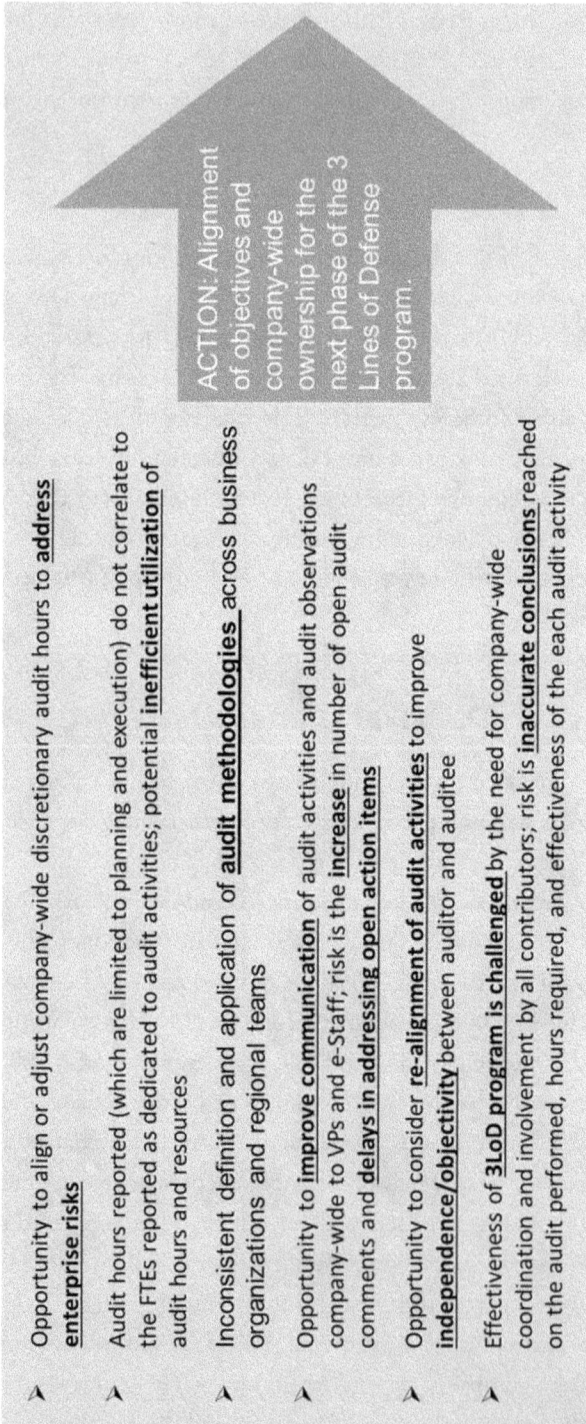

> Opportunity to align or adjust company-wide discretionary audit hours to **address enterprise risks**
>
> Audit hours reported (which are limited to planning and execution) do not correlate to the FTEs reported as dedicated to audit activities; potential **inefficient utilization** of audit hours and resources
>
> Inconsistent definition and application of **audit methodologies** across business organizations and regional teams
>
> Opportunity to **improve communication** of audit activities and audit observations company-wide to VPs and e-Staff; risk is the **increase** in number of open audit comments and **delays in addressing open action items**
>
> Opportunity to consider **re-alignment of audit activities** to improve **independence/objectivity** between auditor and auditee
>
> Effectiveness of **3LoD program is challenged** by the need for company-wide coordination and involvement by all contributors; risk is **inaccurate conclusions** reached on the audit performed, hours required, and effectiveness of the each audit activity

ACTION: Alignment of objectives and company-wide ownership for the next phase of the 3 Lines of Defense program.

Figure 13.4 Lines of defense—key takeaways

Project

The project began with the Overview and Objectives as shown in Figure 13.5.

Overview of 3 Lines of Defense Activities
- Obtained and analyzed audit hours and audit comments reported by COMPANY teams across the organization, which includes:
- Assessment of audit hours, specifically the association with each line of defense and required vs discretionary
- Assessment of FTEs reported to audit hours planned for the fiscal year
- Assessment of audit hours vs enterprise risks
- Identified and analyze opportunities to reduce audit hours (due to overlap)

Objectives of 3 Lines of Defense Program
- Improve communication of audits impacting eStaff (and their teams)
- Provide details regarding required and discretionary audit activities (and the areas/risks in which they address)
- Evaluate opportunities to reduce "audit fatigue".
- Increase effectiveness and efficiency of audit programs.
- Communication of audit issues to enable timely closure and high level assessment of audit observation themes

Figure 13.5 Overview and objectives of three lines of defense

Another element that was captured for these 3LoD audit hours were related to whether the audit hours were **required** *(compliance oriented)* or **discretionary** *(based on internal performance need)*. Figure 13.6 shows the total hours by function and a breakdown of required versus discretionary.

Nearly all of the Operations Department hours and the third line of defense Internal Audit Department hours were viewed as discretionary. Although one could view the Internal Audit hours might be required (compliance oriented), the audit team viewed it as discretionary for this project because it was not fulfilling any particular legal regulatory compliance commitment.

Actual to FTE Count

The next step was to analyze the auditor efforts and efficiency for the year in each of these areas. The team had the audit hours reported (as you remember) of 36,150 (Figure 13.6). The next step was to compare that to the actual full-time equivalent (FTE) of employees who worked in those particular departments that were assigned to this audit activity (see Figure 13.7).

Overview of the audit hours by the e-Staff directing the audits

Lines of Defense

First Line   [3,152 Hours (9%)]
Second Line   [27,231 Hours (75%)]
Third Line   [5,767 Hours (16%)]
Total Reported Hours 36,150

Audit Committee — 5,767
Marty Neese — 3,152 / 7,774
Doug Richards — 7,958
Chuck Boynton — 11,499

Discretionary vs. Required

Discretionary   [17,042 Hours (47%)]
Required   [19,108 Hours (53%)]

Audit Committee — 5,767
Marty Neese — 10,926
Doug Richards — 28 / 2,672
Chuck Boynton — 65 / 11,475

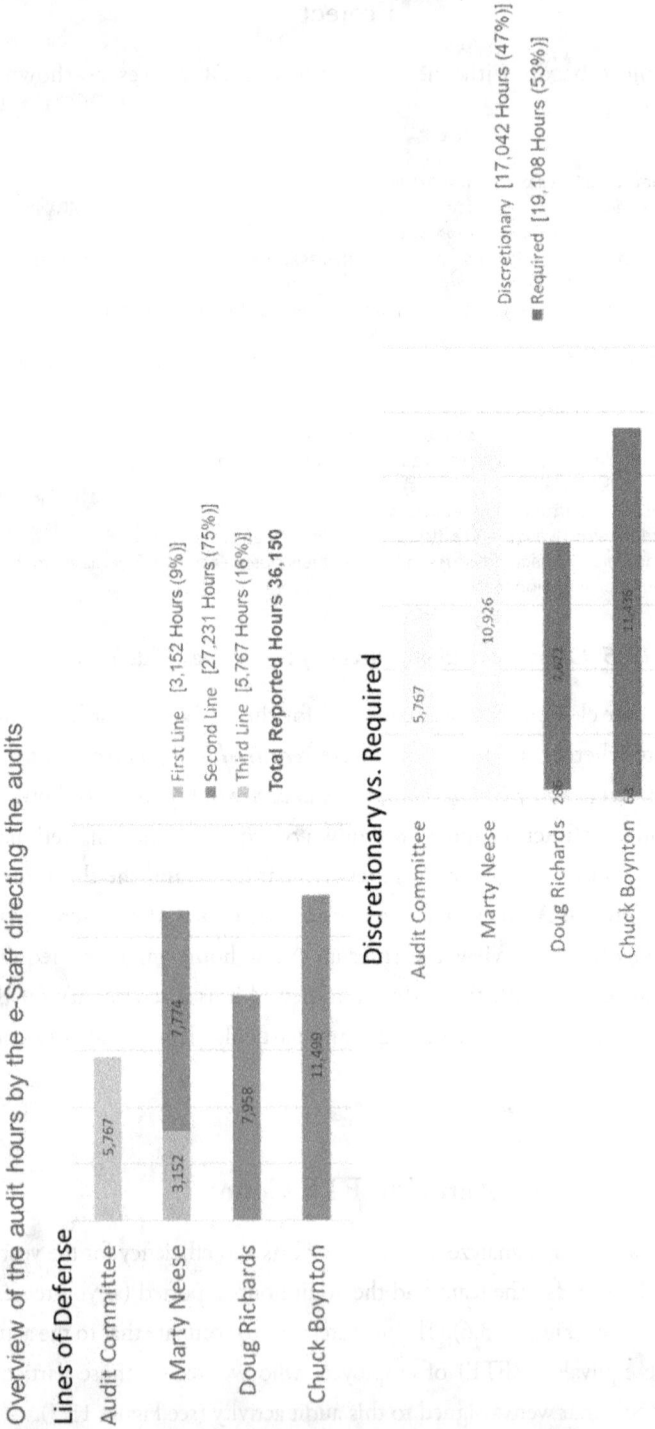

Figure 13.6 Audit hours

Department	Direct Manager	VP	e-Staff	Audit Type	# of Auditors (FTE)
Quality Assurance – SPML	NAME	NAME	NAME	Process Compliance / IMS	8
Quality Assurance – SPMM	NAME	NAME	NAME	Process Compliance	3
Quality Management System - NA	NAME	NAME	NAME	Process Compliance	1
Quality Management System - EMEA	NAME	NAME	NAME	Process Compliance	2
Quality Management System - SPMX	NAME	NAME	NAME	Process Compliance / IMS / Certification	3
Downstream Quality	NAME	NAME	NAME	Supplier Quality	3
Upstream Quality	NAME	NAME	NAME	Supplier Quality	1
Upstream Quality	NAME	NAME	NAME	Supplier Quality	1
EH&S	NAME	NAME	NAME	EH&S	1
EH&S (Construction)	NAME	NAME	NAME	EH&S	6
Continuous Improvement (GBFS)	NAME	NAME	NAME	Process Compliance	1
Global Audit	NAME	NAME	NAME	SOX	6
Global Audit	NAME	JNAME	Audit Committee	Value-Add Audit	4
				Total	**40**

Figure 13.7 *Audit-specific FTE reported*

The reported actual audit hours worked being the planning and field work only, which came back to the 36,150 hours. The audit team made an assumption that each of these employees would also incur roughly 20 percent administrative time for training, holidays, vacation, and so on. Multiplying the full number of employees assigned to these audit functions (40 per above) by 2,080 hours per year equaled the total number of hours (83,200) that had to be accounted for, related to all the employees who were assigned in each of these audit areas.

As the team layered in the actual hours devoted specifically to the tasks, it generated a comparison of the total 83,200 devoted headcount hours to the 36,150 actual hours devoted specifically to auditing. See the following Figure 13.8.

The results indicated that there was a substantial amount of efficiency opportunity particularly in the Operations Department. Less than 50 percent of the Operations Department employee's hours were fully dedicated to their direct audit function activities. Obviously, they were doing many other things, perhaps following up on audit comments, possibly helping to design processes for the mitigation of the issues and reporting. However, those activities were not captured and most likely would not consume nearly that much time.

One would typically expect an audit department to have a model distribution of at least 70 percent allocated to audit planning and field work hours. The other remaining elements would include the 20 percent administration and 10 percent miscellaneous activities. If that allocation is compared to the functions noted, then Operations has more than 50 percent of the employees doing miscellaneous activities. Human Resources (EH&S) was roughly 25 percent absorbed by these more miscellaneous activities.

Just to emphasize the assumptions used, the audit team interviewed department heads in all departments in all functions, and the full head count numbers that came from the organization charts and confirmed those to be fully dedicated employees to the audit activities. They used the actual hours and reported them for field work and planning of audits. Then the audit team just plugged in the 20 percent administration.

The bigger picture assessment of the 45,000 hours did not account for any efficiency opportunities in audit planning and field work, which can represent significant man-hours.

A component of the 3 Lines of Defense program included evaluating the required FTEs compared to the audit hours reported.

➤ Audit Hours Reported => Hours reported for planned audit engagements (planning and fieldwork only)

➤ Admin Hours => PTOs, trainings and other administrative tasks (calculated as 20% of FTEs)

➤ Efficiency Opportunity => Although these hours may include audit specific activities, such as issue monitoring and analysis, follow-up actions, continuous improvement efforts, customer (auditee) support, and others; there is an opportunity to evaluate the hours incurred that are not directly associated with planning and fieldwork.

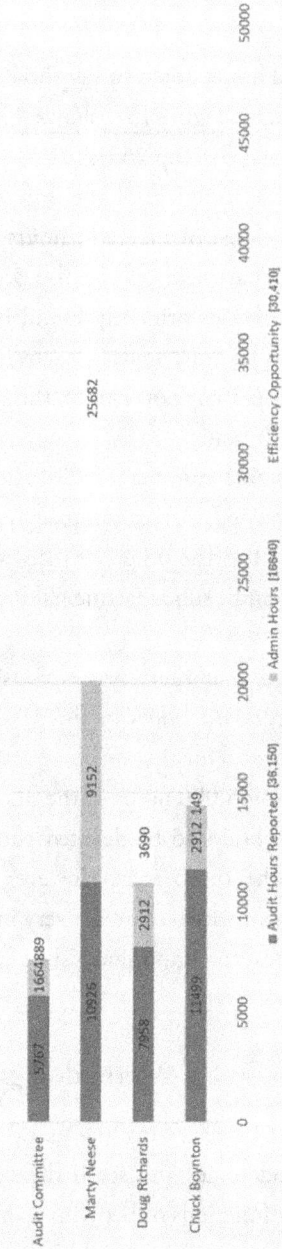

Note:
- FTE's were obtained by the audit area /owner. No specific assessment regarding accuracy of data provided was performed.
- Admin hours were calculated as 20% of the total hours of an FTE (2080 hours).
- FTE used assumes they are 100% dedicated to audit work.

Figure 13.8 Auditor efficiency analysis

ERM Matching

As mentioned earlier, the audit team already implemented the ERM program and had a Top 25 enterprisewide risks that the company would be remediating.

Those 45,000 hours noted earlier should ideally be allocated to larger risks of the company. Figure 13.9 shows the annual audit hours that were attached to auditing the Top 25 risks.

As you can see, only six of the Top 25 risks had any audit hours applied to them. Most of the audit hours applied really came from the Internal Audit Department on the Top 3. The audit team excluded the required audit activities primarily found in the EH&S and finance for SOX as they must be done anyway, regardless of whether they have a risk that falls in the Top 25 or not. Hence, this analysis was only composed of discretionary audit hours.

The only notable number of discretionary hours from the 3LoD audit activities related to risk number 16, the product design quality. So what happened to the other 19 risks, which received zero emphasis from the various audit subdepartments throughout the 3LoD within the company?

This indicated that there was a massive mismatch between available discretionary audit hours in the 3LoD against the largest risks of the organization.

With a total of 45,000 hours in the 3LoD, one would expect a higher number of those hours to be devoted particularly to the Top 10 risks, or preferable to the Top 5 risks. However, that was not the case in this particular company, which created a very inefficient use of precious audit resources to address the important risks of the company.

Methodologies

Another element of reviewing the audit activity for all 3LoD was to assess the methodologies and see if there were inconsistencies between the various audit functions or between team members who have the same function or by location. This would help to understand how structured the audit activities were.

Comparison of audit activities to the Top 25 Enterprise Risks

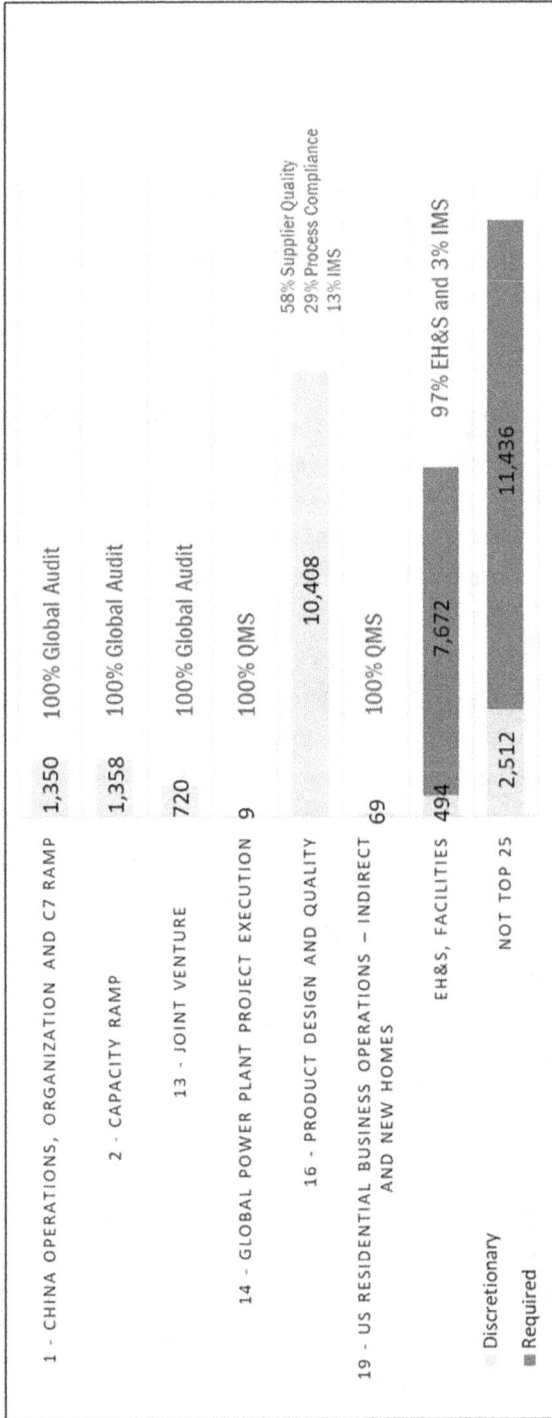

	Required	Discretionary	
1 - CHINA OPERATIONS, ORGANIZATION AND C7 RAMP	1,350	100% Global Audit	
2 - CAPACITY RAMP	1,358	100% Global Audit	
13 - JOINT VENTURE	720	100% Global Audit	
14 - GLOBAL POWER PLANT PROJECT EXECUTION	9	100% QMS	
16 - PRODUCT DESIGN AND QUALITY	10,408		
19 - US RESIDENTIAL BUSINESS OPERATIONS – INDIRECT AND NEW HOMES	69	100% QMS	
EH&S, FACILITIES	494	7,672	97% EH&S and 3% IMS
NOT TOP 25	2,512	11,436	58% Supplier Quality 29% Process Compliance 13% IMS

Discretionary
Required

Figure 13.9 Audit hours by ERM risk

The audit team noted that the most hours attributed to audit activities were Quality Management Systems (QMS) Function Quality Management Group, Operations Group, Quality Team and Procurement Supplier Audits. Figure 13.10 shows the results of the review, which are explained in more depth later.

The audit team looked at the planning fieldwork reporting and validation metrics and found that the programs were generally unstructured and inconsistent. There were some fragmented approaches by region. There was not an overview of the overall audit plan to determine if it was addressing the right areas of concern of management.

The methodologies of audit announcements, clearing recommendations or action plans, conducting the fieldwork, use of checklist versus a more in-depth process reviews, and reporting of issues was much different as well. Most reporting did not go outside of their internal department, and very few were escalated to the executive team of the organization.

None of the 3LoD functions, except Internal Audit, had a validation of their work by use of metrics.

It became obvious that there were a lot of methodology issues that would create more efficiency if they were similar in nature. There was not even a tracking of all audit comments by all of the groups.

The next step was to work with all these audit functions to come up with the number of audit comments that were open (not addressed by auditees) as well as those that were closed throughout the year. Each of the functions had their own methodology of rating audit comments as high, medium, or low as to importance in risk, with differing definitions of the ratings. There was not a consistent application of those ratings to ensure that auditees or business management were putting remediation time in the right place to correct the higher impact management action plans, which was another imbalance in the inefficiency of the organization team members.

The audit team pulled this information together (shown in Figure 13.11) of all the 3LoD audit activities or audit functions, which collectively had 1,508 audit comments for the year. Only 51 comments were ranked as a high-risk exposure to the organization, with 607 at a medium-risk rank, and 850 ranked as low risk.

Looking at the higher risk column of the 51 that were reported, 31 (or 61 percent) came from the Global Audit Department. Generally, the

Audit Methodologies were provided; which initial assessments yielded inconsistencies between teams and location.

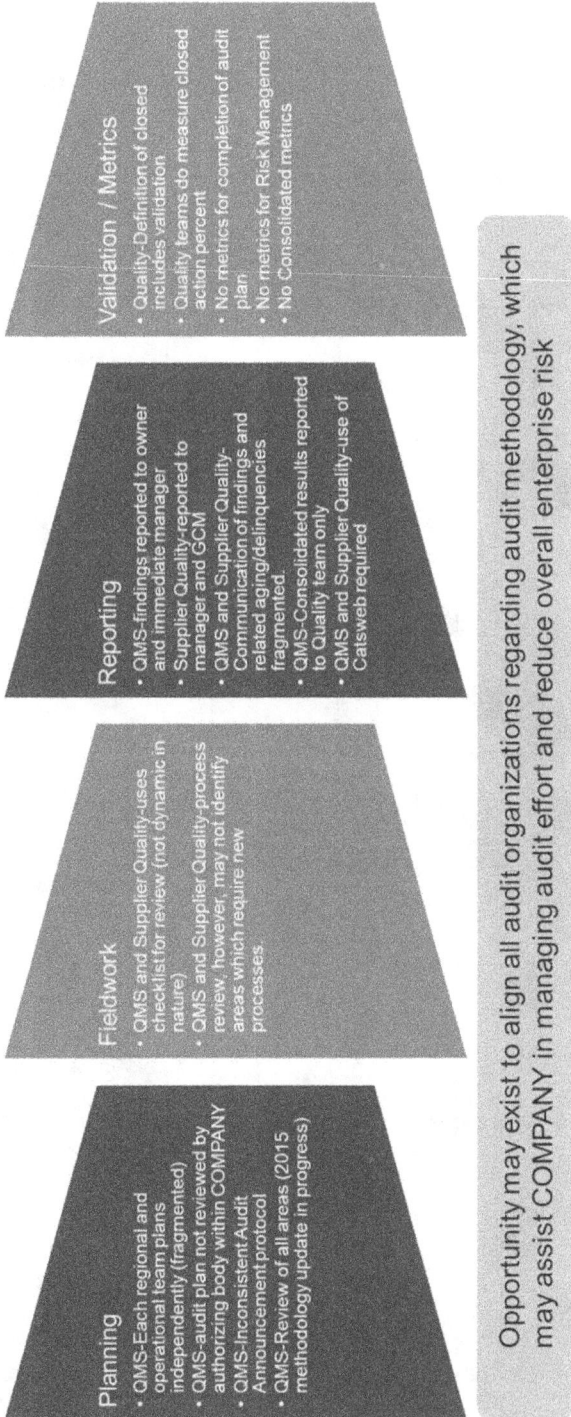

Planning
- QMS-Each regional and operational team plans independently (fragmented)
- QMS-audit plan not reviewed by authorizing body within COMPANY
- QMS-Inconsistent Audit Announcement protocol
- QMS-Review of all areas (2015 methodology update in progress)

Fieldwork
- QMS and Supplier Quality-uses checklist for review (not dynamic in nature)
- QMS and Supplier Quality-process review, however, may not identify areas which require new processes.

Reporting
- QMS-findings reported to owner and immediate manager
- Supplier Quality-reported to manager and GCM
- QMS and Supplier Quality-Communication of findings and related aging/delinquencies fragmented.
- QMS-Consolidated results reported to Quality team only
- QMS and Supplier Quality-use of Catsweb required

Validation / Metrics
- Quality-Definition of closed includes validation
- Quality teams do measure closed action percent
- No metrics for completion of audit plan
- No metrics for Risk Management
- No Consolidated metrics

Opportunity may exist to align all audit organizations regarding audit methodology, which may assist COMPANY in managing audit effort and reduce overall enterprise risk

Figure 13.10 Audit methodology assessment

Overview of the open and closed audit comments

Auditors	High	Medium	Low
Operational Audit	31	40	28
Product Compliance	8	10	1
Supplier Quality	6	265	239
ISO Process Compliance	3	127	239
EH&S	2	8	61
Direct Labor	1	140	273
SOX		17	7
Certification			2
TOTAL	51	607	850

1508 Audit Comments were communicated:

˄ **High** - 51 comments (61% attributed to Global Audit)

˄ **Medium** - 607 comments (44% attributed to Supplier Quality)

˄ **Low** - 850 comments (60% attributed to each Process Compliance, Product Compliance and Supplier Quality)

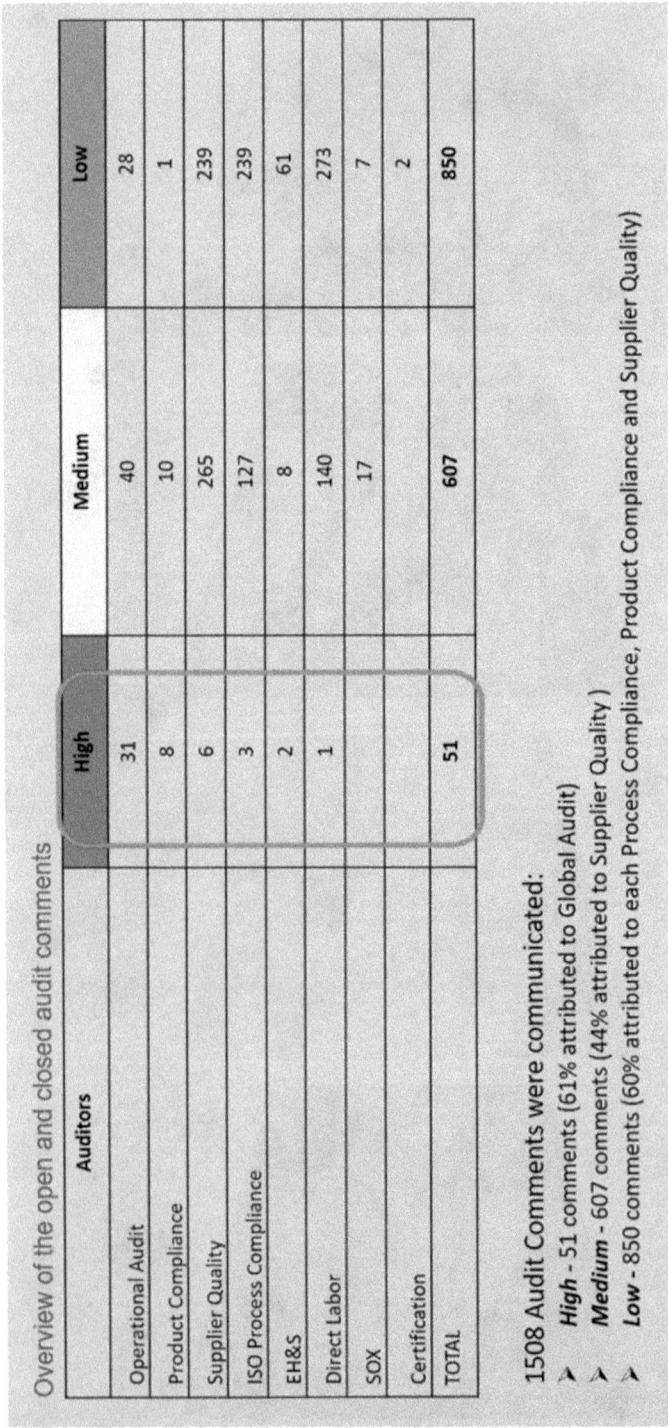

Figure 13.11 Overview of the open and closed comments

smallest department identified the largest number of risks. Within the medium category, the biggest contributor was the supplier audits and the quality audits performed by direct labor on the manufacture line, and the ISO process compliance. Most of the 850 low ratings came from supplier audits, ISO process, and the direct labor quality auditors. Only 99 came from the Global Audit Department.

Looking at the lines more closely, you can tell that the Global Audit Department had a stronger focus on higher risk areas. Thirty-one (or 30 percent) of the audit comments by Internal Audit Department were in a high-risk category, with a higher percentage in medium and a much lower percentage in low. This is more like the expected distribution if the organization was employing risk-based methodology through all lines of defense audit activities.

It was obvious that the ISO process compliance, supplier quality, and the direct labor quality were only finding issues that were of very low risk to the company by their definition. Keep in mind those that are the same three groups that represent over 50 percent of the discretionary audit hours. The obvious theme that was starting to generate.

Prior to obtaining all the open/close comments in the three risk categories, the audit team only had to make the methodology consistent on defining high-, medium-, and low risk to the company. They worked with each of these 3LoD audit functions and developed a common methodology to assign the risk of each of the comments that they currently had, open and closed. This made sure that the audit team looked at the comparison of all the closed and open comments with a consistent application of impact and likelihood.

The next step was touching a very sensitive area. The intention was to consider realigning the reporting of the second line of defense into the Global Audit Department. Based on peer group companies, the trend has been to integrate the second and third lines of defense, where possible, either as an execution agent or an oversight function. See the following Figure 13.12 showing the trend.

After assessing all of the information and data in all of the interviews, the audit team developed a next steps proposal to the Executive Team. In Figure 13.13 you see the overview of the proposal, which includes

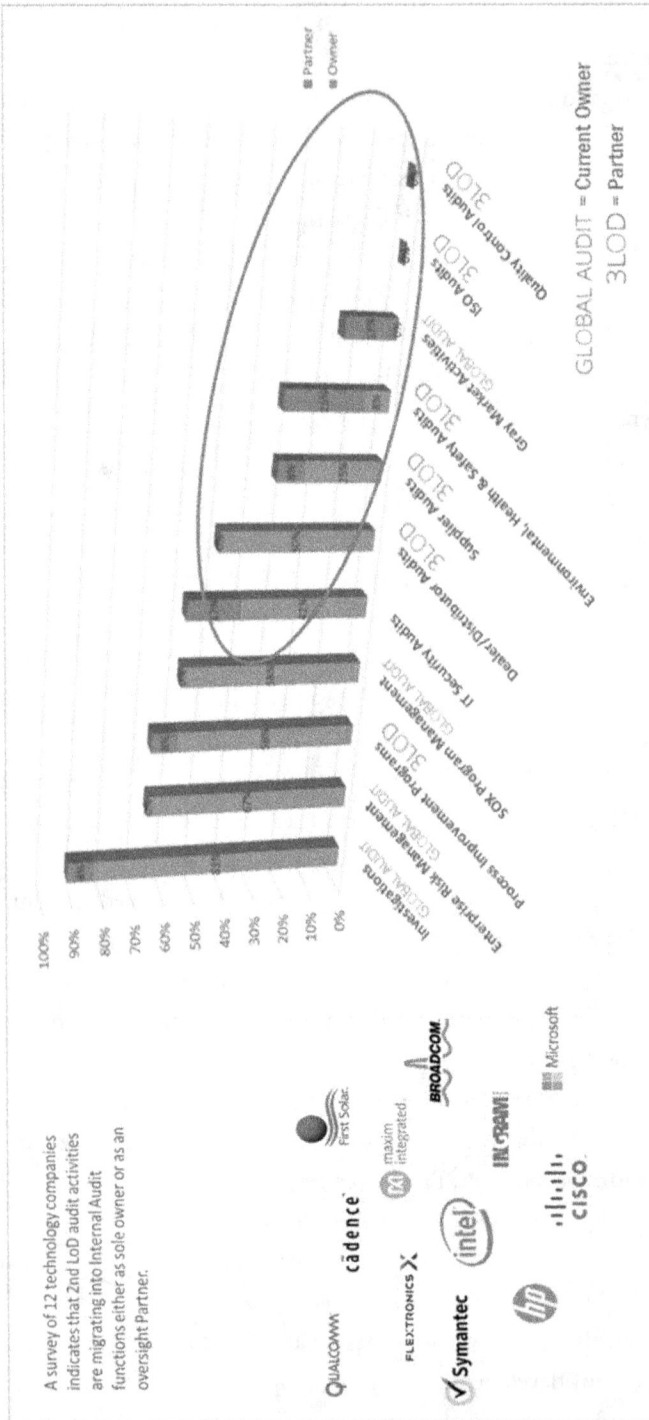

A survey of 12 technology companies indicates that 2nd LoD audit activities are migrating into Internal Audit functions either as sole owner or as an oversight Partner.

GLOBAL AUDIT = Current Owner

3LOD = Partner

Figure 13.12 Internal audit direction—company comparison

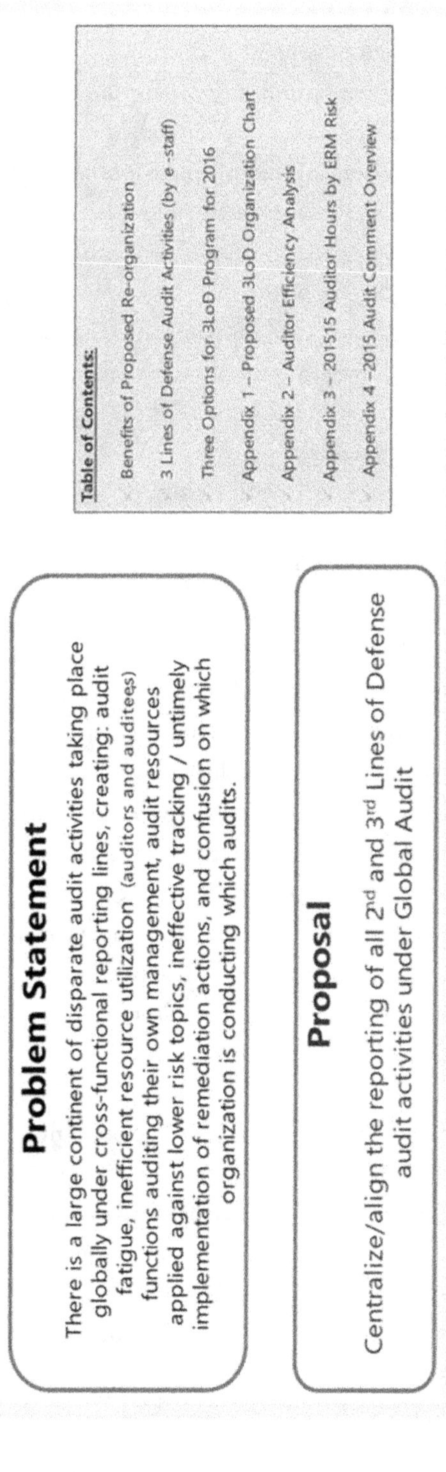

Problem Statement

There is a large continent of disparate audit activities taking place globally under cross-functional reporting lines, creating: audit fatigue, inefficient resource utilization (auditors and auditees) functions auditing their own management, audit resources applied against lower risk topics, ineffective tracking / untimely implementation of remediation actions, and confusion on which organization is conducting which audits.

Proposal

Centralize/align the reporting of all 2nd and 3rd Lines of Defense audit activities under Global Audit

Table of Contents:

Benefits of Proposed Re-organization

3 Lines of Defense Audit Activities (by e-staff)

Three Options for 3LoD Program for 2016

Appendix 1 – Proposed 3LoD Organization Chart

Appendix 2 – Auditor Efficiency Analysis

Appendix 3 – 201515 Auditor Hours by ERM Risk

Appendix 4 –2015 Audit Comment Overview

Figure 13.13 3LoD next steps

primarily the problem statement and the ultimate proposal of where the team needed to reach at some point in time.

The problem statement confirmed where the concerns were at the very beginning. There were a lot of audit activities taking place globally in the cross-functional organizations. There was audit fatigue, a highly inefficient utilization of audit resources, and a lack of any kind of level of objectivity or independence—people were auditing their own function. A large preponderance of the man-hours of auditing were actually applied to low-risk audit topics of the company. The audit comments that were identified were reportedly tracked and remained open for a very long period of time. There continued to be confusion of which organization was conducting which audits.

In the next section, you'll see the story pulled together as how the audit team brought this to the next level.

Some of the recommendations that are shown in the next few pages will require moving the second line of defense auditors into the third line of defense audit group and could raise some conversation about whether or not the line between second and third was being blurred specifically from an accountability standpoint and independence. Additionally, there were a lot of nonaudit-oriented people who were conducting second line of defense, which would stay intact. Only those who were conducting actual physical audits with recommendations in assessing risk would be folded under the larger umbrella of Global Internal Audit, the third line of defense. It is very important to clarify that to make sure everyone understands that, the audit team considered the value of independence and objectivity in this process, which would ultimately give much better efficiency and end results.

As you see in Figure 13.14—Lines of Defense Strategy—Opportunities, the audit team had to identify and express the opportunities it saw to the Executive Team, CEO and his staff, as to why this made sense to consider. Normally, management teams are very protective of their own employees and the teams they have built within their group to improve their own quality in a more siloed effect. It was a difficult conversation to have with all the executives to convince them of the value-add brought to the organization.

The audit team focused on four different elements that would improve the overall program:

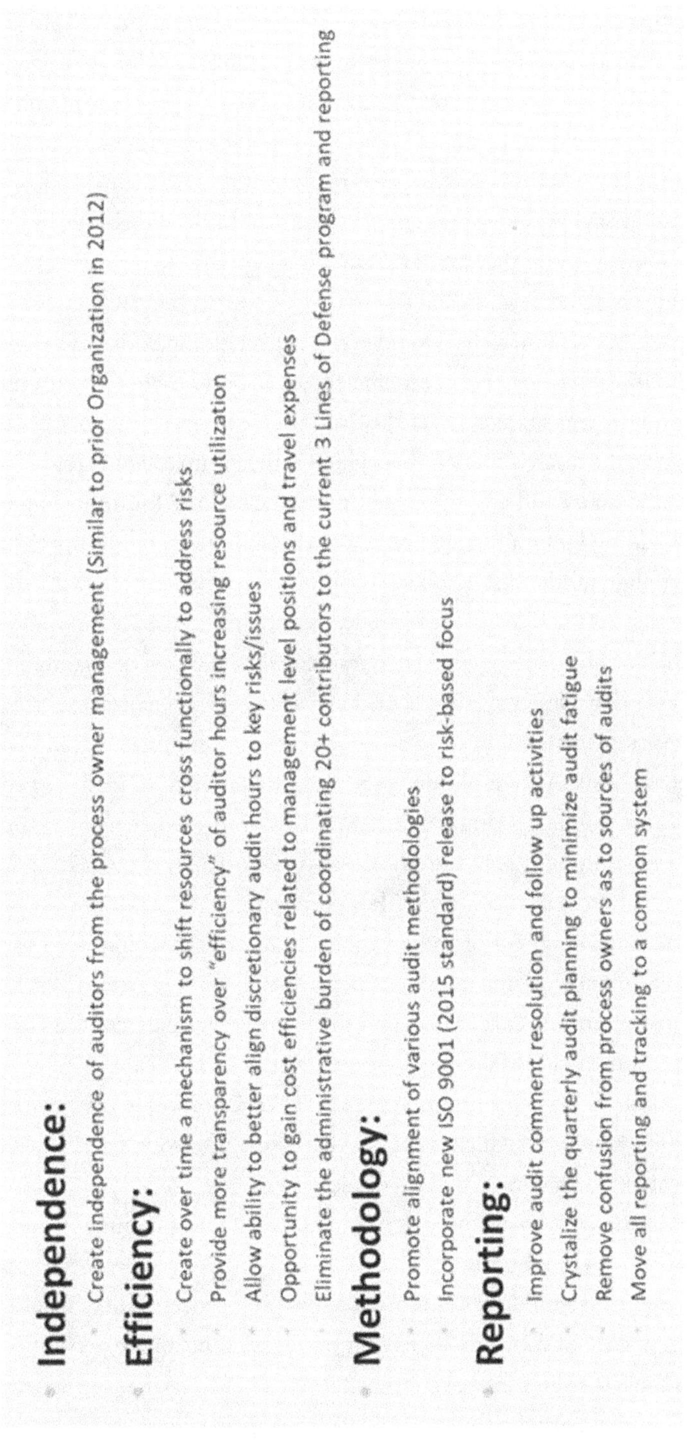

Independence:

- Create independence of auditors from the process owner management (Similar to prior Organization in 2012)

Efficiency:

- Create over time a mechanism to shift resources cross functionally to address risks
- Provide more transparency over "efficiency" of auditor hours increasing resource utilization
- Allow ability to better align discretionary audit hours to key risks/issues
- Opportunity to gain cost efficiencies related to management level positions and travel expenses
- Eliminate the administrative burden of coordinating 20+ contributors to the current 3 Lines of Defense program and reporting

Methodology:

- Promote alignment of various audit methodologies
- Incorporate new ISO 9001 (2015 standard) release to risk-based focus

Reporting:

- Improve audit comment resolution and follow up activities
- Crystalize the quarterly audit planning to minimize audit fatigue
- Remove confusion from process owners as to sources of audits
- Move all reporting and tracking to a common system

Figure 13.14 Lines of defense strategy—opportunities

1. **Objectivity and Independence**: By consolidating the second line of defense auditors into one group, the auditors would no longer be auditing the processes owned by their boss or own team members. That would create a stronger effectiveness and reporting of issues and bring more transparency of the concerns that were mentioned.

2. **Efficiency:** As time progressed, there would be the ability to shift resources from the subcross-functional groups to other teams to address higher level risks. Prior to that, of course, there would be a fair amount of training that would take place including both business and auditing training. From an efficiency perspective, this would create far more transparency over the utilization of the audit hours, particularly the discretionary hours, which is the group of hours that is not well defined and also the largest percentage of the full-time employees doing these audits. It would give the audit team the ability to better align all the discretionary audit hours to the ERM Top 25 risks, which are the risks that really need the attention. Also, there would be the opportunity to gain synergies related to the cost of maintaining these departments. There currently were several management-level positions that would ultimately be able to be eliminated along with travel costs. Also duplicate costs currently required to maintain each group would be eliminated. And lastly under efficiency, it would just simply eliminate the administrative burden of coordinating 20+ contributors to the current 3LoD program.

3. **Methodology:** All of these various audit groups would need to be fully aligned on how they conduct audits, how they assess risks, how they determine exceptions, and the value of those exceptions before recommendations are made in each of the various categories of risk exposure. It would improve the ability to incorporate the new ISO 9001 standard, which requires that the ISO work be risk-based, which is a change in that methodology.

4. **Reporting:** Management action plans with audit comments would be much easier to resolve and follow-up activities easier to monitor. Reporting would also improve the planning process. There would be an update of quarterly plans sent out to all appropriate personnel to be able to minimize audit fatigue. And the audit team could schedule all audits centrally for all 3LoD in the organization.

Also under Reporting, the team would remove the confusion from everyone as to the source of individual audits being conducted. There would be one person to contact who manages the entire audit plan.

And lastly, under Reporting, all the tracking and reporting activities would be placed under a common system to gain efficiency and accuracy.

Those were the four major elements of support to accept and implement this program.

The next Figure 13.15 shows a timeline of what it would take to pull this program together under one reporting structure. It certainly would not happen immediately and would most likely take two to three quarters to be fully implemented. Most of the benefits would be incurred after at least three quarters and maybe even four quarters. It is a very involved process, and a lot of planning would need to take place before starting the implementation.

Of course, it is always good when you are selling a project or a program to have a quick win to show as an example. Therefore, the audit team overlapped the internal audit work, particularly in the SOX program, and the budget hours for the Quality Management Team related to the budget hours for SOX in the Finance Team (see Figure 13.16).

As the team looked at the overlap over a three-year period, it was clear in just this one isolated comparison that there could be close to 1,200 man-hours reduction identified over three years. That would eliminate 64 QMS audits that would be consolidated into other audits, 42 of their audits could be coordinated with Internal Audit Department, thereby reducing stakeholders' interaction. And there were 39 audits that QMS was doing that really supported the Sarbanes–Oxley or the SOX function. Those could be completely eliminated since there is a robust SOX program in place. This excludes the time devoted to the audits by the auditees and management, which would drive the savings much higher. By just comparing that one isolated area, it was clear that a lot of audits could be eliminated or consolidated, and many hours reduced between these two audit groups.

After presenting the objectives and the opportunities and the timeline and the quick win, the audit team proposed three different options for the Executive Team to consider.

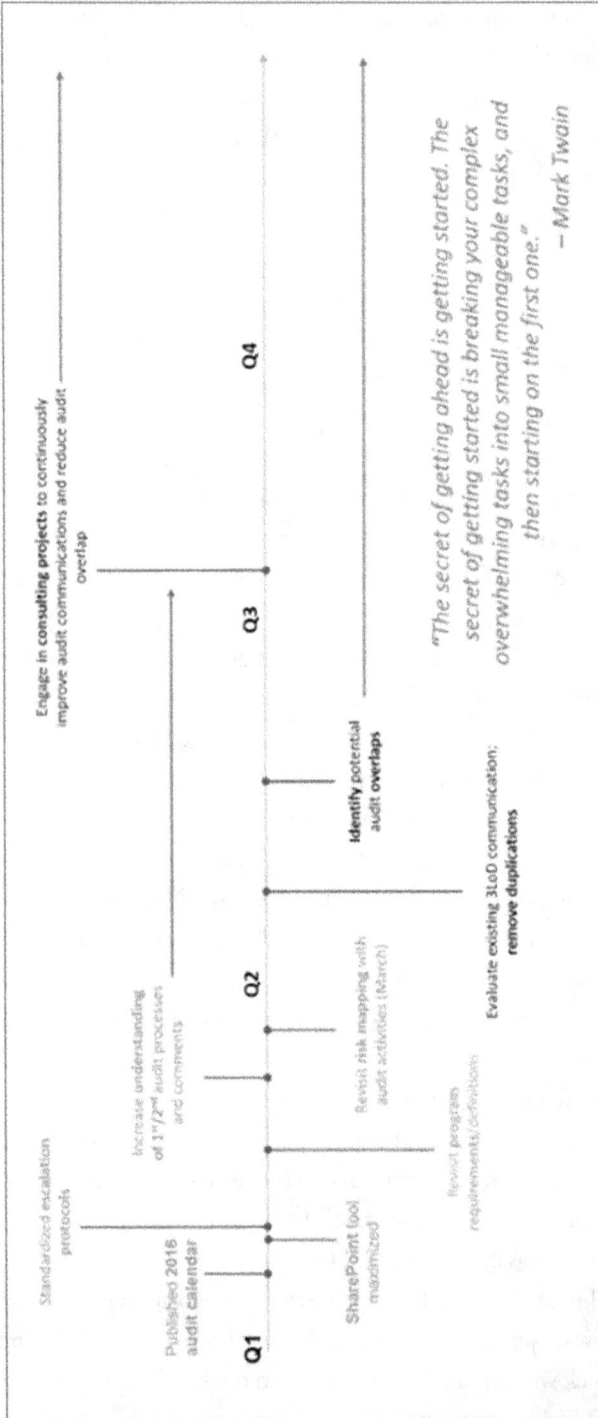

Figure 13.15 Next year objectives

An evaluation of the audit overlap was performed between QMS and SOX

Budgeted Hours for QMS Audits (2016-2018)

Audit Reductions identified over 3 years: 145 Audits (1,160 hours)

✓ **64 QMS** audits were consolidated based on departments / regions in-scope

✓ **42 Audits** will be coordinated by Global Audit and QMS (reducing stakeholders interaction)

✓ **39 SOX** were identified as overlap with SOX. Proposed reliance on results of SOX compliance testing

← 1,160 Hours →
SOX
SOX & QMS
QMS
QMS Planned

Planned   Consolidated

4500
4000
3500
3000
2500
2000
1500
1000
500
0

Collaboration between Quality Team and Global Audit potentially yielded 1,160 hours reduction over 3 years

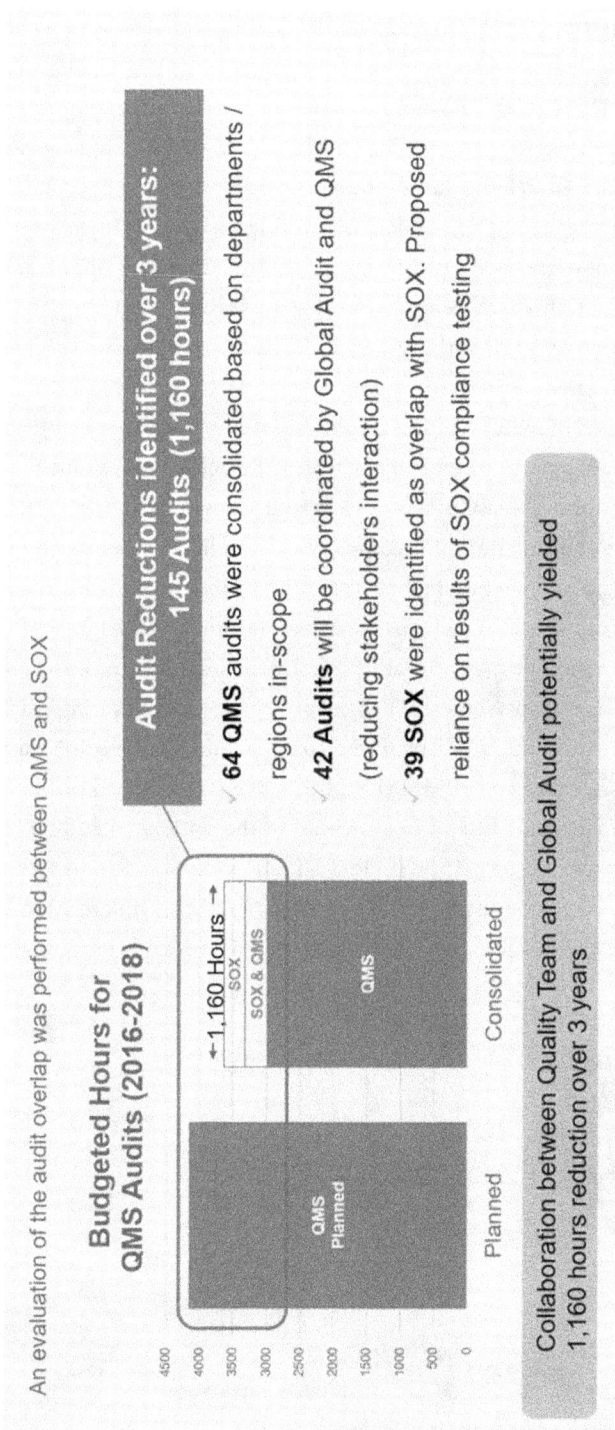

Figure 13.16 QMS audit reduction evaluation

The first option which was Internal Audit's preferred option (ReOrg) is shown in Figure 13.17.

This preferred option would be to conduct a reorganization. Even that could be defined with two possible options: one would be to simply create a second line of defense audit group organization, and the second would be to have the second line of defense audit groups report into the existing third line of defense Global Internal Audit function. This option gave the management an alternate direction if they did not want to go with the Global Internal Audit as the owner, but at least consolidate all second line of defense activities into one group.

This level of reorganization would gain nearly all the benefits discussed from establishing independence between the audit groups and the business functions; the ability to deploy staff cross-functionally; providing a stronger coordination of a companywide audit schedule for improved alignment; a more simplified process for communication and reporting; and lastly, allow audits to focus on companywide ERM risks.

There were not many negatives associated with this recommendation other than perhaps some challenges of separating or carving out these employees from the business. There could potentially be some misalignment of strategies and risks if they did not report to the Global Internal Audit Department. But all in all, either of the options including reorganization would be an improvement.

The second proposal (No Change) (digital copy—in green) in Figure 13.18 was to basically keep the organization as it is with no change.

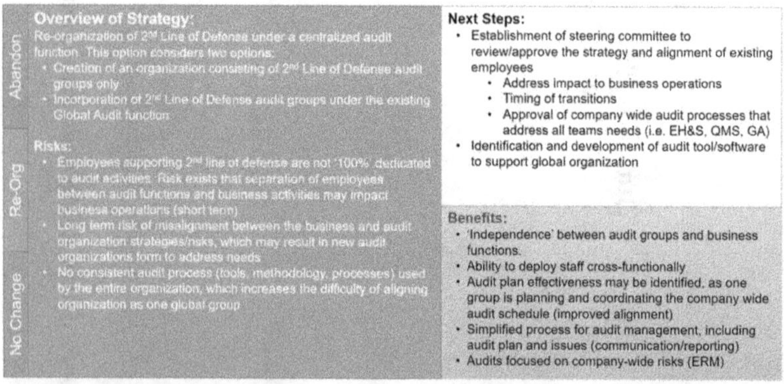

Figure 13.17 Three lines of defense—beyond

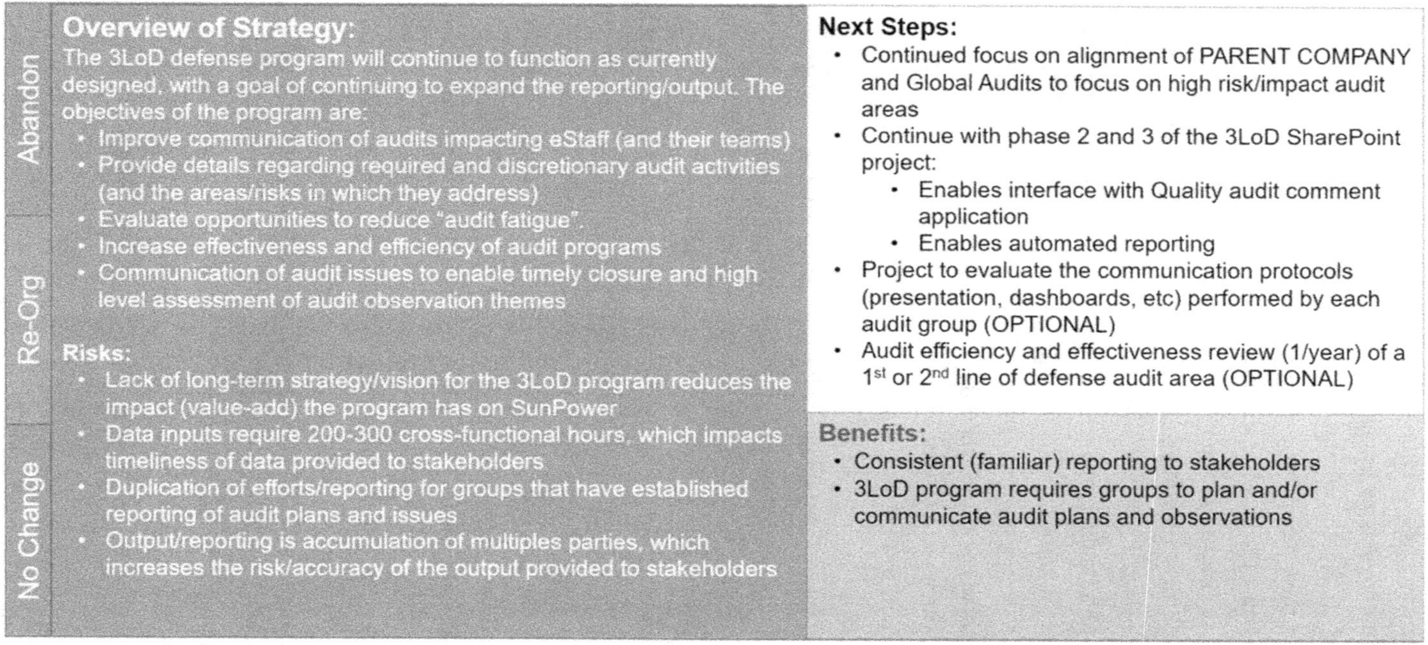

Overview of Strategy:
The 3LoD defense program will continue to function as currently designed, with a goal of continuing to expand the reporting/output. The objectives of the program are:
- Improve communication of audits impacting eStaff (and their teams)
- Provide details regarding required and discretionary audit activities (and the areas/risks in which they address)
- Evaluate opportunities to reduce "audit fatigue"
- Increase effectiveness and efficiency of audit programs
- Communication of audit issues to enable timely closure and high level assessment of audit observation themes

Risks:
- Lack of long-term strategy/vision for the 3LoD program reduces the impact (value-add) the program has on SunPower
- Data inputs require 200-300 cross-functional hours, which impacts timeliness of data provided to stakeholders
- Duplication of efforts/reporting for groups that have established reporting of audit plans and issues
- Output/reporting is accumulation of multiples parties, which increases the risk/accuracy of the output provided to stakeholders

Next Steps:
- Continued focus on alignment of PARENT COMPANY and Global Audits to focus on high risk/impact audit areas
- Continue with phase 2 and 3 of the 3LoD SharePoint project:
  - Enables interface with Quality audit comment application
  - Enables automated reporting
- Project to evaluate the communication protocols (presentation, dashboards, etc) performed by each audit group (OPTIONAL)
- Audit efficiency and effectiveness review (1/year) of a 1st or 2nd line of defense audit area (OPTIONAL)

Benefits:
- Consistent (familiar) reporting to stakeholders
- 3LoD program requires groups to plan and/or communicate audit plans and observations

Abandon   Re-Org   No Change

Figure 13.18 Three lines of defense—beyond

To implement a common program throughout all of the individual second lines of defense groups mean there would be a common language and more consistent communications. It might help to an extent the audit fatigue if there were overlapping consideration of audits, and certainly could increase the effectiveness and efficiency of the programs in general. This recommendation or proposal was presented as a compromise. There would still be a continued lack of long-term strategy or vision for the 3LoD program. It would continue to have duplication of cross-functional hours and administrative efforts, and the output and reconciliation of management audit comments would tend to lag. While there would be benefits to this option, it certainly would not maximize the process.

The third option (Abandon) (orange where available) shown in Figure 13.19 , which was the least desirable, was to simply abandon the notion of the 3LoD related to the auditors conducting the work within their organization.

There were some benefits at least bringing forward awareness if there could be some consistency of audit scheduling put in place, reduce audit fatigue, and maybe continuity in reporting issues through remediation. But the overall planning of audits to help address the primary company risks from the ERM program would be minimal. This option was by far the least beneficial of all the three proposals, but nonetheless an option. This option was the least intrusive to organizations and an option, should management not have an appetite to bring forward such a sweeping change to the program.

What happened? As we all know, timing is everything. There was no immediate decision by executives as to which direction a company would go. There were some underlying changes coming up within the organization and business models that would impact any kind of structural change that would be taken over the next six months.

However, the audit team immediately implemented several of the recommendations to remove audit fatigue and do some centralization of reporting of the audit plan accumulating at each quarter and avoiding overlaps and duplication. They also incorporated a semiconsistent methodology of high-, medium-, low-risk ratings and facilitated the reporting to executives of this open management action plans to help get the remediation closed timelier.

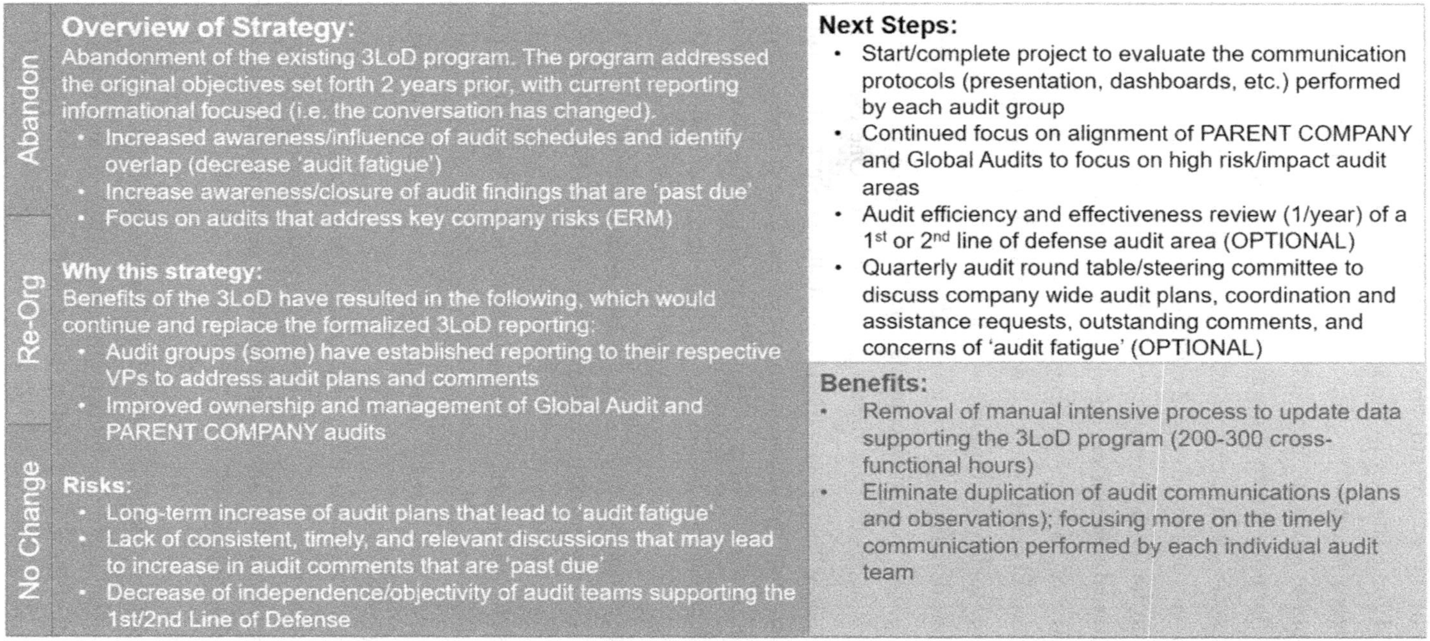

Overview of Strategy:
Abandonment of the existing 3LoD program. The program addressed the original objectives set forth 2 years prior, with current reporting informational focused (i.e. the conversation has changed).
- Increased awareness/influence of audit schedules and identify overlap (decrease 'audit fatigue')
- Increase awareness/closure of audit findings that are 'past due'
- Focus on audits that address key company risks (ERM)

Why this strategy:
Benefits of the 3LoD have resulted in the following, which would continue and replace the formalized 3LoD reporting:
- Audit groups (some) have established reporting to their respective VPs to address audit plans and comments
- Improved ownership and management of Global Audit and PARENT COMPANY audits

Risks:
- Long-term increase of audit plans that lead to 'audit fatigue'
- Lack of consistent, timely, and relevant discussions that may lead to increase in audit comments that are 'past due'
- Decrease of independence/objectivity of audit teams supporting the 1st/2nd Line of Defense

Next Steps:
- Start/complete project to evaluate the communication protocols (presentation, dashboards, etc.) performed by each audit group
- Continued focus on alignment of PARENT COMPANY and Global Audits to focus on high risk/impact audit areas
- Audit efficiency and effectiveness review (1/year) of a 1st or 2nd line of defense audit area (OPTIONAL)
- Quarterly audit round table/steering committee to discuss company wide audit plans, coordination and assistance requests, outstanding comments, and concerns of 'audit fatigue' (OPTIONAL)

Benefits:
- Removal of manual intensive process to update data supporting the 3LoD program (200-300 cross-functional hours)
- Eliminate duplication of audit communications (plans and observations); focusing more on the timely communication performed by each individual audit team

Abandon | Re-Org | No Change

Figure 13.19 Three lines of defense—beyond

As time moved forward, there were some major changes of the company and some changes to the second line of defense reporting structure. It was a very positive project. Management chose to follow in the "compromise proposal" option due to the other surrounding circumstances. But nonetheless, this was a great exercise and each of the organizations specifically addressed inefficiencies. Particularly, the Operations Department addressed the 25,000 discretionary efficiency-oriented type audit hours that could not be pegged to any real risk and gained some internal cost efficiencies within their organization as well.

It did create a lot of positive changes, but it did not get to the full desired level of benefit expected when all audit activities would be highly centralized under the third line of defense or at least centralized under a second line of defense department head.

This project inspired other teams thought out the organization to reconsider their approach to addressing company risks. One executive leader asked the audit team to conduct a management assessment of the standalone department that conducted and managed the Process Improvement Program, which was viewed as a second line of defense function in addressing risks. When issues surfaced in the day-to-day operations in any organization or function, the related group owning the issue engaged the Process Improvement Program group to facilitate this exercise in a very structured manner. The Process Improvement Program utilized the Eight Disciplines approach that was very similar to those more well-known process improvement programs, such as the Kaizen, Six Sigma, or Total Quality Management (TQM).

The Eight Discipline methodology referred to as 8D is a methodology used to assist and identify corrective actions for issues that surface. See Figure 13.20.

The picture of the 8D program shows the beauty in that it never changes regardless of the process being assessed. This program is very similar to other similar process improvement programs. Key elements are discussed as follows:

- The first discipline is to create a cross-functional team that fits right into the ability to make sure problems are corrected where most issues tend to fail—specifically, interdepartmental changes versus intradepartmental activities.

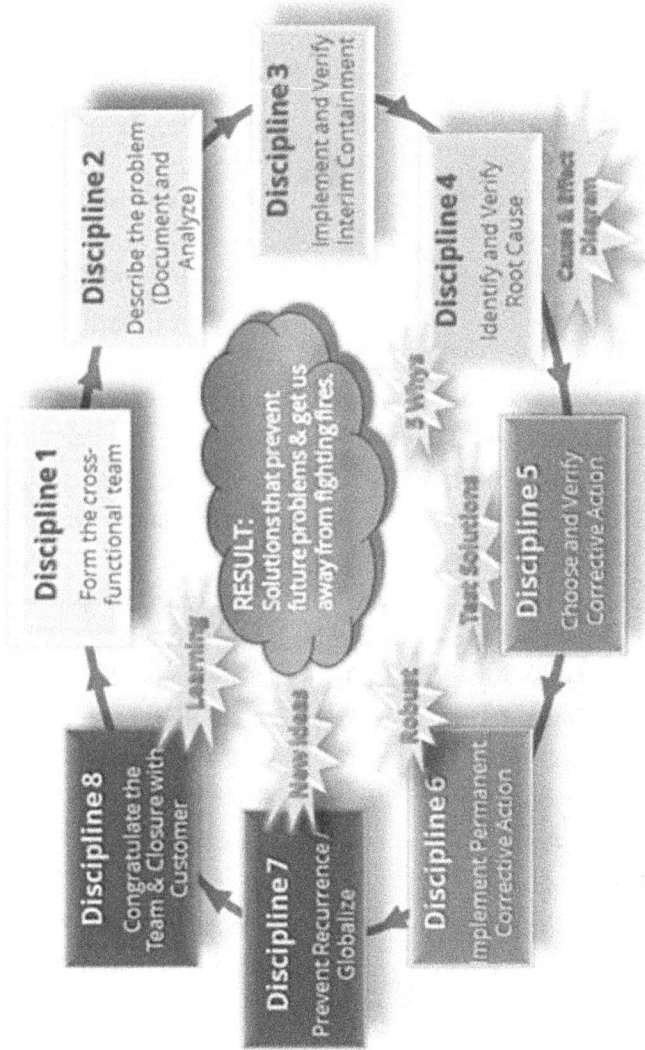

Discipline 1
Form the cross-functional team

Discipline 2
Describe the problem (Document and Analyze)

Discipline 3
Implement and Verify Interim Containment

Discipline 4
Identify and Verify Root Cause

Cause & Effect Diagram

5 Whys

Discipline 5
Choose and Verify Corrective Action

Test Solutions

Discipline 6
Implement Permanent Corrective Action

Robust

Discipline 7
Prevent Recurrence / Globalize

New Ideas

Discipline 8
Congratulate the Team & Closure with Customer

Learning

RESULT:
Solutions that prevent future problems & get us away from fighting fires.

Figure 13.20 Disciplines (8D) process

- The second discipline is to describe the problem statement, which can be a challenge as participants prefer to jump immediately to the corrective action steps.
- The third discipline is to contain the current situation.
- The fourth discipline is to identify and verify the root causes, which is where you ask the "why" question five times.
- The fifth discipline is to identify and verify corrective action.
- The sixth discipline is to implement permanent corrective action.
- The seventh discipline is to prevent recurrence and add globalization.
- The eighth is to congratulate the team and close with the customer.

Some specific examples of issues where this technique is applied frequently relate to product and material or equipment, business process breakdowns, field failures, reliability problems, customer-escalated complaints, safety events, financial reporting accuracy, and environmental and nonconformity problems. These action items are pulled together to address very specific and considerably important issues. It was always the CEO's first go-to direction if an issue surfaced, "Conduct an 8D."

This 8D group was embedded in the quality control function in the Operations Group and was devoted specifically to these projects. To assess the effectiveness of the 8D program, it was tracked for a couple of quarters and then brought the activities into the 3LoD project modifications explained earlier, because it is somewhat consistent with tracking management action plans.

Figure 13.21 shows the takeaways after the initial review of the process around the 8D program. These are action items that were created together to address very specific and significant issues.

The audit team found that not all organizations in the company consistently logged their 8D projects in the primary repository. This created difficulties in tracking the status and the completion of the companywide 8Ds. There were logical reasons for some projects not to be logged in to the central system, such as those that related to legal items where there is attorney–client privilege, key finance strategy items including tax

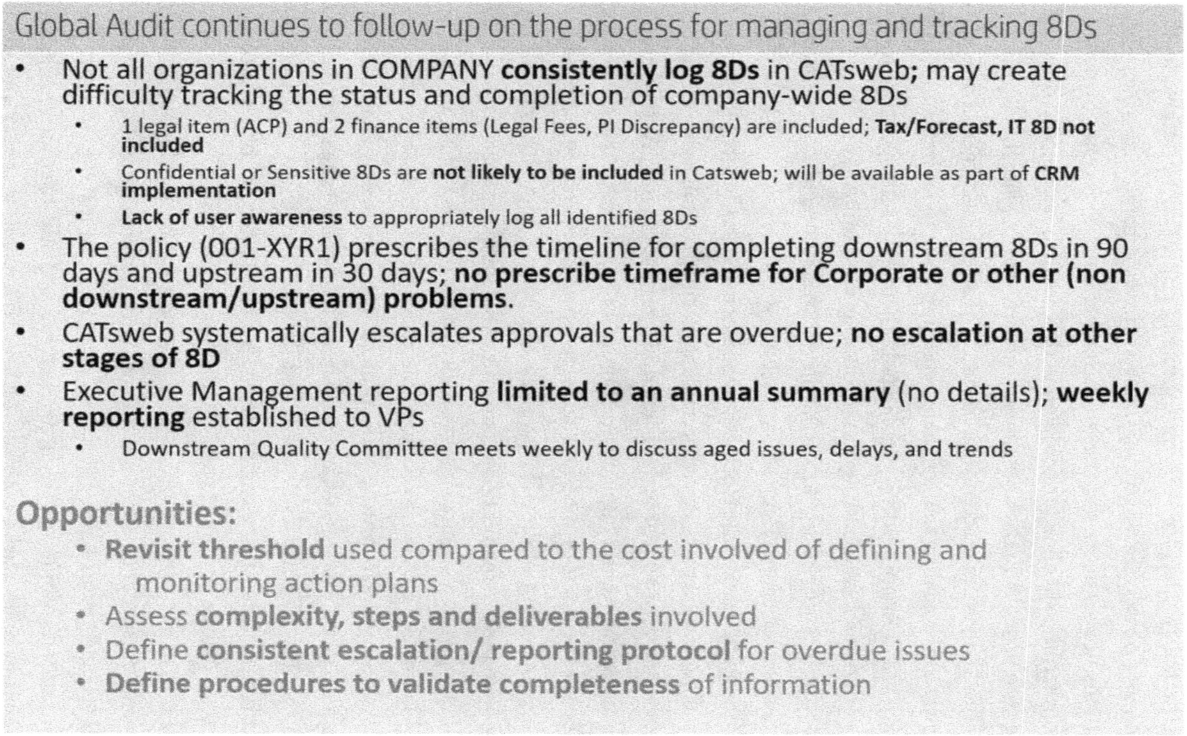

Global Audit continues to follow-up on the process for managing and tracking 8Ds

- Not all organizations in COMPANY **consistently log 8Ds** in CATsweb; **may create** difficulty tracking the status and completion of company-wide 8Ds
  - 1 legal item (ACP) and 2 finance items (Legal Fees, PI Discrepancy) are included; **Tax/Forecast, IT 8D not included**
  - Confidential or Sensitive 8Ds are **not likely to be included** in Catsweb; will be available as part of **CRM implementation**
  - **Lack of user awareness** to appropriately log all identified 8Ds
- The policy (001-XYR1) prescribes the timeline for completing downstream 8Ds in 90 days and upstream in 30 days; **no prescribe timeframe for Corporate or other (non downstream/upstream) problems.**
- CATsweb systematically escalates approvals that are overdue; **no escalation at other stages of 8D**
- Executive Management reporting **limited to an annual summary** (no details); **weekly reporting** established to VPs
  - Downstream Quality Committee meets weekly to discuss aged issues, delays, and trends

Opportunities:

- **Revisit threshold** used compared to the cost involved of defining and monitoring action plans
- **Assess complexity, steps and deliverables** involved
- Define consistent **escalation/ reporting protocol** for overdue issues
- **Define procedures to validate completeness** of information

Figure 13.21 8D takeaways

forecasting, and certain IT projects. However, there was also clearly a lack of user awareness of the requirement to log all identified 8Ds into the common system.

The policy related to 8D was primarily geared for operations in the beginning phases of the program, but as it was expanded to other organizations, it was never updated to include corporate or other owners. It did prescribe a timeline for completing downstream issues in 90 days and upstream issues in 30 days, which continued to stay in place for all projects.

The system did not escalate delays at the various stages of the 8D, nor was any executive management reporting done more frequently than once a year and only with limited detail. There were some periodic meetings of downstream quality committees, but very limited, and there were opportunities to possibly bring this into a second line of defense from a process improvement element.

The audit team worked behind the scenes with the Quality Department on pulling together a more structured approach of consolidating all the 8D projects and reporting of such on a periodic regular cadence. As they modified this reporting and implemented some of the process changes, the team looked at the status of the 8Ds that were currently open in the repository. Eighty-six percent of the 8Ds were past due overall, and 51 percent of the 8Ds were greater than 90 days past due. This indicated that a substantial amount of work took place but got stalled in the process (see Figure 13.22).

Figure 13.22 shows a couple of pie charts. The pie chart on the left-hand side is the static image of the projects at the beginning of the review. The pie chart on the right-hand side shows the status of the same projects two months after the results were highlighted to executive management for the first time. In the beginning there were 82 percent of the projects delayed. A total of 80 were over 90 days past due, with 17 over one year past due. A lot of these projects were substantially overdue while only 27 were on schedule. After monitoring and implementing the new procedures, and reporting to executives, the change in just two months was very positive. While still high, 69 percent was still overdue, while the number of open tracks fell from 127 to 107. While this was a positive sign, it would take a few months to get all the projects caught up.

Figure 13.23 shows the status of the eight steps in the program for the open projects discussed earlier.

Specific consideration was reviewed regarding the progress of prior quarter open 8Ds

8D Aging (as of 3/4/16)

5/1/16 Update of Q1 Items Reported (as of 3/4/16)

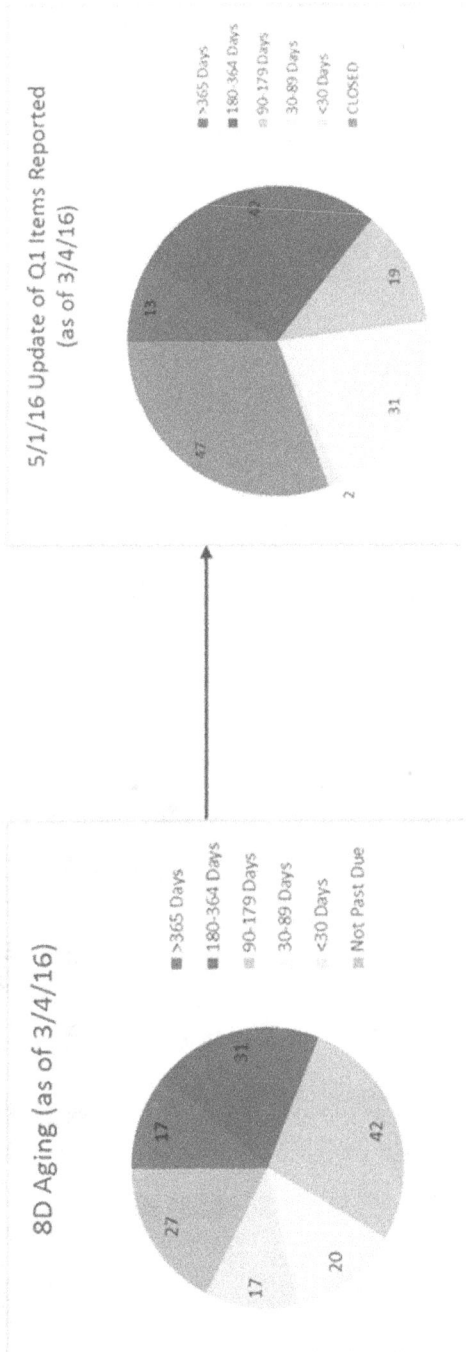

- 47 8Ds were closed (**31% closure rate**); 107 8Ds from Q1 are **past due**
- Average movement of an 8D **1.7 steps** (i.e. D4 to D5/6)
- **46%** (71 of 154) of the 8Ds had **no movement** in the 2 months evaluated

Figure 13.22 8D aging overview

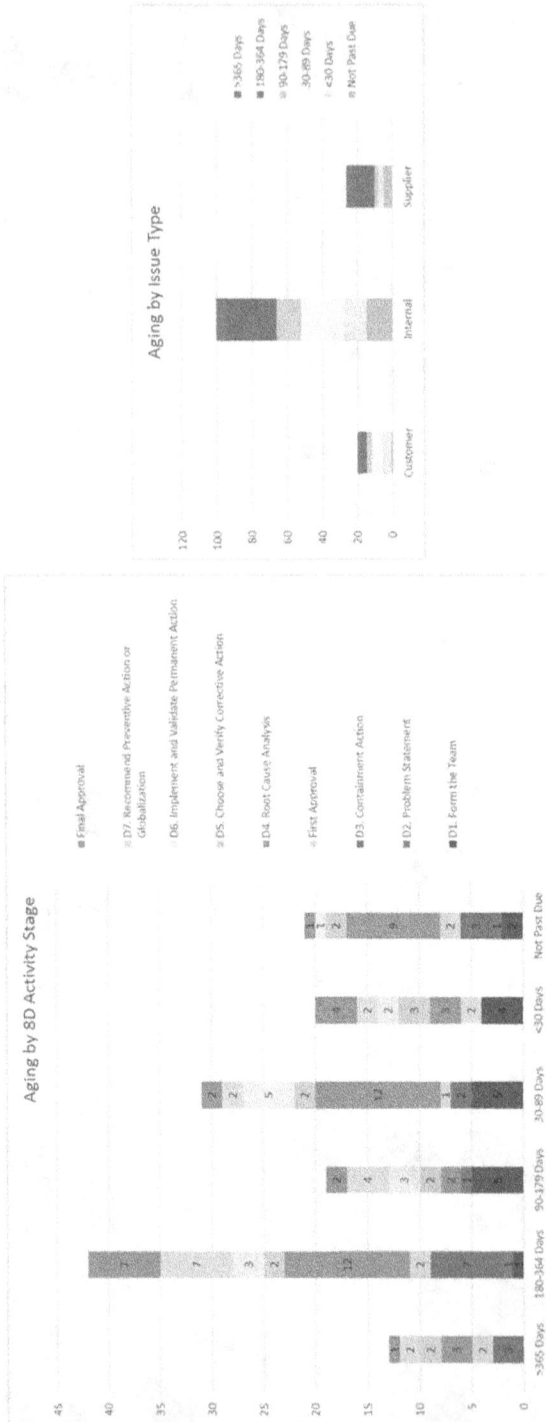

Figure 13.23 8D aging—additional analysis

Once the cleanup is done and the new procedures are consistently followed, this becomes a very useful part of the second line of defense in managing the risks. The point to this section is that it should be an area that is built into the second line of defense in the quality function. It does relate to identified global cross-functional issues, many of which will relate to higher risk elements within an organization.

However, it is so often that without proper supervision and moderation that these programs will fail to produce 100 percent because people stopped a bit early before completion. They accomplished a couple of quick wins, then just move forward. They never knew whether same improvement was experienced once applied globally.

It is all about asking many **why** questions, testing solutions, making sure it is robust, incorporating new ideas and learnings from the process, and finally, making sure it is implemented globally.

CHAPTER 14

Creating and Implementing an ERM Program

Implementing an ERM program in a company can be relatively easy, to nearly impossible. It all depends on various factors, which include the type of industry, the size of the organization, the business model, the geographical footprint, the level of regulations that a company is managed by or monitored by, the culture of the organization, and the resources used to create and implement the program. This chapter will focus on the initial selling of the new ERM program to obtain ELT and Board of Director support and approval to move forward. Subsequently, we will discuss the actual process of implementing the ERM program. Demonstrating the above concept will be based on manufacturing types of companies, specifically a solar company and semiconductor company.

These companies range between US$1.5 billion and US$3.5 billion in annual revenues, with a global footprint covering around 40 countries each throughout the world. These companies have manufacturing operations, some of which are fully in-house while some are heavily outsourced to contract manufacturers. The total number of employees in these companies ranged between 4,000 and approximately 8,000.

Even though this book is based on the experiences at both of technology manufacturing companies of medium size, most of the approaches and methodologies can be applied or adapted to other types of companies and organizations. Even among the companies used as examples in this chapter, there were differences as to the ease of implementing the ERM program.

In the first case, a solar company had no ERM program in place and was only introduced to the enterprise risk management concept by the Internal Audit Department that conducted the normal risk assessment to drive the annual internal audit plan. The value of an ERM program came to forefront and attention of the CEO and CFO only after they saw the results of the risk assessment. Synthesizing the common risk themes created around 50 separate risk topics identified throughout the organization. After reviewing this information, the CEO asked: *Well, what do you do with this information? Do you put it on the bookshelf and revisit it again next year when you want to create your internal audit plan?* The response was that it all depends on the level of discipline the CEO would like his company to have and the rigor built-in around developing a mindset of risk, risk-based processes, and risk-based decisions. These are frequently left on the bookshelf and generally referred to as a resource for internal audit activities. Fortunately, this savvy CEO's response was that he would really like to see a formal and robust ERM program implemented to ensure these risks are being addressed and asked that the Internal Audit Department come back to him in about a month with a proposal for the companywide ERM program. The ERM program was initially sold to the CEO and subsequently to CFO, gaining their full support to move forward, which was essential for the ERM program to be created and implemented.

The second case related to a semiconductor company that also did not have an ERM program in place. However, in this case, the Board of Directors requested the CEO to implement an ERM program, which was the point in time that the Audit Department was being transformed into a value-add audit function. The executive support was already there, at least from the CEO, CFO, and the Board of Directors' standpoint, which made the process of selling the ERM program companywide much easier as the other executives also needed to buy-in to the ERM program to make it fully successful.

The third scenario, a semiconductor company already had an existing risk management program that was administered by a different (not an Internal Audit) function within the company. The ERM program was only updated once every two years with a full bottom-up and/or top-down risk assessment. In the off year, the risk profile was somewhat updated, but very informally. There was no reporting out, no active documented treatment plans, and no structural components. This was shared with the CEO and CFO and demonstrated how the company could benefit from a more robust ERM program.

All three of the programs are slightly different and were initiated with different levels of support. In the last case there was already existing ERM program that was perceived as valuable, yet the executive leadership team was not fully aware of the fully realizable benefits of a more robust ERM program.

While the "selling" approaches were slightly different for each of these scenarios, the biggest difference was primarily in the first step— identifying what needed to be sold to the ELT. The focal point for the initial selling presentations ranged from (1) the first case to build a program from scratch and persuade the other executives to support it, (2) the second case to sell the program from a benefits standpoint to support the needed investment, and (3) the third case to rebuild the existing program into a more robust one with added resources requirements.

Since some level of ERM programs are widely deployed in most companies today, we will focus primarily on the third scenario, which is a company that already had an existing low-level ERM program in place. The content of the "selling" presentation will be discussed knowing that it can be adapted to fit either of the other two cases mentioned earlier. Once the need for the robust ERM program is successfully sold to the executives, the processes and methodologies become relatively similar moving forward. Another reason to focus on the third scenario is because it is also the most current example and a company's Board of Directors' view of ERM programs were more up to date and different from five years ago.

The first step in this journey is to develop a presentation suitable for a company that will address major components of the message. As examples of approaches, included in this chapter are excerpts from the presentation made to the third company's CEO and CFO. The agenda is shown as follows; however, only the topics that are most relevant for a typical situation will be discussed further:

- ✓ ERM Objectives
- ✓ ERM Program Adds Shareholder Value
- ✓ Typical ERM Infrastructure
- ✓ ERM Program Leading Practices
- ✓ ERM Program Benchmarking
- ✓ Why is Change Needed Now?

✓ Why Internal Audit?

✓ What Does This Mean?

✓ Opportunities to Improve over Current Program

✓ ERM Implementation Plan

✓ ERM Calendar

✓ Proposed Implementation Timeline

✓ ERM Implementation Road to Success

✓ Checklist for Implementing ERM Program

ERM Objectives

For the best result, start the presentation by discussing the ERM objectives as shown in Figure 14.1, which illustrates four primary benefits that can be discussed at a very high level.

The first point is to **balance risk exposure against opportunity to best create, preserve, and ultimately realize value for the company.** Earlier in this book, Figure 2.1 illustrated "What an ERM Program Is," and "What an ERM Program Is Not." This first point really focuses on that concept. Many times, risks can be turned into opportunities or can be exploited as an opportunity. All of which would certainly generate value for the company. But there needs to be a balance of the risk exposure and the cost benefit for choosing to either accept the risk or manage it in other ways. An ERM program will also encourage risk owners to recognize the future potential benefits of the risk from a strategic standpoint.

- Balance risk exposure against opportunity to best create, preserve, and ultimately realize value for the Company.
- Develop residual risk improvement plan to monitor and measure effectiveness of risk mitigation activities.
- Embed ERM activities in normal business operations and management decision-making processes to encourage balanced risk/reward mindset.
- Identify and monitor implications of emerging risks.

Enterprise Risk Management (ERM): A process, effected by an entity's board of directors, management and other personnel, applied in strategy setting and across the enterprise, designed to identify potential events that may affect the entity, and manage risk to be within its risk appetite, to provide reasonable assurance regarding the achievement of entity objectives.

Figure 14.1 ERM objectives

The second point is to **develop a residual risk improvement plan to monitor and measure effectiveness of risk mitigation activities**. This is frequently where many ERM programs can falter and become more of an "ERM Lite" program. It usually happens when companies may do a good job in identifying and recording risks and developing a risk register, yet stumble on developing, measuring, monitoring, and reporting actions to mitigate the risks. For an ERM program to be effective, the risks must be monitored very closely and must include key performance indicators (KPIs) as discussed earlier about risk treatment plans. This is where the value of a robust ERM program is generated. Moreover, this monitoring, measuring, and reporting must be done frequently enough to adapt to the risk profile of the industry for a specific company.

The third point is to **embed ERM activities in the normal business operations and management decision making to encourage a balanced risk–reward mindset**. ERM should not be viewed as a project, but rather as a process. It should be a process that is embedded in virtually every decision made by the company's management—whether at its executive level, or high, medium, or lower management level. There must be a mindset in place throughout a company that there are risks to every decision, which must be considered, and understanding the costs for implementing the risk mitigation plans in place. In other words, this thought process must become a part of the normal day-to-day operations. The effective decision making must always consider the strategic direction and risks associated with the decision.

The fourth point is to **identify and monitor implications of emerging risks**. This area was considered in ERM programs for all example companies discussed in this chapter. However, the velocity at which emerging risks can become a significant factor can accelerate rapidly (as experienced with the COVID-19 pandemic as an example). At this point in time, emerging risks became almost a separate subcomponent of the ERM program, not just an afterthought of showing some industry risk slides to executives. Emerging risks have become a much more critical element in every ERM program.

As a refresher of the definition of ERM: it is a process effected by an entity's Board of Directors, management, and other personnel, and applied in companywide strategy setting, designed to identify potential events that may affect a company, and manage risk within a company's risk appetite, and to provide reasonable assurance regarding achievement of a company's objectives.

It is always good to have a list of high-level objectives, just to align the executives' mindset, as the presentation will most likely be made to the CFO and CEO, and possibly the audit committee chairman. Therefore, it should be one of introductory information presented. Experience has proven that it is better to present such introduction content to a company's CFO first to obtain his or her input before presenting it to the CEO. Once the CFO is sold on the message, the team should listen to the CFO's thoughts and opinions about how to present this material to the CEO. The presentation materials should be refined after the meetings with the CFO and CEO, addressing their input and any requirements in reporting to the audit committee chairman or the audit committee in full attendance.

ERM Program Adds Shareholder Value

After the objectives of an ERM program are established, the next step is to emphasize how ERM programs create shareholder value (as shown in Figure 14.2). The content will be different per an individual company but there should be similarities to the main messages emphasizing the important benefits.

It is very important to set the stage for the rest of the ERM program presentation by continuing to sell its benefits before going further into

✓ Firmly implemented and successful after 18 months in duration
✓ Model proven at Company, subsequently adopted by Parent Company, utilized by HP
✓ Centralized administration with decentralized risk solicitation and Treatment Plan execution
✓ Continuous program with quarterly updates to the Audit Committee
✓ Risk results incorporated in the annual Presidents Strategic Planning (PSP) program
✓ Risk results incorporated in the Annual Operating Plan (AOP) process
✓ Risk Treatment Plans incorporated in executive Quarterly Operations reviews
✓ Risk Treatment Plan deliverables linked to quarterly bonus incentive program
✓ Combines both short term and long term risk drivers with treatment plan prioritization
✓ Incorporates external and emerging risk sources
✓ Low cost administration – 2 ½ Full Time Equivalent (FTE) headcount to administer/monitor

Figure 14.2 *ERM program adds shareholder value*

discussions about the structure, infrastructure, investment, and so on. The 11 points shown in Figure 14.2 are good topics to cover at early stages.

The first bullet emphasizes that it may take from 12 to 18 months to implement a successful ERM program with continued and persistent benefits being measured and derived.

The second bullet lists companies where this ERM program and model has been proven and that this model was successfully implemented (with customized elements) at both the semiconductor and solar industries, with the approval of the major investors (i.e., Board of Directors, audit committee members, as well as company executives). This is a major selling point because it shows that ERM programs clearly added shareholder value.

The third bullet speaks to the fact that this ERM operates most effectively if there is a centralized administration of the program, containing a decentralized structure for risk solicitation and treatment plan execution. In some cases, various departments from within a company create their own ERM program, modeling it after the corporate-level program. Departments such as the tax department, the legal department, and R&D department are real examples of implementing scaled-down ERM program versions. This actually makes it easier and efficient to roll up their risk profile into the corporate-level program. Because departmental levels have much smaller thresholds than at the corporate level, these departments are able to identify and resolve many risks before they make it to the Top 25 at a corporate level. All those departmental ERM programs generally have similar treatment-plan-level type of execution, which improved operations within the individual departments. The summation of all those individual efforts is a dramatic gain to a company and added shareholder value.

The next bullet points out the need for a continuous program with quarterly updates to the executives and the audit committee. In the technology industry, as well as many others, risks and businesses are changing so frequently that there must be at least quarterly, if not a continuous monitoring of risks. In one of the above scenarios, the sense of urgency was accentuated in an audit committee meeting where the members saw a risk for the first time without any prior exposure or notification. From that point forward, any risk in the Top 10 risk profile had to be discussed at the board-level meetings. This particular experience was learned only six months into the new ERM program and highlighted to the ERM Administration Team that they need to ensure that executives are aware of any new risks immediately. This approach was also seen as a strong value-add to the shareholder community, making sure the board is aware of all risks in a very early fashion.

The next bullet points out that any robust ERM program incorporates the risk profile incorporated in a company's annual strategic planning whether it is the two-year plan, five-year plan, or even 10-year plan. There is typically at least an annual if not semiannual meeting at the executive level discussing strategic planning. The results of the ERM program provide a solid input to the strategic planning. The ERM program calendar must consider timing of these strategy planning meetings to provide the updated reporting and results.

The next bullet emphasizes that the risk profile results should be incorporated in the annual operating plan process or the annual budget process. If there are mitigation efforts for the risks identified in the risk profile that require either operating expense or capital expense, this must be included in the annual financial plan. Building risk mitigation into the financial plan avoids unbudgeted surprises or there will be a delay in the mitigation progress until funds are available. Similar to the strategic planning process, the risk profile needs to be updated immediately prior to the annual operating plan process kickoff.

The next bullet emphasizes that the Risk Treatment Plans should be incorporated in the executive Quarterly Operations Reviews. Regardless of the name and frequency, every company has these types of operations reviews where the core leadership will discuss the business elements of the recent quarter, as well as future expectations for at least the next quarter and possibly the rest of the year. All of the companies shown in the above examples required that the status of Top 25 risks is incorporated in the Quarterly Operations Reviews, which were held with the CEO and the other leaders of a company. This was ultimately a requirement made by the CEO at different stages of maturity of the ERM program, but eventually all of them required the updates.

The next bullet suggests that the risk treatment plan deliverables should be linked to management's bonus incentive and compensation programs. In the case of all these companies, the quarterly bonus programs and quarterly goals were set and measured. Bonuses were paid based on the accomplishment of specific goals each quarter. This was a strong incentive for the executives to be on top of the formal risk treatment plans, which include KPIs, deliverables, tracking of actions, ownership, just like any well-managed project. Bonus incentive programs that are tied to quarterly objectives nearly always have some type of linkage with goals of other departments. The performance interdependency exists for most of the risk statements and helps to hold multiple departments jointly accountable. In these situations, indirect pressure can be applied to the interdependent departments when the cross-function team is lagging, causing a delay in the accomplishment of success. This is one of the strongest motivators of making sure everybody is operating at the same pace. There also must be a strong and frequent open dialogue and communication among the various departments to be able to view the statuses in the middle of the quarter and correct the course as needed. This also drives shareholder value and profitability to the business.

Another example of the ERM program creating shareholder value is that a robust ERM program combines both short-term and long-term risk drivers and requires treatment plan prioritization. Longer term risks are not always specifically considered in many ERM programs but based on the speed or velocity at which the risk could occur, this consideration will drive how quickly management should start addressing the longer term elements in the near term. This helps to drive short-term goals with attention to longer term strategy and ultimately shareholder value.

Another element that creates shareholder value is to incorporate both external and emerging risk sources. External and emerging risks could be the same type of risk or quite different risks. Both components need to be covered differently in developing the risk profile and reporting. However, the key takeaway here is that there is a need to make sure that all external risks for which the company has a restricted amount of ability to influence is identified. Management should start dealing with those external risks quickly to minimize the impact to the business model. Similarly, most boards today are more interested about knowing what they do not know. That basically means, they want to know any potential risk before it happens. They want to know what is emerging, whether it is emerging in the industry or in a company only, is it emerging in the global economy, and if this emerging risk is more of a geopolitical type of risk. In 2020, the emerging risks from COVID-19 pandemic were not known or even expected. However, many companies were better situated because they had other risks coverage implemented that helped relieve the issues caused by the pandemic. For example, some companies already had a pandemic policy in place, including having a crisis team in place, which facilitated a timely and effective implementation, or had a disaster recovery plan and business continuity plan, as well as backup plans associated with having sole and/or single suppliers. Their ability to avoid the surprises that could take down a manufacturing plant or impact their resourcing certainly had an impact on shareholder value.

The last point for adding shareholder value is the cost of having an infrastructure and resources in place to manage an ERM program. A robust program with frequent reporting can be resourced without incurring huge costs, especially when it is compared to the staggering benefits that can be realized from the program. In all the example companies, once the program got up and running, the administrative element to run, coordinate, monitor, and report the ERM program took approximately two and one-half FTE head counts. That is not a lot of expense considering millions and billions of dollars of risk.

Typical ERM Infrastructure

While it's extremely important to share the benefits and the objectives of an ERM program with the ELTs, it is equally important to share the expected size of the program. How many people should be involved? What is the coverage, breadth, and the amount of work that must be accomplished on recurring basis and without failures? Figure 7.3 was shown earlier, but it is shown again here (Figure 14.3) as a reference to reaffirm the executives that this program is a board-level program with a high level of visibility and transparency.

Figure 14.3 shows the required participation and the responsibility of each participant. The risk committee oversees the overall governance and will be composed of specific key executives who drive the business model

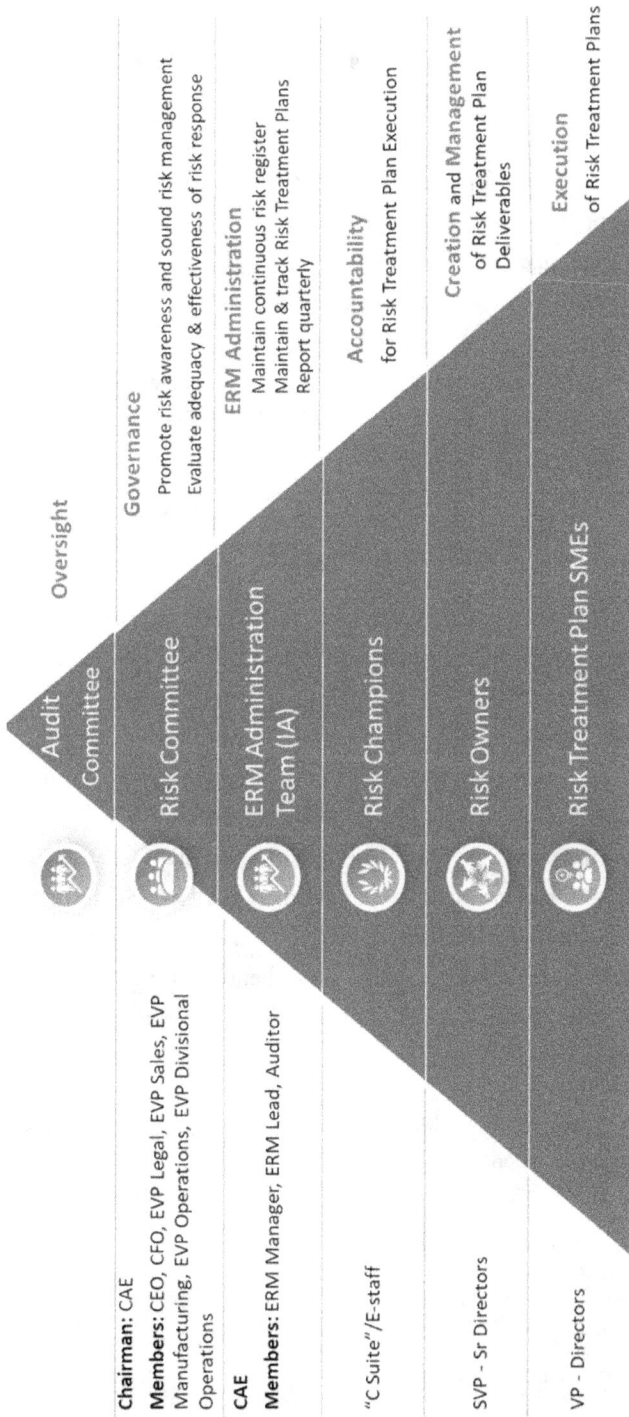

Figure 14.3 Typical ERM infrastructure

from a bigger picture perspective. There is also the ERM Administration Team, although small, to drive the program and report the progress. There are Risk Champions assigned to the Top 25 risks who are usually a C-suite or E-staff level person for accountability. The Risk Owners are the people who own the Top 25 risks and are responsible for the creation and managing of the risk treatment plan deliverables. Finally, there are the risk treatment plan Subject Matter Experts (SMEs), who are typically the director to vice president level management. They are responsible for the execution of the risk treatment plans. You can also include several participants, to make it very clear how many people are involved in this robust ERM program. For example, the number for one of the example companies was 84 people from top to bottom.

ERM Leading Practices

Figure 14.4 shows the leading practices of ERM programs within companies of a specific size. The benchmarking results were obtained from the Gartner ERM Study.

The benchmarking was done for each of the example companies, but the statistics discussed here were specifically obtained for the third scenario—a semiconductor company, as they are most recent. The results were based on answers to questionnaires from ERM peer groups and from other professional organizations such as Gartner, which specialize in risk management topics. Later, we will show the detailed examples of the benchmarking and show the results of the benchmarking, which pertains to the model, size, and footprint most similar to the three companies referenced in this book.

> • Based on ERM Peer and Professional Groups Benchmarking:
>   • ERM Annual Spend: $310,000 (50th percentile)
>   • Headcount designated to ERM Administration: 1.5 (50th percentile)
>   • ERM reporting relationships: CFO (majority)
>   • ERM programs in place by Company size in revenue: Even <$1B
>   • ERM programs that use KPI Indicators: Trend is to use them.
>   • Frequency of Enterprise risk Assessments (ERA): Varies
>   • Synergies of Risk Reporting to the BoD: IA Highest %

Figure 14.4 What are ERM program leading practices?

The first bullet shows the annual ERM spend to be about US$310,000, at the 50th percentile of all the companies that were interviewed.

The second bullet is the number of designated headcount to administer the program, again at the 50th percentile. It was 1.5 full-time equivalents (FTEs). While the benchmarking shows 1.5, experience shows that it may be closer to 2.5 FTE headcount. The difference is driven by the varying approaches used when conducting the risk assessments. Specifically, sending out surveys versus visiting locations for face-to-face meetings will be more resource consuming. Experience has also shown that the face-to-face interviews may be the most beneficial and productive way to develop the risk profile, as discussed earlier in this book.

The third bullet shows the reporting relationships and that 50 percent of the ERM teams report to the CFO.

The fourth bullet shows the size of the company's annual revenue. Note that ERM programs are in place even in companies less than one billion dollars in annual revenue. The trend is that the number of companies implementing ERM programs is increasing, regardless of size. Historically, only larger companies had these programs in place.

The fifth bullet is the number of ERM programs that use KPIs. While it sounds very basic, statistics show that many treatment plans are not driven with KPIs. However, most recent trends show them to be included and used as part of the risk treatment plans.

The sixth bullet shows that the frequency of the actual risk assessments whether bottom-up, top-down, or in both directions varied. There did not seem to be one practice more dominant over the other.

The last bullet indicates that there were more synergies of reporting risks to the Board of Directors when the program was administered by the internal audit department. Very few other departments have their primary mission and scope as being a risk-based organization that highlights, identifies, and reports, high-risk issues. The synergies were more dominant when the program was reported to the internal audit department. That does not mean that the recommendation was made for the ERM program to report to the CFO but was rather just a spotlight of showing the common or leading practices.

Benchmarking for Leading Practices

Figure 14.5 shows specific benchmarking information related to dollar spend, head count reporting, and company size.

These are summaries of the benchmarking study that were then brought forward to the summary shown in Figure 14.4 that was just reviewed.

Also in Figure 14.5, pay attention to the chart in the upper right-hand corner titled "Head of ERM Characteristics." While it was a desire for the internal audit department to have ERM program under its control, the CEO and CFO should be the ones making that decision as there was enough information provided to help them to make an educated decision based on how other companies were doing it. Generally, the Head of ERM sits within three or four primary department: (1) internal audit department, (2) finance department, (3) legal department, and (4) treasury department, or maybe a company has its own individual ERM department. This table does show that internal audit seems to include the primary work experience for the largest percentage of the Head of ERM roles. Specifically, the ERM reported to the CFO (and through the chief audit executive through the CFO) 38 percent of the time. The CFO is the top leader who has the direct administrative reporting responsibility. The Head of ERM frequently includes other roles and the most frequent other roles include internal audit, followed by business continuity planning disaster recovery, then ethics and investigations, and finally internal

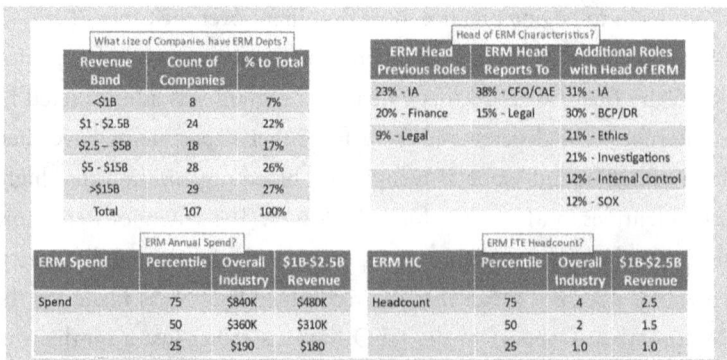

What size of Companies have ERM Depts?

Revenue Band	Count of Companies	% to Total
<$1B	8	7%
$1 - $2.5B	24	22%
$2.5 - $5B	18	17%
$5 - $15B	28	26%
>$15B	29	27%
Total	107	100%

Head of ERM Characteristics?

ERM Head Previous Roles	ERM Head Reports To	Additional Roles with Head of ERM
23% - IA	38% - CFO/CAE	31% - IA
20% - Finance	15% - Legal	30% - BCP/DR
9% - Legal		21% - Ethics
		21% - Investigations
		12% - Internal Control
		12% - SOX

ERM Annual Spend?

ERM Spend	Percentile	Overall Industry	$1B-$2.5B Revenue
Spend	75	$840K	$480K
	50	$360K	$310K
	25	$190	$180

ERM FTE Headcount?

ERM HC	Percentile	Overall Industry	$1B-$2.5B Revenue
Headcount	75	4	2.5
	50	2	1.5
	25	1.0	1.0

Figure 14.5 ERM benchmark: Spend, headcount, reporting, and company size

control and Sarbanes Oxley (SOX). Those types of roles indicate that the leading practice or the most frequent practice is for the ERM function to report up through the internal audit department to the Finance (CFO). The table on the bottom right side of Figure 14.5 is also important because it shows the span or range of FTE headcount devoted to the ERM administration. Companies in the US$1 billion to US$2.5 billion range are closer to the example companies we referenced before and have a range from one to two and one-half people. As mentioned earlier, that is probably most frequently driven by the approach used to conduct the risk assessments and the frequency of reporting.

Figure 14.6, showing ERM Benchmarking Program Elements, relates more to the benchmarking associated with the infrastructure and the makeup of the program.

The upper left chart shows data about ERM programs that use KPIs. There is a staggeringly high volume of companies that do not use KPIs, notably around the 54 to 56 percent mark, while only around 27 or 28 percent of companies use some level of KPIs for at least 50 percent of their risks. A small percentage (single digit) have KPIs for the entire profile population. The chart also shows whether companies use predictive risks or lagging risks indicators. Certainly, both types of indicators are probably the most effective way to address the program. The upper right corner table shows the frequency of enterprise risk assessments being conducted. About 45 percent are done annually, which is normal. About 21 percent is done semiannually, which is more in line with the volatility of the global

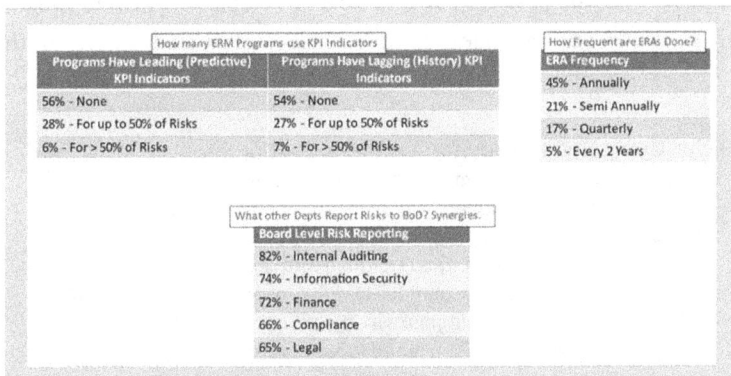

How many ERM Programs use KPI Indicators		How Frequent are ERAs Done?
Programs Have Leading (Predictive) KPI Indicators	Programs Have Lagging (History) KPI Indicators	ERA Frequency
56% - None	54% - None	45% - Annually
28% - For up to 50% of Risks	27% - For up to 50% of Risks	21% - Semi Annually
6% - For > 50% of Risks	7% - For > 50% of Risks	17% - Quarterly
		5% - Every 2 Years

What other Depts Report Risks to BoD? Synergies.
Board Level Risk Reporting
82% - Internal Auditing
74% - Information Security
72% - Finance
66% - Compliance
65% - Legal

Figure 14.6 ERM benchmarking program elements

environment. Our experience has shown that a semiannual frequency is preferred. One being a full blown, top up and top down, grassroots type of exercise, while the second one being more of a refresh. And there are about 70 percent of the companies surveyed that do this quarterly, which is moving more in line to a continuous monitoring type of risk management program. This is the direction of the future but requires either more resources or more automation. Lastly, only 5 percent do the Enterprise Risk Assesment (ERA) every two years, which is too long inbetween for nearly all industries.

The bottom chart shows the leading practice and benchmarking results related to where the correct reporting relationship is for the ERM function. The referenced companies used in this book made the decision to have ERM reporting to the internal audit department. In the latter case, the function was moved from the Legal department to the internal audit department.

Why Is Change Needed Now?

Depending on your success in selling the ERM program, it may be advantageous to add some commentaries about why the changes to the ERM are needed in your company. After all, ERM program does cost money and time, even though the benefits are significant.

Figure 14.7 is showing some ideas why the changes are needed now, which can be presented to a company's CEO.

The benchmarking provided the justification for a more robust ERM program when compared to the one currently in place, which is updated only every two years and clearly not the best-in-class model. Some of the

✓Our Company is ready for a more robust program:
- Size of $1.4B, 40+ countries, 3000+ Employees
- Industry is an environment with high velocity of change
- Major organization alignment and bringing in new executives
- Continues to be a turnaround situation with great momentum
- Ready for a focus on accountability with formality of measurement
- Need a focus on emerging risks in the industry and environment
- Need more centralized/structured focus of risk at enterprise level

Figure 14.7 Why is change needed now?

points that should be brought forward to the CEO and CFO should focus on:

- The size of a company, the number of countries included in its footprint, and the number of employees even without having manufacturing employees in the mix. The population is large enough to create workforce risks.
- The industry is in an environment with a very high velocity of change even prior to the pandemic with normal routine business. Geopolitical risks have grown dramatically over the past few years needing continuous attention as to how they affect the way of conducting business.
- A company is going through a major realignment including several new executives at the CEO direct report level. This type of change brings in a new perspective of conducting business and changing priorities and goals, all of which can create risk associated with an environment of change.
- A company has been executing through a turnaround situation with great results, but still needing a careful oversight to maintain the strong positive momentum the company is experiencing.
- A new organization realignment and the changes in the business model emphasizes the need for additional focus on accountability along with formality of measurements of success.
- The need for additional focus on emerging risk in the industry and environment. That element is seldom brought forward within any other process other than an ERM program. The focus on emerging risks as noted earlier has escalated particularly since the pandemic and global political unrest.
- A need of a more centralized and structured focus on the ERM program at an enterprise level to ensure that the decentralized efforts are in sync and are experiencing synergies that are possible throughout the organization.

While this may not be completely new information for a CEO and CFO, it does pull everything together into a theme highlighting the

importance of acting now and ensuring there is an effective ERM program in place to monitor and mitigate risks to the company.

Why Internal Audit?

The next topic of discussion with the CEO and CFO is to provide enough
information for them to decide on the reporting structure of the ERM
program. While it is their decision, it is prudent to share recommendations or at least provide the facts that would drive their decision. In the
third scenario example (a semiconductor company), the ERM program
was already placed within the legal department. In this specific instance,
there was a need justify the need for the more effective reporting structure
that could be achieved by placing the ERM program with an internal
audit department (see Figure 14.8).

This Figure 14.8 is used merely to pull together everything that has
been discussed so far and help solidify the final decision. One of the key
points is related to the level of independence that Internal Audit has
from the company operations. Such level of independence provides an
environment that ensures there are no biases or leniency toward any of a
company's groups or organizations, and that the reporting of results and
progress is straightforward. The following three points are supported by
the benchmarked information. Specifically, they reinforce that the back-
grounds of ERM heads are generally more Internal Audit and Finance
driven, with the reporting structure typically to Finance organization.

> • IA's primary mission is Risk Management, and has
>   independence/objectivity from Company Management and
>   Operations
> • ERM blends better with other risk areas of investigations, SOX,
>   Audit, Internal control, etc. [benchmark]
> • Background of ERM Heads is more predominantly IA/Finance,
>   not Legal [benchmark]
> • Reporting practice is more predominantly to Finance, not Legal
>   [benchmark]
> • IA is the most predominant dept for reporting of risks to the Board
>   for added synergies [benchmark]
> • IA has a "pool" of auditors to manage the peaks of ERM needs.

Figure 14.8 Why internal audit?

Additionally, the Internal Audit Department is in any respect the most dominant department that already generates most of the risk reporting to the Board of Directors.

The last point discussed in Figure 14.8 is the big benefit of the Internal Audit Department having a pool of auditors to manage at the peaks of ERM needs. Having two and one-half equivalent headcount does not mean the department has two halves and one-half fully dedicated people to ERM program, but it means there could be at least one person fully devoted to the ERM program with the other one and one-half made up of hours contributed from several other auditors, as needed in the peak time for the risk assessments or reporting.

At this point, the CEO and CFO should be clear at least with respect to the general direction of the ERM program, should agree to move forward with a more robust ERM program, and change the reporting structure from Legal to Internal Audit Department and ultimately to the CFO.

What Does This Mean?

After having the CEO and CFO acknowledgments to move forward with the ERM program, it is now appropriate to discuss what it really means as shown in Figure 14.9, to draw parallels between expectations and deliverables.

Since there was already an existing ERM program in place within the Legal department and a new risk register had just been recently developed, it makes sense to confirm that the changes will be introduced during the implementation period. The second bullet indicates that there should be

- Utilize Legal's existing program through the implementation period
- Refresh Risk Profile with new methodology before June Strategic Meeting
- Staff 1.5 designated to "head/execute" the effort (In 2022 AOP)
- Utilize the IA pool of team members to gain synergies
- Transition period to implement program will cover 4 quarters once resource is available
- Implement in piecemeal so as not to overwhelm anyone
- Integrate program format into existing processes
- Train, train, train, train.....ongoing

Figure 14.9 *What does this mean?*

a refresh of the risk profile with the new methodology before the next (in this example, June) strategic long-term planning meeting.

The third bullet confirms that it would take one and one-half employees (FTEs) to create and execute the program during 2022 with a ramp up in 2023 with an additional headcount. This assumes that the transition period to implement the ERM program would cover four quarters after the initial resources were made available and onboarded. Additionally, the ERM program would be implemented in a piecemeal method to avoid overwhelming everyone with the amount of work and changes that will be taking place. It is also important to note that the new program should integrate any type of efficient program formats that might already exist to minimize "changes" where possible.

Finally, the last bullet indicates that everyone should expect a new language related to enterprise risk management and that necessary training would be provided every step of the way. Some retraining would happen multiple times throughout the implementation period.

Figure 14.9 helps to put the executives at ease, demonstrating that this would be a methodical, well-managed approach, and that any incremental financial cost for the program would be incurred over a two-year period. This would be a better match with the costs at the time when a company could start seeing some benefits. It is important to conclude the executive pitch and buy-in on such a positive note. There can be other data points presented and made available in the appendices if needed. The following section shows some illustrations that may be included as appropriate. In the case study, these slides were included in the appendix as back, but were not needed to seal the deal.

Opportunities to Improve Over Current Program

Figure 14.10 shows the benefits of having a more robust ERM program to help sell the program if needed or to clarify what might be seen for the foreseeable months to come and during the transition.

Several of the items note that the existing ERM program could be substantially improved by focusing the dedicated resources and efforts on the program and minimize the need for the temporary external resourcing.

✓ Only Bi-annual ERA (needs to be at least annually and preferable Semi-annually)
✓ Questionnaire Only (Needs to have a higher blend of in person conversations to get full feel of risks)
✓ Sends predetermined questions (needs to have no prescribed guidance on topics blank sheet of paper)
✓ Does not quantify risks (can't manage what is not measured)
✓ No formal Treatment Plan in place (need a Treatment Plan with KPIs, action owners, action steps, dates, etc.)
✓ Non - Employees synthesize the risk statements (needs to be internal folks who learn the business and know the business better)
✓ No Cadence to monitor progress of Treatment Plans
✓ There is no focus on Emerging Risks
✓ There is no comparison of our risk profile to competitors or to our own quarterly reporting
✓ No formal reporting to the Board on a quarterly basis
✓ Rating criteria is very judgmental without detailed rationale supporting the rating

Figure 14.10 Opportunities to improve over current program

The most immediate change would be an increase in the frequency of the risk assessment updates, which was previously done only every two years. Leading practices require that a risk assessment should be done annually at a minimum, and preferably semiannually.

The second improvement is the approach used to obtain the risk statements during the assessments. The previous approach was predetermined questions based on a questionnaire lacking any supplemental conversations and as a result, lacking a full understanding of the risks potentially gained from having in-person conversations. There are benefits to be realized to start with a blank sheet of paper and no prescribed guidance on suggested topics. Additionally, the previous ERM program did not quantify the risk statements, which made it very difficult to get a good risk profile ranking. The ranking was purely based on judgment of impact and likelihood obtained as part of the questionnaire. There were no formal treatment plans in place including normal project management elements such as owners, action steps, dates, or KPIs to drive the remediation of the risks.

Another improvement related to implementing the more robust ERM program was in using internal experts and resources going forward. The previous ERM program relied on an external firm that was hired to synthesize the risk statements utilizing its offshore employees. This firm had no knowledge of the company's business and lacked the access to the employees to ask follow-up questions to clarify the context of the statements or to better understand the acronyms, and so on. Nor was there a cadence to monitor progress of the remediation. As a result, there was no focus on emerging risks or even external risks that were called out specifically for comparison to existing risks and for further thought by the executive team. There were no comparisons made of the company's risk profile to the risk profile of competitors or to the risks that are reported in the company's quarterly and annual financial reporting filings (10Qs and 10Ks.) It also lacked a reporting to the Board of Directors on a quarterly basis, but rather only once per year. Lastly, the rating criteria was very judgmental without any rationale supporting the ratings.

It was clear that the previous ERM program and resulting risk profile could be incomplete if not misleading under the existing program, and therefore required to be changed.

ERM Implementation Plan

In anticipation of possible questions about implementation, it is prudent to have a high-level draft of the ERM plan as shown in Figure 14.11.

This implementation plan is from the previously mentioned semi-conductor company's project and reflects a three-quarter exercise. ELT wanted it in place very quickly to start recognizing the benefits as soon as possible. The time period is a little shorter than would be ideal, but the audit team met their expectations. The resources were hired and put in place at the very beginning of Q2. During Q2, the resources ramped up their familiarity with the multiyear strategic financial plan and the goals and objectives of the executives and stakeholder expectations. The Enterprise Risk Management Charter including the supporting framework was created with focus on topics such as:

- How to work with short-term and long-term considerations;
- Qualitative and quantitative factors;
- Establishing the risk committee and charter; and
- Other elements discussed in earlier chapters such as the templates.

During the second three months (Q3) the training began, as well as communicating awareness of the goals and expectations to the broader management audience. During that same period, the first risk assessment

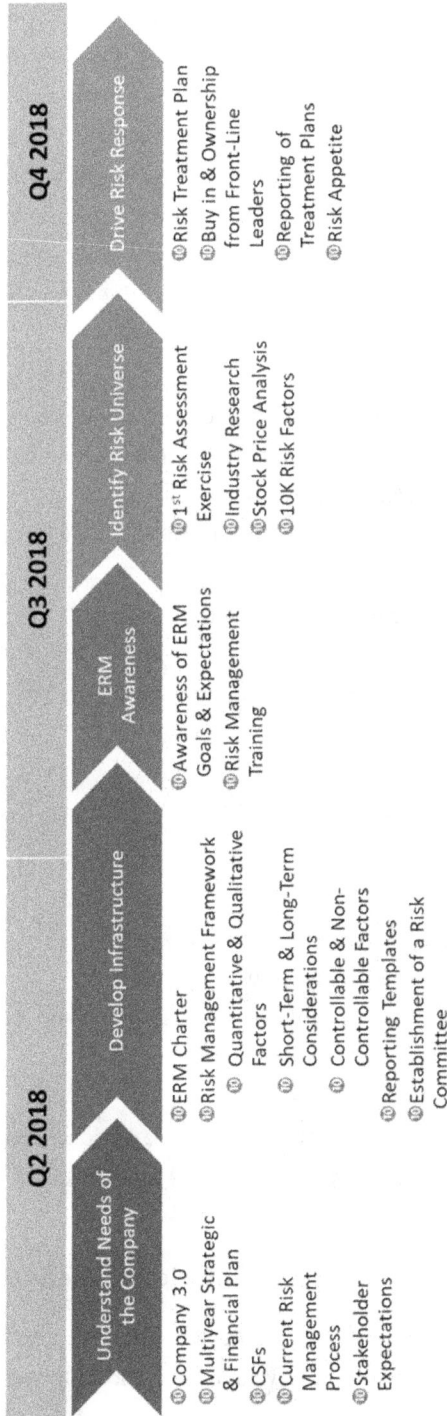

Q2 2018

Q3 2018

Q4 2018

Understand Needs of the Company
- Company 3.0
- Multiyear Strategic & Financial Plan
- CSFs
- Current Risk Management Process
- Stakeholder Expectations

Develop Infrastructure
- ERM Charter
- Risk Management Framework
- Quantitative & Qualitative Factors
- Short-Term & Long-Term Considerations
- Controllable & Non-Controllable Factors
- Reporting Templates
- Establishment of a Risk Committee

ERM Awareness
- Awareness of ERM Goals & Expectations
- Risk Management Training

Identify Risk Universe
- 1st Risk Assessment Exercise
- Industry Research
- Stock Price Analysis
- 10K Risk Factors

Drive Risk Response
- Risk Treatment Plan
- Buy in & Ownership from Front-Line Leaders
- Reporting of Treatment Plans
- Risk Appetite

Figure 14.11 ERM implementation plan

exercise was conducted from both a bottom-up and top-down, along with concluding industry research such as reviewing the 10K risk factors from competitors. These were high-volume focus activities that consumed far more than the 1.5 FTE headcount during this three-month period. The extra resources were pulled from the operational audit team. Lastly in Q4, risk treatment plans were created for the Top 10 risks and reported out for the first time.

ERM Calendar

To supplement the Implementation Plan, it is important to provide a visual of the normal ERM program calendar over a regular year after full implementation as seen in Figure 14.12.

The calendar of events shows the sequence of activities such as:

- Quarterly risk committee meetings;
- Quarterly audit committee meetings;
- Annual multiyear strategic planning;
- The annual operating budget creation.

These quarterly events, are then followed by other key events such as:

- The risk assessment;
- The emerging risk assessment;
- The risk factor mapping to the 10K and 10Q;
- The creation of treatment plans in assessing; and
- The creation of the stock price analysis.

This provides an overview of when the various events happened during the normal yearly cycle.

Proposed Implementation Timeline

To support a broader timeline of implementation and calendar, an implementation timeline should be developed at a monthly level as shown in Figure 14.13.

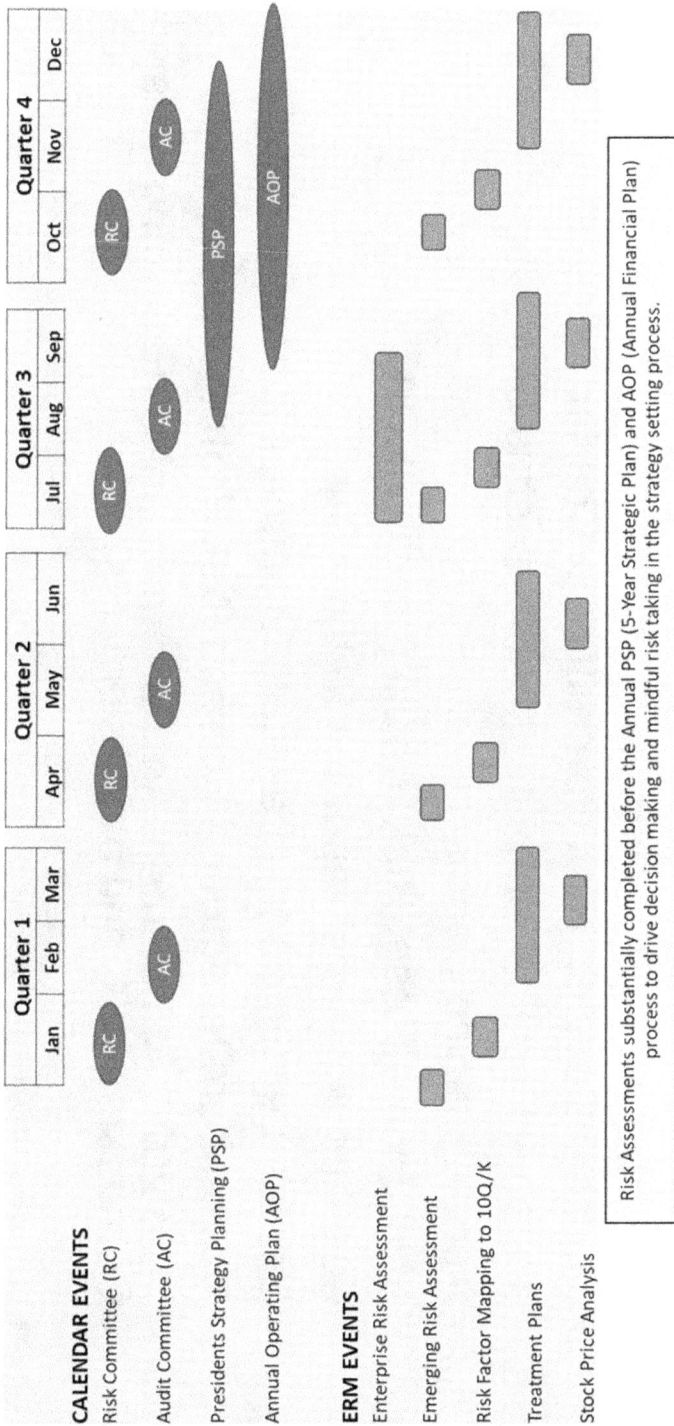

Figure 14.12 ERM calendar

✓ January/February – Hire open requisitions

✓ March – Develop Risk Committee & Charter

✓ March – Develop templates that fit existing processes

✓ April – Training Begins

✓ May/June – Reset Risk Profile (conduct ERA)

✓ July/August – First reporting to the AC

✓ September/October – Facilitate Treatment Plans for Top 10

✓ November/December – Refresh Risk Profile

✓ Year 2023 – Implement Ancillary mechanics (Emerging risks, Competitor 10K, and other elements)

Figure 14.13 Proposed implementation timeline

This schedule is not discussed during the initial executive buy-in presentations, but it is important later on during the implementation trainings.

The timeline (as shown in Figure 14.13) is an actual timeline used in one of the companies as an example. It was successful and resulted in decisions to support the ERM program with an accelerated schedule.

The following sections will discuss the implementation period.

ERM Implementation Road to Success

This section will discuss **ERM implementation, Road to Success** as shown in Figure 14.14. Even in the best of business cultures, implementing an ERM program can be extremely difficult, so it is beneficial to create the ERM implementation checklist. Let's start with some general comments relative to positioning a company and the ERM Administration Team for success. There are many factors that can complicate a successful implementation of an ERM program, most of which can be eliminated or dramatically reduced by considering and addressing the following concerns.

As with any companywide program, an ERM program also requires the ongoing **support of the executive level and the Board of Directors** to be successful. ELT typically understands the incredible benefits and of implementing a successful ERM program although they may not

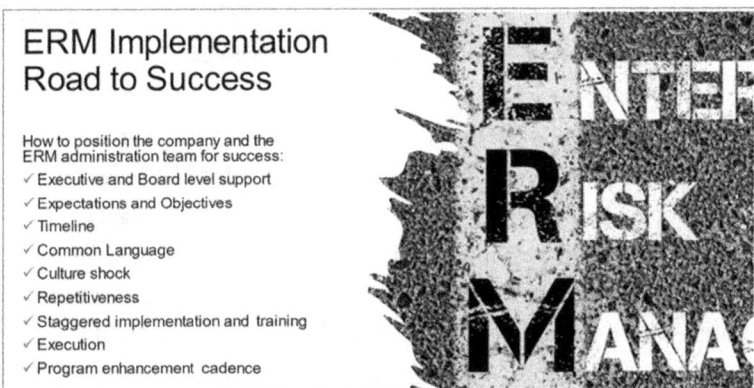

Figure 14.14 ERM implementation road to success

necessarily understand or inquire about the administrative efforts or time required of company personnel to generate the end results.

If there is a way to have the ERM program introduced to the management level immediately below CEO, specifically being a CEO direct reports, then the chances of succeeding will be much greater. Normally, this would be done after the CEO/CFO presentation. The ERM Administration Team should create a separate presentation showing the agreed-upon **objectives and expectations** to the next executive-level reporting. The best time for sharing the proposed ERM program would be at an important strategic-setting meeting or prior to developing of the annual operating plan. This timing will help leverage the necessity of applying whatever support is needed for a strong strategic meeting and a strong annual operating plan. Such presentation or level of support may depend on who requested the implementation of the ERM program. If it was the Board of Directors, then the CEO is best to convey this message to his or her direct reports. If the CEO requested the ERM program implementation, then he could still be the primary person to deliver the message; however, it can be equally as important if the Head of ERM or the CFO were to deliver the message to the C-suite or E-staff level of the organization, preferably with the Head of ERM in the meeting.

In the situations where ERM program is presented by the Head of Internal Audit or other similar functions, then the head of that function should expect to be the primary driver and even introducing the program to the executive team. As long as the right people are in the room and as long as the CEO and CFO support the program, it becomes the Head of the ERM Administrative Team to assume the responsibility and execute the plan to make the ERM program successful.

Most companies have internal mechanisms that track project management of initiatives, or they at least have some level of cadence from which employees are used to creating and presenting performance results. Similarly, it is to the best interest of the Head of ERM to try to incorporate any existing processes or any existing templates that may already be in place within the company to lessen the amount of additional work or perception of additional work that the employees may need to do. This will also improve the effectiveness of the training programs.

The **timeline of implementation** is also an area that can help ensure the success of the program. In the three companies used as examples, the length of time it took to implement the program varied. When the program was initiated by the Head of Internal Audit, it took nearly two years to implement the ERM program and get it stabilized so that it was an ongoing part of everyone's day-to-day operations. Conversely, with one of the semiconductor companies, the Board of Directors requested the new ERM program and the timeline mandate for implementing the ERM program from beginning to end was only nine months. At the end of the ninth month, the risk register had been created, all the infrastructure documents, templates, policies, and charters had been created, as well as results of the treatment plans were communicated, while presenting the risk profile to the Board of Directors happened after the first six months of implementation. If given the opportunity to implement the program over a different timeline, it would be better to extend the implementation period longer than nine months. The sweet spot would be between four and six quarters, and preferably no longer than six quarters. The main reason is that this would provide enough time to build the infrastructure, to train management, implement the templates, and train and train and train. Once the management team sees the results, they become more excited about the application of the ERM program and the resulting benefits.

Another element for success of ERM program would be teaching everyone a **common risk management language**. What this means is that risk management terminology should become very prominent in the conversations and the terms should mean the same thing for everyone who is discussing the ERM program. "Risk treatment plan" should be called the "risk treatment plan" by everyone. There should not be any other terminology for the risk treatment plan. As these terms are not part of day-to-day conversation especially at a lower management and employees' level, it is better to establish a list of common language terms, and even document definitions of terms and the acronyms for use during the training sessions in the very beginning, as well as any refresh trainings that happen subsequently.

Similarly, to introducing a common language there is another element called **culture shock**. If the culture of the organization is not accustomed to this type of oversight, coordination, and execution required for effective enterprise risk management, they could hinder the implementation progress. This is yet another reason to include the management team in the development of the ERM processes, procedures, and governance models, as they are the ones on the ground. While they are not a part of the senior management team, they are the people who will be creating risk treatment plans and executing the steps within the risk treatment plants. This frontline ownership will certainly carry over into the effectiveness of the initial program, as well as post implementation of the ERM program and operations. A successful implementation will be difficult without involving the frontline management. In the checklist to be discussed later, recommendations will be provided on the best practices and advice on how to avoid some of these common pitfalls.

Another element to help ensure "Road to Success" is to instill repetitiveness as often as possible. **Repetitiveness** means that the same process is used consistently. There must be policies that drive the same procedures, even down to the point of creating the risk profiles and risk rankings. This repetitiveness will also need to be carried over into how the results are reported to the risk committee, to the executives, as well as to the audit committee of the board. It is better to also use a standardized deck during the quarterly presentation of these results. These decks should be in standard formats and templates. This helps the audience get familiar with the identical format and will make it easier for them to digest the information and results being communicated.

This leads to the next point, which is implementing and training at a staggered interval. When talking about a **staggered implementation** concept, it is to ensure that the various levels of the company are trained thoroughly. Different levels of a company will require different levels of training. For example, the departments that already have or are creating their own ERM program within the individual department, should be preferably trained after the primary programs are implemented at a company level using the same philosophies, terms, and templates.

Another element of success is to maintain the same repetitiveness in communicating and adding any **program enhancements at a regular cadence**. For example, once the primary ERM program is implemented, the ERM Administrative Team should set a target to make at least one improvement per quarter. In that fashion, the audience is familiar with the ERM baseline and only must adapt to understanding one new concept per a quarter. This creates incentive for the ERM Administrative Team to keep thinking of new ways to improve the effectiveness of the ERM program. Experience has shown that a solid goal is to implement new enhancements every quarter for as long as the program lasts. Yes, there may be some quarters where there is simply nothing significantly new to introduce; however, there is always room for an improvement or refinement even if it is as basic as new reporting or data aggregation templates.

ERM programs have changed dramatically from what they were 10 years ago, and they will continue to change and evolve dramatically in the future. New tools and new sources of information will become available. The concept of heat maps and risk ranking will undoubtedly change as well, and the use of artificial intelligence can certainly impact how the ERM program model will look in the next five years. Therefore, it is important to keep enhancing the ERM program on a regular basis, while not adding too many radical changes at once.

Lastly, the road to **success depends on execution**. There must be a solid execution from the first quarter and forward. Quarter after quarter, there must be a demonstrated yield in benefits and progress for each of the risk topics. If the program becomes stale and the Top 25 risks do not change over time (new risks being added and old risks falling off the list due to remediation), the program will not succeed. Solid execution on a consistent basis is required for the program to be successful and remain successful moving forward. Regardless of the industry or the nuances of the ERM program, make sure the "Road to Success" guidelines stay in the forefront of thought.

ERM Implementation Checklist

This section includes a dialogue around a quick reference checklist for implementing an ERM program. Each of the primary steps included in the checklist will be discussed individually by phase.

In Figure 14.15, the **Phase 1** is **Selling the Program**.

This phase is the preliminary work (**Step 1**) that needs to be done prior to presenting to executives to obtain their buy-in. Preparation for

Ref	Phase	Action Description
1	Selling the Program	List what is important to your company and start developing information to present to executives. (tailored) 1 – Research the company goals and business objectives over net 24 months. 2 – Gather company statistics (geography, headcount, financials). 3 – Research for Benchmarking stats for companies like yours. 4 – Determine objectives for the program (be company specific). 5 – Develop specific benefits expected (be company specific). 6 – Consider availability of resources to implement and maintain. 7 – Assess cost impact and timing of such (labor, systems, etc.). 8 – Determine who are the decision makers and anticipate any obstacles.
2	CFO Presentation	Create a presentation deck for the lower-level decision maker (usually CFO) 1 – Utilize the comments in this book to develop the deck outline. 2 – Determine the message to be conveyed. 3 – Compile a complete deck with detail as needed (put extras in appendix). 4 – Present to CFO and note the take-a-ways in preparation for CEO deck.

Figure 14.15 *Quick reference checklist for implementing ERM (steps 1–2)*

developing and selling the ERM program can be quite exhaustive as it must be done with full knowledge of the organization to ensure the program is tailored to the company's dimensions. Most companies have missions, goals, and objectives published on its intranet site. The ERM team must match the ERM goals to those goals and objectives, both short term and long term. Frequently, the quarterly goals of a CEO and his or her direct reports are made public through a company's goal system, which makes it much easier for the ERM team to understand company direction.

Step 2 item under "Selling the Program" is to make sure that all company statistics are gathered in support of the ERM program coverage. Specifically, there needs to be accurate information about the company's geography, its footprint, number of locations, number of countries, global regions, and different financial statistics. All these data points will help drive the necessity of an ERM program and should be used to sell the program.

Step 3 under "Selling the Program" is to research the benchmarking statistics, particularly for companies within the same industry and a comparable footprint and statistics. Usually, the benchmarking studies have this information broken down by industry and by different annual revenue figures.

Step 4 under "Selling the Program" is to determine the actual objectives of the program for the company. The objectives will differ between banking, manufacturing, and services companies. The team has to develop the objectives tailored specifically to the designated company.

Step 5 under "Selling the Program" is to identify specific benefits that a company should expect from the ERM program. This list can be refined or expanded after the initial conversations with the CFO and CEO, and the benefits will continue to be refined and used in the training decks later.

Step 6 under "Selling the Program" refers to the preparation in discussing the cost of the ERM program, not only the cost to implement but also cost to maintain the program. It needs to consider the dedicated resources, as well as any existing resources to be utilized on a part-time basis during the peak periods. It must consider the company structure and footprint, where employees are located, and where executives are located. There is a very strong possibility that the ERM Administrative Team could reside in a low-cost location. Conducting further assessment of the cost impact (**Step 7**) and specifically the timing of incurring those costs to implement the ERM program and maintaining the program should include systems or automated tools to facilitate the administrative efforts.

Step 8 is the last step under "Selling the Program." This is a necessary step to determine the decision makers in relation to implementing the ERM program and anticipating any obstacles or pushbacks that may be received. The ERM team needs to anticipate these obstacles and prepare additional information for the appendix, if needed.

In summary, the first phase—"Selling the Program"—is all about collecting the information related to the company internally and externally, which will help develop the sales pitch that is tailored specifically to the company and requires the buy-in of the CEO and CFO.

Phase 2 is the **CFO Presentation**. This presentation should be prepared for presenting to the "one level lower decision-maker," generally the CFO. While the CFO would be very crucial in the decision making, the ultimate decision would still likely rest with the CEO or the Audit Committee. This presentation will not only cover higher level areas that have been previously discussed, but it will go into more detailed elements of the program. **Step 1** is important as a CFO is typically more adept at digesting detail to understand the facts, repercussions, and benefits.

Step 1 is to utilize the Road to Success and other materials shown in this book, as well as the presentation that was prepared for the CFO.

Step 2, as with any presentation, is to determine the message to be conveyed.

Step 3 is to "over-prepare" for the CFO. This means create several presentation materials anticipating selling the ERM program to the CFO. Anticipate that a CFO could very easily request to go deeper into the detail for certain parts of the program. Have this information available but place it in the appendices as a reference.

Step 4 of the CFO presentation phase is to take notes and takeaways from the conversation and absorb any comments or direction the CFO suggests in preparing a similar deck for the CEO. The CFO knows the CEO much better than most Heads of ERM and will likely know what is more important for CEO to keep him focused.

Figure 14.16 shows **Phase 3**, which is the **CEO presentation**. This presentation should be different and should be geared toward a higher level of messaging.

Since a CEO will usually be the final decision maker, step 1 is to decide on the message conveyed to the CEO using the input/guidance from the CFO. Step 2 is to remember to reduce the level of detail and reduce the size of the presentation as CEOs usually have a limited time for any conversations about *how the soup is made*. Step 3 after the CEO presentation is to capture any takeaways from the CEO presentation in preparation for the Audit Committee presentation. In certain situations, it may be wise to include the CFO in the CEO presentation. It is a choice that the ERM team will need to make and get CFO's participation confirmation. Where the CEO is the decision maker, step 4 is to obtain a confirmation of the direction for next steps.

Ref	Phase	Action Description
3	CEO Presentation	Create a presentation deck for the higher-level decision maker (usually CEO) 1 – Determine the message to be conveyed (based on CFO input). 2 – Elevate the level of detail with fewer slides. 3 – Present to CEO and note take-a-ways in preparation of Audit committee. 4 – Get direction for next steps, obtain decision if possible.
4	Executive/ Board approval sign off	Ensure the executive and board level approvals are documented even if by sending confirming email 1 – No surprises during phase. Do not over promise. Set up for success.
5	Detailed Implementation Plan	Create a detailed implementation timeline for implementation consistent with the messages in the selling presentations 1 – Establish a realistic time frame consistent with the current conditions (1-2 years). 2 – Segregate timeline for each phase until full program is implemented. 3 – Isolate the "nice to haves" until later in the program. 4 – Month by month in a logical approach considering interdependencies.

Figure 14.16 Quick reference checklist implementing ERM (steps 3–5)

Phase 4 is the **Executive Board Approval Sign Off.** Approval from the Board of Directors or the audit committee is not always required. However, it is beneficial to share the ERM program information during the Audit Committee meeting and obtain their confirmation during the meeting. The decision should be documented in the meeting minutes. Where the Audit Committee approval is not required, the ERM team should consider sending a confirmation e-mail to the CEO and the CFO as to the agreed-upon decisions. This chain of decision and approvals needs to be well documented so that there are no surprises during the implementation and future phases. Keep in mind—"do not over promise." Make sure the ERM program is set up for success and that the ERM Administrative Team is set to deliver the success.

Phase 5 is called the **Detailed Implementation Plan.** Once the required approvals have been obtained and documented and the next steps agreed upon, a detailed implementation plan must be created. It will consist of messaging from the CEO and CFO "buy-in" presentations as well as a timeline for the overall program. In this phase, **Step 1** is to establish a realistic timeline consistent with the current conditions of the company and the culture of the company. Timeline was discussed earlier in the context of the "Road to Success." Just to reiterate, the timeline would generally be somewhere between one and two years to get the program fully operational and stable and yield some benefits of the remediation efforts. The program may be implemented in stages. In such case, the ERM team needs to segregate the timeline for each of the stages until the full program is implemented (**Step 2**). The timeline could cover a two-year period with a month-to-month detail of the expectations.

Step 3 is to isolate the nice-to-have elements and defer it to later stages of the program. Sometimes, it is better to add those nice-to-haves during the second year or even third year, after program has been established; however, the key is that it may not be in the best interest of the ERM program to ask for everything at full cost if it has not yet been fully proven. The detailed implementation plan should be updated regularly. It is critical that the implementation plan follows a very logical step-by-step approach (**Step 4**). While there are only four steps within the detailed implementation plan, they take a considerable amount of time to develop and obtain the required executive signoffs.

Ref	Phase	Action Description
6	Resource Requirements	Determine the required resources to implement and to maintain the program considering the first 3 years 1 – Consider the full-time dedicated resources required. 2 – Identify any part time resources that will be available for peak times. 3 – Create the requisitions for the primary lead with experience. 4 – Consider a secondary person with less experience to assist. 5 – Hire employees with ERM experience is recommended. 6 – Consider a centralized vs. decentralized structure. 7 – Consider existing offices in low-cost regions as appropriate.
7	Infrastructure	Create the infrastructure and gain concurrence and approvals to set the program in the beginning 1 – Create a Risk Committee with company executives. 2 – Create a Risk Committee Charter. 3 – Develop ERM policies and procedures. 4 – Create standard templates for ERA, Treatment Plans, etc. 5 – Identify a system/tool to assist in the administrative portion. 6 – Develop a calendar staging timing of primary meetings and deliverables

Figure 14.17 *Quick reference checklist for implementing ERM (steps 6–7)*

Phase 6 is **Resource Requirements** and is shown in Figure 14.17. Although, this has been discussed to some extent earlier, the following section will go into more detail.

It is essential for the ERM team to determine the required resources to implement and maintain the ERM program especially for the first three years. Once the team determines the parameters of the overall ERM program and knows the geographic footprint and the layout of a company, it should be able to determine how many full-time dedicated resources would be required (which was **Step 1**).

Step 2 is to consider any requirements for the part-time resources that could be pulled in from other departments or other groups within the ERM department or internal audit department. There will be peak times, especially during the risk assessment phase, that will require multiple headcounts availability to conduct the interviews, synthesize the risk topics, and consolidate in the final risk profile list. Typically, there is a very short time period to complete these tasks and it can take multiple FTE headcounts.

Step 3 is to create the personnel requisitions for hiring the primary ERM program lead. This is usually the first person hired, as this person will help build the rest of the team/department. The ERM lead person should have prior experience of running ERM program as there really is not any time to learn about ERM while developing, training, and implementing the ERM program.

Once the ERM lead is hired, **Step 4** deals with the requirement for a second person to potentially be fully dedicated to the ERM process, or at least a majority of their time. This person can have less experience but should be able to assist in some of the more detail-oriented work, while the lead ERM person is primarily focused on the strategic tactical elements of the ERM implementation plan.

Step 5 involves hiring employees with ERM experience. To improve the likelihood of ERM program success, it is always better to find candidates with ERM experience within the same industry. To implement a robust ERM program, the ERM Administrative Team needs to be well-versed in the business model and products of the company. Bringing in experienced people within the same industry will help short-circuit the training time required.

Step 6 is to consider a centralized versus decentralized structure for the ERM Administrative Team. Experience shows that a centralized approach is the most efficient in the early phases of the ERM program. As the ERM program develops, there may be a preference to have a partially decentralized structure, especially when the executive levels are in other global locations.

Step 7 under resource requirements is to give consideration to the existing company offices/locations, particularly those in low-cost regions and with executive presence. Keeping the cost of the ERM program low especially in the beginning is very important, since the early stages of the program must yield results and show the cost efficacy. This phase is primarily dealing with the personnel resource requirements. There are also other resources, which will be discussed later.

Phase 7 is called **Infrastructure**. As the ERM Administration Team develops the infrastructure and gains concurrence and approvals from the executive management, **Step 1** is to create a risk committee comprising of company executives. The composition of the Risk Committee will vary by company, industry, and culture but the members should always include the CEO, the CFO at a minimum, and preferably their direct reports. For example, in a semiconductor company, the head of sales, the head of research and development, and the head of manufacturing or operations should also typically be members of the Risk Committee.

Step 2 is to create a Risk Committee Charter. This charter will govern the roles and responsibilities of the Risk Committee. Components of a Risk Committee charter were discussed in a previous chapter.

Step 3 relating to the infrastructure phase is to develop ERM program policies and procedures. These policies and procedures will change over time as the program continues to evolve. These base-level policies and procedures need to be well documented to facilitate the efficient training.

Step 4 is to create standard templates for the ERM program. Preferably, the summary or entity-level templates should be the same as allowing the risk owners to use a consistent level of detail and project tracking as commonly used for other company projects. It is however important to keep all the entity-level summary documents the same for all risks report, including the risk treatment plans, risk report cards, risk heat maps, even risk presentations.

Step 5 of the infrastructure phase is to search for systems or tools that can help with the administrative elements of the ERM program. Preferably, these should be tools that are already purchased and implemented within a company so that additional implementation costs will be minimized. The tools or systems need to support the ERM process, not drive the ERM process. This does not necessarily mean that these tools should be utilized right from the beginning. In many cases, the ERM process should be developed prior to an automated tool being acquired or utilized. Often, the automated tools are implemented in year two, or even year three after the ERM program is defined and implemented.

Step 6 is to develop a calendar staging the timing of primary meetings and required deliverables. Risk Committee meetings should normally be held on a quarterly basis and should be booked in advance to accommodate executives' schedules, which are very difficult to coordinate on a short notice. The calendar should also identify other key dates for meetings such as the dates of the executive strategic meetings with the CEO and his or her staff, as well as the annual operating plan/budget submissions because ERM results should have input into both of those efforts. There should also be quarterly updates to the Audit Committee which should be clearly defined in this calendar. To emphasize again, the ERM program must be developed in a manner where the output is predictable and timely to support all the objectives of the program to benefit the company.

Ref	Phase	Action Description
8	Training	Create a training deck to address the different levels of participants. Hold trainings with refreshers periodically 1 – Training materials should be available online to all participants. 2 – Training sessions should be higher level initially for executives. 3 – Trainings session should be more detailed for middle management. 4 – Offer multiple sessions to accommodate different time zones. 5 – Enlist executives for introductions/kick offs to emphasize importance. 6 – During risk assessment exercise, present training slides again.
9	Risk Assessment	Set the initial kick-off of the ERM program by conducting a multi-purpose risk assessment 1 – Determine best approach of risk assessment (Survey, interview, workshop). 2 – Live sessions are better for at least initial assessment. 3 – Review training materials in each interview. 4 – Create a short list of questions to show desired thought pattern. 5 – Synthesize results as the sessions are held and accumulate topics. 6 – Confirm the messages shared by the respondent/interviewee. 7 – Obtain an initial judgmental rating by the interviewee.

Figure 14.18 Quick reference checklist for implementing ERM (steps 8–9)

Phase 8 is **Training** as shown in Figure 14.18. Training is probably the most underestimated step when implementing an ERM program.

Since a large amount of information and new processes must be conveyed to the company's management, the training programs will require a lot of time and effort. There should be different training materials for the various levels of audiences.

Step 1 is to develop and maintain the training materials online, so they are readily available to all participants.

Step 2 is to create training programs that initially have a high level of detail for the executives.

Step 3 is to create the training materials for the middle management, which generally have more detail because middle management will be the risk SMEs and the risk treatment plan developers.

Step 4 is to ensure that there are multiple sessions available to accommodate the working schedules and different time zones. Absorbing the training of ERM program concepts requires the audiences' full dedication and attention. Therefore, it is always better to have the training meetings during the audiences' normal workday in each of the primary offices' regional time zones.

Step 5 under the training phase is to enlist executives who will volunteer to kick off the meetings and introduce the ERM program to elevate and emphasize the importance of the ERM program, and to help ensure cooperation from everyone in the intended audience.

Step 6 is to retrain the intended audience as often as necessary to accommodate the different phases of the implementation program. Training for creating risk treatment plans in the first month of the ERM program is of little value since the risk treatment plans will not actually be implemented until a few months later, and all the knowledge passed on will likely be forgotten. A good time to refresh the training materials is during the initial risk assessment exercise. In the three companies used as examples, face-to-face meetings were usually held once a year to refresh each company's risk profile. These sessions, whether individual one-on-one or work group sessions, were the perfect time to reintroduce the updated training materials. It normally did not take long and were well-worth the few minutes spent on refreshing the audiences.

Phase 9 is called **Risk Assessment**. This stage of the ERM kickoff is most important to ensure its completeness as a multipurpose risk assessment. Multipurpose means an opportunity in these one-on-one or work-group sessions to establish relationships with all the personnel, to refresh the training materials, and to respond to very specific questions from the management team in the audience.

Step 1 in conducting the risk assessment is to determine the best approach of the risk assessment. There are many options including questionnaire surveys, face-to-face interviews, video interviews, workshops, and the list goes on. Different approaches may work better in different cultures. Experience has shown that the most effective risk assessments are conducted with one-hour face-to-face interviews (versus surveys) to establish a back-and-forth dialogue to dig deeper into the answers provided for the initial questions. This will avoid follow-up interviews, which are normally required using a survey approach. Workshops also work very well. The main difference is that there are just more people in the room, so it takes a bit more time to conclude. However, it takes less time to have 10 people in the room for a couple of hours than to have 10 individual meetings for an hour each; hence if done well, the workshops can be very effective.

Step 2 refers to the live sessions that are generally better at least for the initial assessment. There may be a need to modify the approach after these initial assessments based on the learnings from the live sessions, as to what works the best for the existing company culture.

Step 3 is to obtain and customize training materials for the individuals who will be interviewed. The customization might relate to the geographic location specifics such as cultural sensitivity, and so on, or the type of business or product and service that is being managed.

Step 4 is to create a short list of questions to help initiate the desired thought pattern. A short list was shown in earlier chapters of this book as an example. In general, this short list of questions would include the goals and objectives of the department as well as the actual risks that are in the forefront of the specific interviewee's mind.

Step 5 of the risk assessment process phase is to synthesize the results from the one-on-one sessions. It pays off to document each of the session immediately and follow up with an e-mail to confirm the ERM Administration Team's understanding of the responses provided during the session.

Step 6 is to provide and document the ERM Administration Team's cleansed responses from these interviews.

Step 7, during the interviews, is to obtain an initial judgmental rating for each of the risks that the interviewees surfaced. This will help in the initial draft quantification and/or prioritization ranking for all the risks that have been identified. Normally, talking to 100 people will generate around 450 individual risk statements. Those 450 individual risk statements will then be synthesized to probably around 50 to 60 common themes. If the initial judgmental rating is obtained from the interviewees who surface the risk, it will help in understanding where that risk might fall in the full population list of risks, and whether it might be in the Top 25.

Phase 10 is called **Prioritized Risk Profile** and is shown in Figure 14.19.

Ref	Phase	Action Description
10	Prioritized Risk Profile	Create a first pass of a prioritized risk profile to segregate obvious lower-level risks. Finalize to a draft prioritized rated listing 1 – Synthesize the individual topics into common risk themes. 2 – Categorize risks into Strategic, Operational, Financial, and Regulatory. 3 – Apply rating criteria to determine rating from a mathematical standpoint. 4 – Identify possible Top 25 risks for quantification. 5 – Review ratings with executives to ensure general confirmation. 6 – Identify initial possible risk owners to prepare for next steps.
11	Risk Treatment Plans (RTP)	Assist risk owners in creating the first attempt at Risk Treatment Plan (RTP) for the Top 10 risks initially. This is a learning process and will improve over time. 1 – Share the template with the risk owners and hold training sessions again. 2 – Assist risk owners in creating KPIs to measure progress of remediation. 3 – Identify the appropriate finance support team to assist in quantifications. 4 – Listen to the risk owners as to any sub-program in place and integrate. 5 – Share the Report Card template so the risk owner is aware of it. 6 – Ensure the risk owner obtains approval of the RTP from their manager. 7 – Ensure the risk owner understands the quarterly cadence for updating.

Figure 14.19 Quick reference checklist for implementing ERM (steps 10–11)

Conduct a first pass to prioritize the risk profile to segregate the obvious lower level risks and finalize to a draft prioritized rated listing.

Step 1 is synthetizing the individual topics into common risk themes as discussed.

Step 2 is categorizing these risk topics or themes into the categories of strategic risks, operational risks, financial risks, or regulatory risks. This will be used later in reporting the risk profile of the organization.

Step 3 is to apply the predefined rating criteria to determine the approximate ranking from a more mathematical standpoint. This will help in preparation for the next step.

Step 4 is to identify Top 25 risks for quantification.

After the Top 25 risk list has been drafted move to the next step.

Step 5 is to review the ratings with executives to ensure a general concurrence is obtained. There will be differences for all the ratings; however, sometimes judgment is necessary and is logical in categorizing or ranking the risk topics.

Step 6 is to identify the initial possible risk owners for the Top 25 risk statements who will be tasked for preparing the Risk Treatment Plans. These owners may change over time, but at least it is a starting point.

Phase 11 is **Risk Treatment Plans**. Treatment plans in the first phase should normally be created only for the Top 10 risks. There is a learning process that will improve over time. The Risk Administrative Team will probably need to assist the risk owners in creating the first attempt at the Risk Treatment Plan.

Step 1 of this phase is to share the treatment plan template with the risk owners and again, hold training sessions.

Step 2 is to assist the risk owners in creating KPIs that will measure the progress of remediation.

Step 3 is to identify the appropriate support personnel, typically from finance, who can assist in quantifying risk exposure.

Step 4 is to converse with the risk owners to understand if any subprogram already exists. If so, integrate the results of those programs into the enterprise level as much as possible.

Step 5 of the Risk Treatment Plan is to share the report card templates, so the risk owners are aware of it and understand that the report card will be created in the future once the program has been established and in place for two or three quarters. The risk report cards are very transparent and create a high-level visibility of the performance of the risk owner.

Step 6 is to ensure that the risk owner reviews their Risk Treatment Plan with their immediate manager and obtains approval of the direction. Sometimes the risk owners operate in of a vacuum and present the treatment plan only to find out that their manager knows of conditions that may change the direction of the treatment plan completely.

Step 7 is to ensure that the risk owners understand the quarterly cadence for updating the Risk Treatment Plan and that they own the responsibility to update the treatment plans. Normally, the ERM Administrative Team will hold meetings on a quarterly basis with each risk owner to discuss this cadence and help update the templates as appropriate.

Phase 12 category is **Emerging Risks** as shown in Figure 14.20.

The ERM team needs to create a process to identify and monitor the emerging risks within the industry as well as external to the industry and organization. Emerging risks can be of so many different varieties and are usually difficult to identify.

Step 1 is to identify experts in the specific industry to garner insight to the emerging risks. Ask for the CEO and CFO to offer the experts from the organizations of which they are members.

Step 2 is to identify experts in the professional community that provides studies. Several examples were shared earlier in the book. Create relationships with these peer groups to set the stage for open dialogue.

Step 3 is to match the results of these SMEs with the risk profile from the first risk assessment and do so each quarter, moving forward.

Ref	Phase	Action Description
12	Emerging Risks	Create a process to identify and monitor emerging risks both within the industry and external to the industry and organization 1 – Identify experts in the industry to garner insight to emerging risks. 2 – Identify experts in the community that provides studies. 3 – Match the results of these experts with the risk profiles from the first risk assessment and quarterly moving forward.
13	Corporate Risk Trend	Develop the methodology for creating a Top 25 total company risk quantification 1 – Implement this reporting after the ERM program has been embedded for at least 3 full reporting cycles. 2 – Be able to track the Inherent and Residual risk quantifications.
14	Treatment Plan Report Cards	Develop a report card for each RTP and be able to roll up the results for the entire company 1 – Implement this reporting after at least 3 reporting cycles. 2 – Create a method that can be utilized to help measure success against any incentive programs or goals.

Figure 14.20 Quick reference checklist for implementing ERM (steps 12–14)

Emerging risks can change very frequently as well, and Audit Committee members are requesting this information more often.

Phase 13 is **Corporate Risk Trend**. After the ERM program has been stabilized, is helpful to show the executives the total company risk quantification for the Top 25 risks.

Step 1 is to implement this reporting after the ERM program has been embedded for at least three full reporting cycles. The quantification process is difficult and can take a few iterations to become accurate.

Step 2 requires the ability to track both the inherent and residual risk quantifications. This corporate risk trend can be cumulative or a rolling four-quarter trend. Experience has shown that a rolling four-quarters trend will level out the peaks and valleys, but it really depends on the audience, organization, and industry.

Phase 14 is **Treatment Plan Report Cards**. The ERM team must develop a report card template and then create a specific report card for each risk treatment plan. These will need to be suitable for consolidating at a company level.

Step 1 is to implement this report card after at least three reporting cycles are in place with some stability in the program.

Step 2 is to create this report card using a method that can best utilize existing programs that help measure success against incentive programs or goals. As noted earlier in this book, the most productive ERM programs exist when components are tied directly to compensation incentive programs.

Phase 15 is **Risk Factor Reconciliation** that is shown in Figure 14.21.

Ref	Phase	Action Description
15	Risk Factor Reconciliation	Create a quarterly process to reconcile the risk profile to the risk factors reported in the quarterly and annual public filing 1 – Implement this once the Risk Profile has become stabilized. 2 – Monitor the risk factors of competitors.
16	Leading/Lagging Indicators	Create reporting formats that will show trends of actual to previous and to predicted ratings 1 – Implement this process after the RTPs have gone through at least 3 cycles.
17	Competition Risk Factors	Allocate a cadence within the ERM Team to monitor public information about the industry and competitors 1 – Report successes and failures of competitors related to bankruptcies, class action lawsuits, etc.
18	Risk Opportunities	Maintain a separate register of risk and cost reduction opportunities that can also supplement the risk benefits 1 – Include this step in the risk assessment interviews/surveys.

Figure 14.21 Quick reference checklist for implementing ERM (steps 15–18)

Step 1 is to create a quarterly process to reconcile the risk profile to the risk factors as reported in the quarterly 10Q and annual 10K public filings. It should be implemented once the risk profile becomes stable, which may mean at least two reporting cycles. Usually, the public reporting of risk factors is the responsibility of the legal department. Share the results of the current risk profile with the appropriate team at least two weeks prior to the filing date (and before the executive Disclosure Committee if one exists).

Step 2 is to monitor the risk factors of competitors to ensure that the risk profile portfolio as well as the current public filings are commensurate. Risk factors from other companies will be a great benchmark to compare against for the quality of the public reporting.

Phase 16 is **Leading/Lagging Indicators**. This phase shows requirement to create reporting formats that will show trends of actual to previous and to predicted ratings. This relates to leading and lagging indicators. Lagging indicators are normally used in the initial ERM program. Refinement of the leading indicators will typically be introduced into the program at least two reporting cycles from the beginning. Once the risk owners are familiar with thinking about leading performance indicators for each risk profile, it will become much easier to incorporate leading indicators to predict the subsequent quarter's results.

Phase 17 is **Competition Risk Factors** refers to allocating a cadence within the ERM team to spend a certain amount of time each week to monitor publicly available information about the industry and competitors.

Step 1 is to report successes and failures of competitors, which may include bankruptcies, class action lawsuits, and successes. The public information can create some independent and real data points that should help executives think about those events within the organization. The results of other competitor companies' successes and failures may also be used to track against the risk profile of the current company. It will typically confirm the blend of risk events between the various categories of strategic, operational, financial, and regulatory.

Phase 18 is **Risk Opportunities** refers to maintaining separate registers for each: risk and profit maximization opportunities. These can supplement the benefits of the ERM program. **Step 1** is to include this question in the risk assessment interviews and surveys just to start the

Ref	Phase	Action Description
19	Risk Appetite/Tolerance	Develop risk appetite and risk tolerance program that applies at a risk level and company level as appropriate 1 – Implement these elements only after the program has been fully embedded for at least 3 quarters.
20	Share Price Tracking	Create a timeline that follows stock prices and indicate events that occurred at the same time frame 1 – Implement this step within two reporting cycles, but do not report out on it for at least 4 quarters of full program.
21	Departmental ERM models	Convince and support the creation of departmental ERM programs 1 – Implement this step once the RTPs have been embedded for at least 3 cycles.
22	Professional Peer Groups	Get engaged with as many peer groups as possible as quickly as possible 1 – Cover professional, academic, and industry connections.
23	Automation	Assess the options to automate the administrative elements 1 – Once the process is fully embedded for at least 3 cycles, explore new tools with a provable payback.

Figure 14.22 Quick reference checklist for implementing ERM (steps 19–23)

initial list of opportunities. Certain opportunities can also result in a potential risk.

Phase 19 is **Risk Appetite and Tolerance** shown in Figure 14.22.

Developing a risk appetite and risk tolerance program applicable at the risk statement level and at company level is important as well. This is a very difficult process and is not always well accepted. **Step 1** is to create and implement these elements only after the program has been fully embedded for at least three to four reporting cycles. Trying to implement this in the beginning will be nearly impossible as risk appetite and tolerance depends on the type of risks being considered. Risk tolerance and appetite will be a combination of individual risk topic level with company level. For example, there may be a very low appetite to accept a risk that could affect the company's reputation.

Phase 20 is **Share Price Tracking**. The ERM team needs to create a timeline that shows stock price changes and indicate events that have occurred at the same timeframe. **Step 1** is to implement this process within two to three reporting cycles, but do not report out on the results for at least four to five cycles of a full program. Training should emphasize that this timeline is not intended to predict share price or justify changes in share price, but to show correlations of events and how the market reacted. It could provide an insight to the future actions of the company and the risk profile.

Phase 21 is **Departmental ERM Models**. As elements/levels of ERM program must be developed at departmental levels, the ERM team needs to sell and support the creation of such departmental-level ERM programs. This is asking certain departments that have an interest in creating its own miniature ERM program and heat map to track its own risk profile. Many of the risks could represent a risk at an entity-level profile. **Step 1** is to implement this process once the risk treatment departmental ERM models' plans have been embedded for at least three cycles. The risk owners and department heads must first get used to the cadence in the day-to-day operational thoughts of risk management. The financial magnitude of these risk will generally be smaller for individual departments compared to the entity-level ERM program but could be quite high risk within its own function.

Phase 22 is **Professional Peer Groups**. The ERM team needs to engage with as many peer groups as possible, and as soon as possible, before beginning the implementation of an ERM program. These peer groups could include professional organizations, academic organizations, or industry connections. It's important to maintain these peer group meetings and sharing of leading practices to continue to be creative in modifying or enhancing the program.

Lastly, **Phase 23** is **Automation**. Assessing the options to automate the administrative elements should be considered as it may significantly increase the efficiencies of the ERM program. **Step 1** is using what was learned in the initial pre-implementation phase. Consider when it makes sense to purchase and implement new automation tools. Normally, it takes at least three cycles before the ERM programs will show tangible benefits and that is the time to introduce a request to purchase automation tools and provide a provable payback. ERM tools are improving as technology for ERM becomes more of a focus.

In summary, this checklist for implementing an ERM program is not exhaustive but does include all the major steps and some consultation points at a detailed level.

CHAPTER 15

Case Study

As we mentioned in earlier chapters, the real-life examples in this book were mostly from our own experiences in implementing ERM programs at companies from the solar and the semiconductor industries. For both, ERM programs were implemented from the bottom up. In this chapter, the first case study will be from the solar company. The solar company case study spans over a three-year period, while the second case study related to the semiconductor company and spans over a one-year period. In the case of the solar company, the discussion will be limited primarily to the results and benefits of the ERM program, while the discussion related to the semiconductor company will show the entire journey to success.

The solar industry is one of the most dynamic and volatile industries in the world. Before the Total Corporate Risk trend is shared, there will be an overview of years 1, 2, and 3, setting the stage for the conditions and status of the ERM program.

Figure 15.1 shows the Corporate Risk Trend for the period of implementation beginning in Q1 of year 1 through Q1 of year 3. We will only discuss the first three years with an understanding of the progress and the challenges of the program in this rather unique industry.

In Figure 15.1, the Corporate Risk Trend shows a rolling four-quarter average rating of the Top 25 risks. In the case of the solar company, these were all short-term risks. Longer term risks were not yet identified and included in the ERM program's first year. The corporate risk trend shows the (upper) red line, which represents the inherent risk for the Top 25 risks and the lower (green) line, which represents the residual risk for the Top 25. The wider the spread between the upper (red) line and the lower (green) line, the more successful the remediation plans have been. Also, keep in mind the spread represents a net impact of adding new risks and mitigating other risks. If there is a lot of movement in the Top 25 risk register, the pure progress of increasing the gap between the inherent and

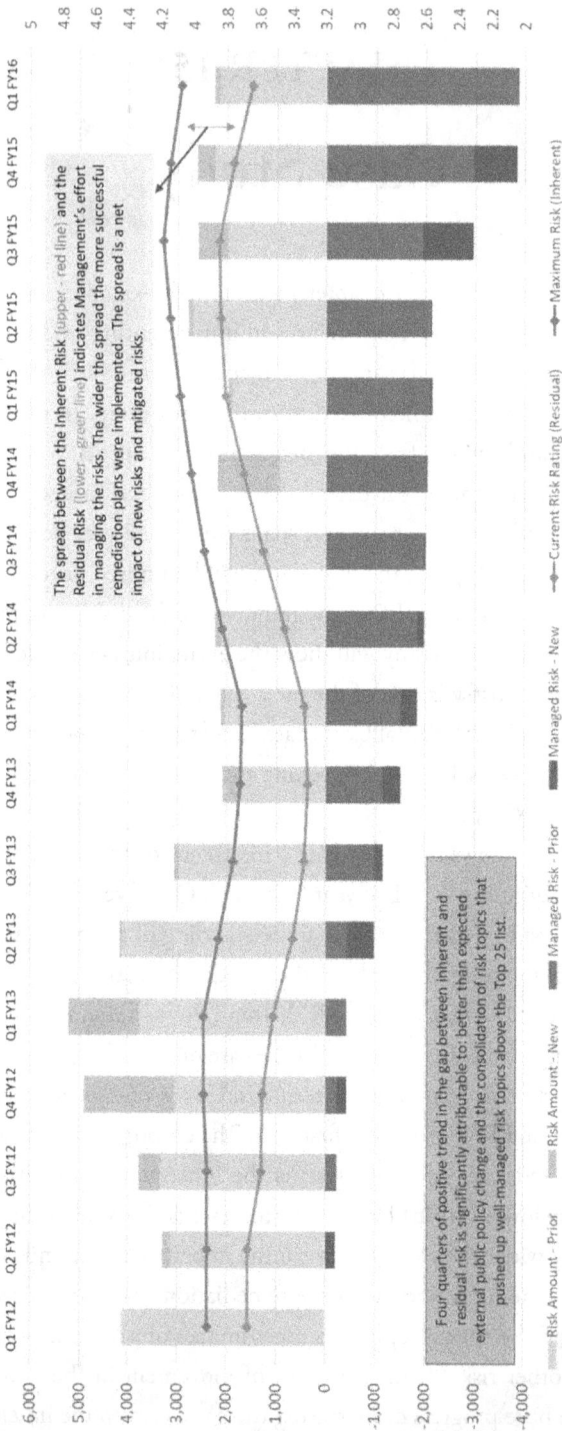

Figure 15.1 Corporate risk trends

the residual risk will not be as dynamic or as great. In this solar company example, the corporate risk trend also reflects vertical bars for each quarter, each consisting of color bars as follows:

- Top Darker Gray (Green)—is the new risk amount added during the current quarter to the Top 25;
- Mid-section light gray above left hand side scale "0" value (Yellow)—the risk amount brought forward from the prior quarter;
- Darkest lowest gray (Blue)—the managed risk for the current quarter; and
- Darker gray below left hand side scale "0" value (Gray)—the managed risk from the prior quarter.

This shows that the managed risk (blue, gray, and green) is greater than the risk from prior quarters ("yellow") indicating a trend of a solid remediation.

However, as noted before, the spread between the inherent and the residual risk is not as great as one would like to see, which is directly related to the frequent quarter-over-quarter movement in the Top 25 risks including additions and mitigations.

Figure 15.2 shows the list of the Top 25 risks at the end of the second year and risk ratings from Q1 through Q4 for each of those Top 25 risks.

As mentioned earlier, the solar industry is extremely volatile and dynamic and so are the risks affecting it. This is demonstrated at the level of risk movement between Q1 and Q4 of the same year in the 2nd year of the program. Note that 11 risks decreased in the ranking between Q1 and Q4, which in general is considered a good result. However, it can also be misleading due to the risk fluctuation. You can also observe that six risks actually increased in ranking, which could be an indication that the risks above these six risks improved and therefore decreased in the ranking, and in doing so pushed the six risks higher in rankings. There were four new risks added to the Top 25 during the 2nd year and there were three risks that fell out of the Top 10 due to effective remediation. There were also three risks that had to be recharacterized into separate risk topics because dynamics changed the characteristics of the risk topic.

Tier	Topic	Champion/s	Q4 '13	Q3 '13	Q2 '13	Q1'13
TIER 1	Solar Contract Requirements & EPC Execution	C-Suite Executive	1	1	1	8
	Customer Satisfaction-NPS	C-Suite Executive	2	NA	NA	NA
	Balance Sheet Lite	C-Suite Executive	3	NA	NA	NA
	Joint Venture	C-Suite Executive	4	9	10	11
	Product Design & Quality	C-Suite Executive	5	4	5	35
TIER 2	Long-Term Poly Silicon Commitments	C-Suite Executive	6	11	3	6
	US Residential Lease- Operations	C-Suite Executive	7	3	4	3
	Public Policy	C-Suite Executive	8	5	7	5
	Cost Roadmap Execution & Cost Estimation	C-Suite Executive	9	RC	6	2
	Back-Leverage Risk	C-Suite Executive	10	NA	NA	NA
	Global Utilities and Power Plants & Distributed Generation Project Execution	C-Suite Executive	11	21	32	36
	Residential Cost Reduction Roadmap & NPV Improvement Program Execution	C-Suite Executive	12	RC	RC	RC
	Capacity Expansion	C-Suite Executive	13	22	NA	NA
	Project Financing	C-Suite Executive	14	2	2	1
	Data & Information Security	C-Suite Executive	15	17	16	20
	Intellectual Property Rights & Infringement	C-Suite Executive	16	10	11	15
TIER 3	Cash Grant	C-Suite Executive	17	6	8	10
	Business Continuity Plan	C-Suite Executive	18	12	13	18
	Inventory Management	C-Suite Executive	19	13	14	7
	Panel Cost Roadmap Execution & Competitiveness	C-Suite Executive	20	RC	6	2
	Warranty (Module and Systems Performance) & Operations and Maintenance	C-Suite Executive	21	20	22	16
	Contract Management & Execution	C-Suite Executive	22	8	9	14
	International Third Party Ownership	C-Suite Executive	23	16	21	24
	Non-compliance to External Laws and Regulations	C-Suite Executive	24	14	15	19
	New Market Entry	C-Suite Executive	25	26	28	26

Extremely volatile and dynamic industry. Frequent movement. Between Q1 to Q4:

- 11 risks went down in ranking
- 6 risks went up in ranking
- 4 new risks were added
- 3 risks fell out of the top 10 risks
- 3 risk elements had to be recharacterized

Figure 15.2 ERM movement trend of risks for the Top 25 during year 2 of ERM program

Figure 15.3 provides a closer look at the highlights in the 2nd year of the ERM program with the outlook for the 3rd year of the program.

The highlights during the 2nd year of the program included:

- Defining and tracking key performance indicators for the Top 25 risks.
- Risk movement and history discussions by each of the executive leadership team members and the four business divisions.
- A longer term risk register was created including time periods beyond 12 months.
- A bottom-up risk assessment refresh conducted at the end of the year.

By the end of the 2nd year, the low light was that some of the risk treatment plans were not fully developed. This was partially due to the volume of risks movement within the Top 25 risks and the actual makeup of a few of the specific risk topics.

The 3rd year outlook included some newly added elements of the program. The outlook was to quantify and prioritize longer term risks with an annual deep dive. As noted earlier, having separate risk registers for short- and long-term risks can be somewhat confusing and probably is not always the best direction. Experience has shown that combining the longer term and shorter term risks into the same heat map gives prioritization and quantification to those elements from a qualitative and quantitative standpoint helping create a solid singular Top 25 risk profile. The 3rd year then shows the total corporate risk register created (retroactively) as was discussed in Figure 15.1.

The next improvement in the 3rd year was that the metrics and measures were defined to assess the maturity level of the risk topics. Another addition was to create a risk heat map per country, per region, as well as a separate heat map for the various lines of business. It became beneficial to create a heat map for each of the lines of business as subrankings had to be managed by the respective executive teams.

Lastly, the expectation was to identify an automated tool to help with the administrative elements of the program. To recap, year 1 was implementation year and a period of learning for everyone in the new program.

Year 2 Highlights / Lowlights

Highlights

- Defined and tracked KPIs for the Top 25 risks
- Discussed risk movement/history by eStaff or business division (4 quarter history)
- Created longer-term Risk Register (beyond 12 months)
- Completed Bottom-Up Risk Assessment at year end.

Low light

- Some Treatment Plans not fully developed due to volume of movement (new/split)

Year 3 Outlook

- Address 2013 low light
- Quantify and prioritize longer-term risks. Deep Dive annually
- Track Collective Corporate risk trends over time
- Define measures / metrics to assess maturity level of ERM
- Create risk heat map per country
- Create risk heat map per business process / cycle
- Continue to refine quantification assumptions and treatment plans
- GRC solution

- Year 1 was implementation year and a period of learning for everyone in the new program.
- Year 2 stabilized the basic elements of the remediation and Quantification activities
- Year 3 began expanding reporting coverage and refining the elements.

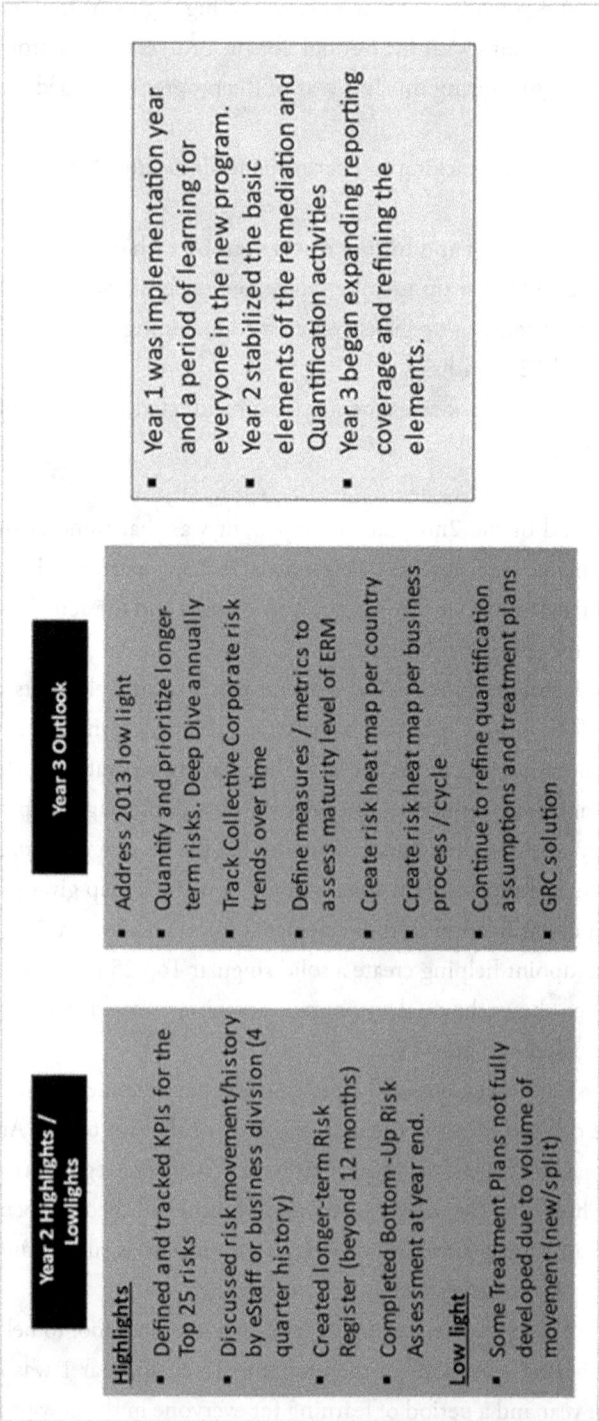

Figure 15.3   Achievements and outlook going from year 2 to year 3 of the ERM program

In year 2, basic elements were stabilized as they relate to the remediation of quantification activities. In year 3, there was expanded reporting coverage and a refinement of the elements within the program.

This concludes the discussion of the benefits from the solar industry organization. For learning purposes, it may be more relevant to cover the semiconductor company ERM program implementation since the industry is more stable than solar and is also a more current approach in risk management.

The next section relates to the semiconductor industry. Figure 15.4 summarizes the benefits recognized after two years of implementation of the ERM program in the semiconductor company.

The above benefits are reflective of the ERM program implemented after lessons learned were experienced from the solar company. Many of the elements that were added in the third and fourth year of the solar company were added during year 1 and year 2 at the semiconductor company. The benefits recognized after the first two years of implementation included the following elements:

- First and most important benefit was that several inherent risks that went through partial or full remediation and recognized over two years totaled roughly $2 billion. This improvement in residual risks took about three quarters to gain the momentum of recognized corrective actions.
- Second benefit was that there were several risks that unknowingly helped prepare the company for the unexpected pandemic, which began in year 2020. There were risks related

---

- Over **$2 billion** of inherent risks remediated over two years
- Identified risks that helped prepare the company for the **pandemic** impact
- Brought forward-looking views with **predictive** risk ratings for next quarter
- Guaranteed Board exposure to rapidly changing risk profile
- Connected risk management to incentive compensation goals
- Provided successful input to strategic summits
- Provided AOP impact (investment) of risks with offsetting impact **(benefits)** of remediated risks
- Risk management embedded into daily management decisions
- Many departments or functions maintained similar ERM program within their own function to manage risks important to the department success

Figure 15.4 Benefits recognized after two years of implementation

to business continuity, disaster recovery, employee staffing, and supply chain. Supply chain management were addressing risks around single versus sole suppliers and lead time with backup facilities for manufacturing. Those efforts eased some of the burden from the pandemic.

- Third benefit is that the program did not just look at current day compared to historical performance like in the solar company case. The semiconductor ERM program brought in a forward-looking view with predictive risk ratings for the upcoming quarter. As the risk treatment plans were updated and reported as of the current quarter end and compared to the prior quarter, it was also compared to the previously predicted ratings for the current quarter. This gave an assessment of how well the risk owners were anticipating the corrective actions and created an accountability if they fell short of the predicted scoring.

- Fourth benefit was that the reporting process guaranteed the board of director exposure to the risks profile on a timely basis as the risks started changing rapidly toward the end. It was expected by the Board of Directors that all Top 10 risks were addressed in the primary board presentation.

- Fifth benefit was the connection of the risk management program accomplishments to the incentive compensation goals. Accomplishments of the goals drove the level of payout for the bonus of the employees. This process generated the need for starting to issue the performance report cards quarterly to the CEO.

- Sixth benefit was that the ERM program was implemented quickly and sustained at a solid depth, that it was useful input to the strategic discussion covering the 10-year strategy.

- Similarly, the seventh benefit was that the updates of the Top 25 risks were refreshed in time to provide input to the annual operating plan/budget with the expectation of planning the costs needed in the upcoming year to help remediate the substantial risks identified during the current year.

- Eighth benefit was that during this short period of time, risk management became embedded into the decision making daily by management personnel at all levels. This was apparent in the dialogues within the operations reviews presented to the CEO.
- The last major benefit was that each department or function tailored a similar ERM program using the same templates and reporting processes for its own individual function or department. This made it particularly easier to refresh and identify new risks because each department was constantly updating its own departmental ERM heat maps using its own level of materiality. Programs were implemented by the Tax and IT organizations, the Research and Development team, and the Legal function.

In the semiconductor case study, before we move into actual implementation story, there should be a few points discussed, which will help make sense of the case study as it progresses through the program. Specifically, the Corporate Risk Trend for the semiconductor program differed from what was shown for the solar company. In the case of the semiconductor Corporate Risk Trend, some of the details around the specific bars were removed and provided the messaging at a higher and more understandable level. The Corporate Risk Trend in Figure 15.5 shows five of the eight quarters, which will be addressed throughout the rest of this case study. Specifically, the third quarter when the program was implemented and reflected the following five quarters.

The above Corporate Risk Trend has both the upper (red) line for inherent risks and the lower (green) line for residual risks. These are computed based on the risk scores for each of the risk profiles for the Top 25 risks. Figure 15.5 shows a steadier state level of Top 25 risks, meaning that the inherent risk did not change dramatically from one quarter to the other. However, the residual risk changed substantially over the five quarters. Additionally, there is a dotted line that shows the predicted risk score. Performance exceeded the predicted risk score for the fourth quarter, and then came back on track in Q1 of the following year. Figure 15.5 shows a tremendous progress in mitigation effectiveness, which began as

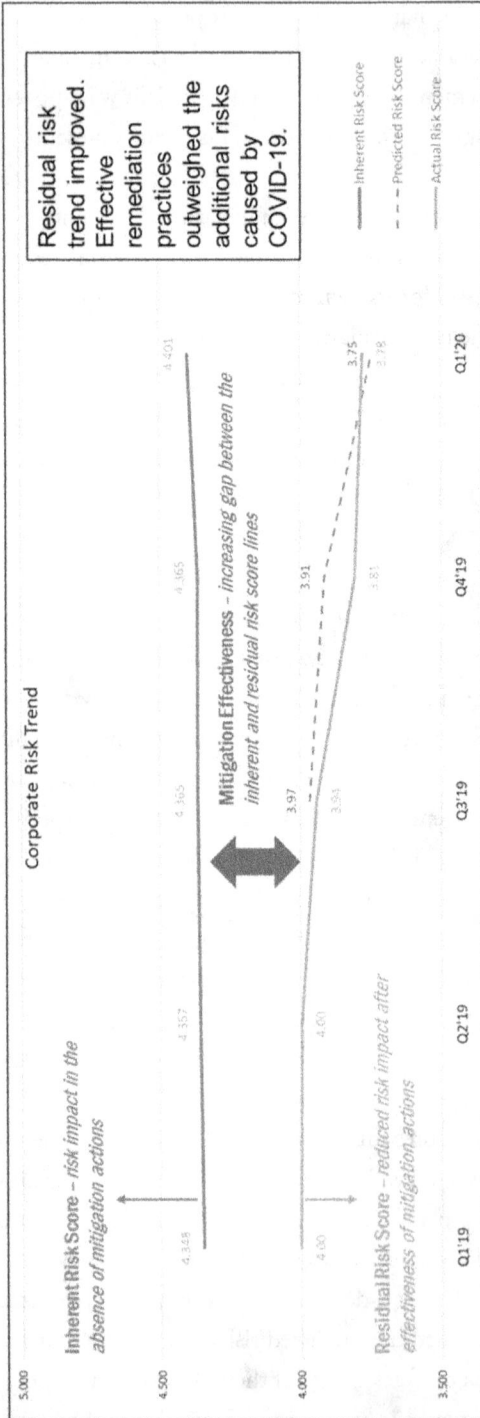

Corporate Risk Trend

Inherent Risk Score – *risk impact in the absence of mitigation actions*

Residual Risk Score – *reduced risk impact after effectiveness of mitigation actions*

Mitigation Effectiveness – *increasing gap between the inherent and residual risk score lines*

Residual risk trend improved. Effective remediation practices outweighed the additional risks caused by COVID-19.

Inherent Risk Score
Predicted Risk Score
Actual Risk Score

ERM mitigation practices prepared Company to better respond to the market volatility in 2019 and the COVID-19 pandemic.

Figure 15.5 Corporate risk trend

early as the second quarter all the way through the following five quarters. This improvement is also noted in Figure 15.6, which is the blended risk heat map.

"Blended" means considering both long-term and short-term risk elements for the Top 25 risks. Figure 15.6 also shows that nearly all the Top 25 risks improved in Q1 versus the prior quarter when compared against its own performance in the prior quarter, while not considering the ranking. This trend is illustrated by the green arrows pointing down. Then in Figure 15.7 there is the same Top 25 ERM blended risk heat map for Q4 of the same year.

Even by just a visual comparison of the risk balls positioning, there is a noticeable shift out of the upper right-hand (red) quadrant down to the lower left-hand (yellow) quadrant. This indicates that remediation is working and that the risks are declining from both qualitative and quantitative perspectives. Even though a few risks remained in a steady state in Q4 versus Q3 of the same year, the overall results from Q1 to Q4 represented tremendous gains for the organization.

Figure 15.8 shows the Tier 1 and 2 risk listings from prior two heat maps and compares the results against each other.

When comparing the Q1 risks listing on the left-hand side to the Q4 risks listing on the right-hand side, there were three out of the Top 10 risks that moved lower into the next 15 because of remediation efforts. Also, between the two listings, the black arrows illustrate that nearly all the risks went down in a ranking except for one, intellectual property, which went up and stayed at a relatively steady state. On the right-hand listing, one risk which is the speed of margin and growth, continued to be the number one risk from a ranking perspective throughout most of the entire year. However, the risk trend rating arrow on the very right-hand side pointed downward (digital copy is the green arrow) shows for this speed of margin and growth improvement risk. The risk score trend history taken from the report card for that risk immediately below that chart shows the dramatic improvement in the actual risk score versus the predicted and from previous quarters. Therefore, while the speed of margin and growth remained the number one risk for the organization, it did show dramatic improvement (downward) from the inherent to the residual risk. It is beneficial for the audience to understand the full story

Tier	Q1	Q4	TOPIC	Trend
TIER 1	1	3	Speed of MXX Margin & Growth	→
	2	1	Product Development Execution	→
	3	4	External Supplier Relationships & Dependency	→
	4	5	Intellectual Property Protection	→
	5	16	Business Continuity & Disaster Recovery	*
TIER 2	6	13	Continuous Pricing Pressure	→
	7	6	New Product Introduction	→
	8	10	Velocity of MCC Market Decline	→
	9	7	Geopolitical Environment	→
	10	15	Short Term Mindset	→

Tier	Q1	Q4	TOPIC	Trend
TIER 3	11	8	Transformational Product Innovation	→
	12	11	Scalability for Rapid Growth	→
	13	18	Customer Centric Mindset	↔
	14	12	Threat of Made in China 2025	→
	15	21	Inventory Management Controls & Systems	→
	16	14	Industry Consolidation	→
	17	2	Cybersecurity Breach	→
	18	25	Effectiveness of Procurement Activities	↔
	19	9	Supply Demand Forecasting Accuracy	→
	20	23	Distributor & Channel Dependency	→
	21	17	Managing Investor Confidence & Activist Investor	→
	22	24	Employee Hiring & Retention	→
	23	19	Financial Reporting Controls (SOX)	→
	24	20	High Customer Concentration (XXX Company, XXX Company)	→
	25	22	Competitiveness & Stability of Mfg Operations	*

Risk Trend

↑ Increased   □ New Risk
↓ Decreased   * Recharacterized
↔ No Change

Development of treatment plans allowed transition to residual risk measurement in Q1'19.

Recharacterized #5, BCP to emphasize disaster recovery plan, and #25 Mfg operations to include longer term competitiveness risk.

Primary Driver of Blended Rating
- Balanced Influence
- Long Term Influence
- Short Term Influence

Likelihood/Qualitative Factors

Financial Impact

Note: See Appendix 1 for the description of risk factors used to prioritize ERM risks.

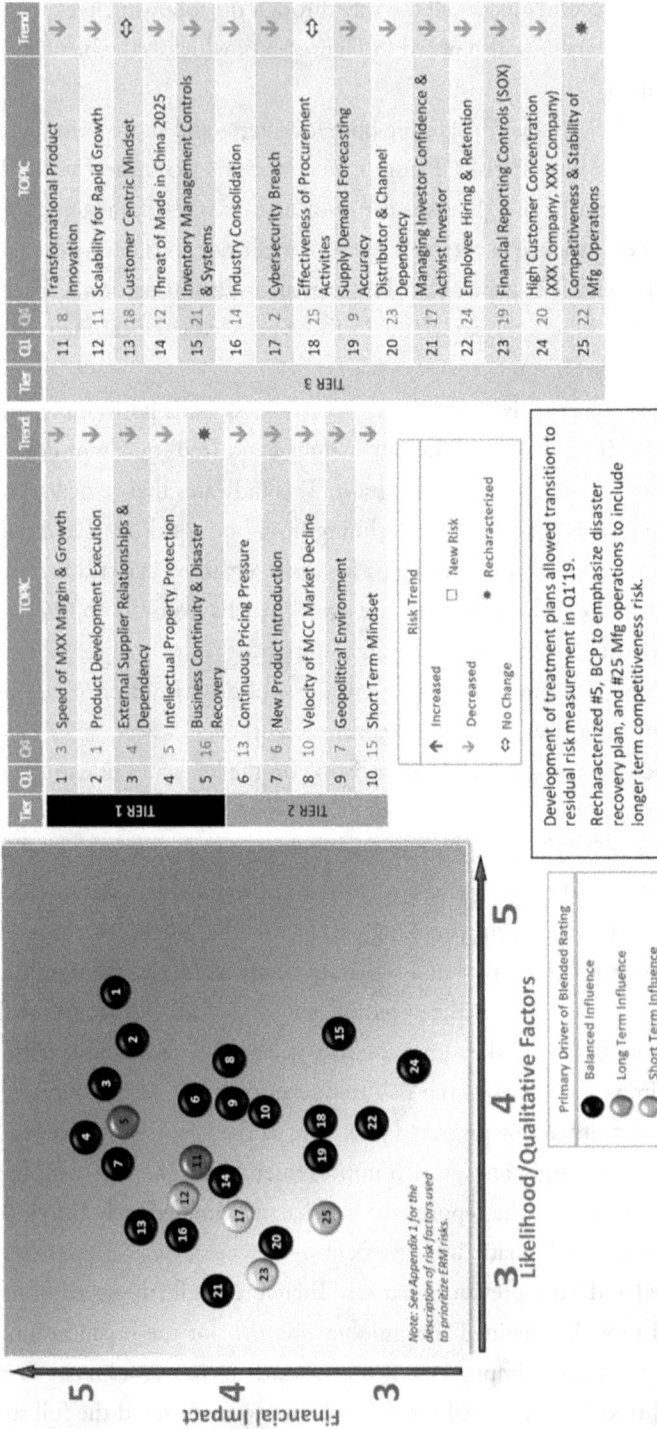

Figure 15.6 Top 25 ERM blended risk heat map Q1 2019

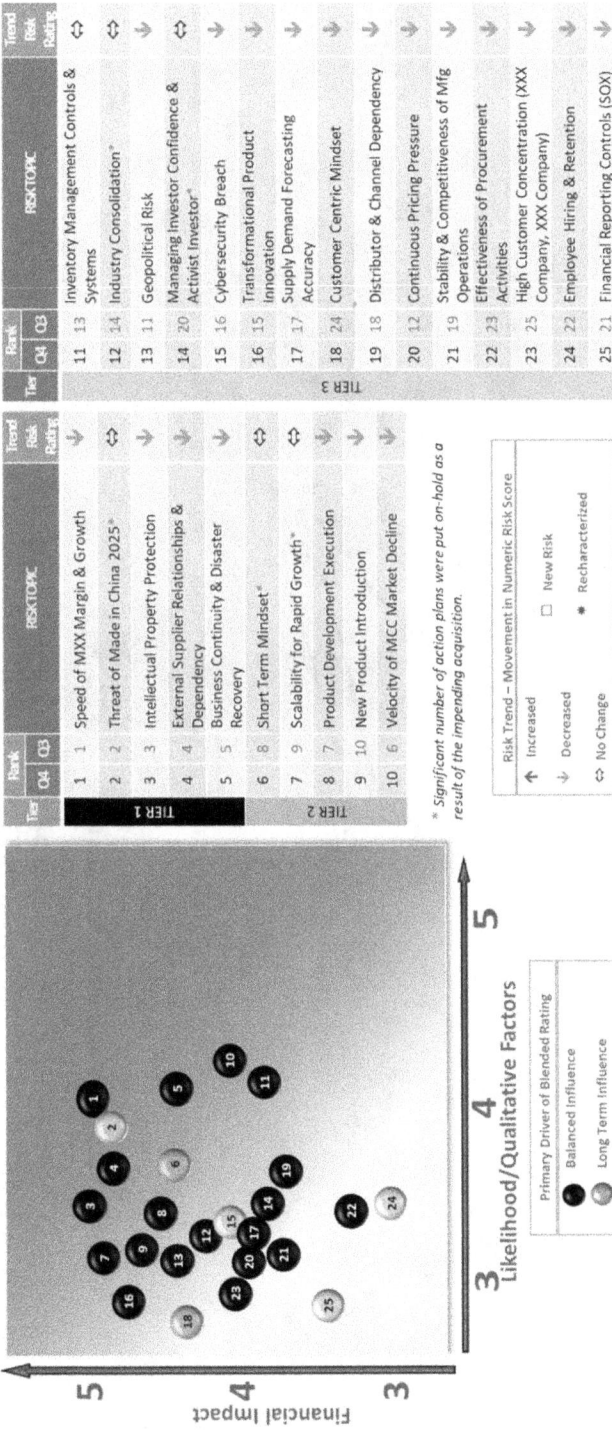

Tier	Rank Q4	Q3	RISK TOPIC	Trend Risk Rating
TIER 1	1	1	Speed of MXX Margin & Growth	→
	2	2	Threat of Made in China 2025*	↔
	3	3	Intellectual Property Protection	→
	4	4	External Supplier Relationships & Dependency	→
	5	5	Business Continuity & Disaster Recovery	→
TIER 2	6	8	Short Term Mindset*	↔
	7	9	Scalability for Rapid Growth*	↔
	8	7	Product Development Execution	→
	9	10	New Product Introduction	→
	10	6	Velocity of MCC Market Decline	→

Tier	Rank Q4	Q3	RISK TOPIC	Trend Risk Rating
TIER 3	11	13	Inventory Management Controls & Systems	↔
	12	14	Industry Consolidation*	↔
	13	11	Geopolitical Risk	→
	14	20	Managing Investor Confidence & Activist Investor*	↔
	15	16	Cybersecurity Breach	→
	16	15	Transformational Product Innovation	→
	17	17	Supply Demand Forecasting Accuracy	→
	18	24	Customer Centric Mindset	→
	19	18	Distributor & Channel Dependency	→
	20	12	Continuous Pricing Pressure	→
	21	19	Stability & Competitiveness of Mfg Operations	→
	22	23	Effectiveness of Procurement Activities	→
	23	25	High Customer Concentration (XXX Company, XXX Company)	→
	24	22	Employee Hiring & Retention	→
	25	21	Financial Reporting Controls (SOX)	→

* Significant number of action plans were put on-hold as a result of the impending acquisition.

Risk Trend – Movement in Numeric Risk Score
↑ Increased   ☐ New Risk
→ Decreased   ＊ Recharacterized
↔ No Change

Primary Driver of Blended Rating
Balanced Influence
Long Term Influence
Short Term Influence

Likelihood/Qualitative Factors

Financial Impact

Figure 15.7 *Top 25 ERM blended risk heat map Q4 2019*

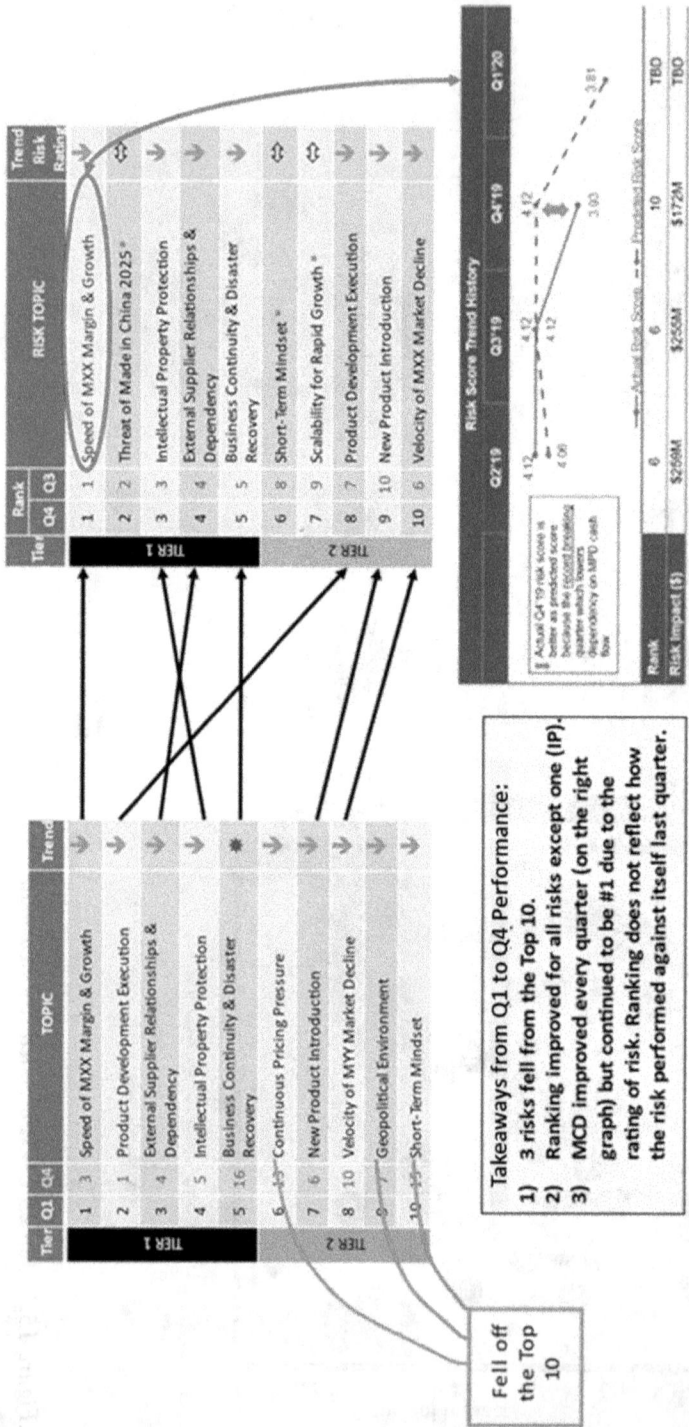

Figure 15.8 Q1 versus Q4 ranking versus rating for the year 2019

of how the risks relate to themselves from quarter to quarter, otherwise the rankings can be a little misleading.

Figure 15.9 shows the complete view of the Risk Performance Report related to the number one risk (Speed of Margin and Growth). Examining the performance report for this particular risk shows why the risk rating improved when compared to itself in the prior quarter.

In the bottom right-hand side, the Overall Action Completion box shows that almost 60 percent of the action items have been completed. No action plans were delayed and about 37 percent have been started but not due yet. That shows that the risk treatment plan was very effective and working quite well.

An easier, more visible reference of the improvement noted during the year of 2019 is shown in Figure 15.10.

The mere positioning of the balls, each representing one of the Top 25 risks, moved substantially from the upper right-hand darker gray corner (in digital copies the red corner) more toward the lower left-hand lighter gray (in digital copies—yellow) corner. This progression means that the risks' likelihood and qualitative factors, including the financial impact, have improved dramatically.

The first few slides illustrated that the ERM program over a simple two-year period was incredibly beneficial to the company, which also indicates that the implementation plan was well thought out, well executed, and well supported by management. This success shows that also the risk owners were serious about the treatment plans while improving the company's performance. To gain this level of benefit during year 1 or 2 is difficult to obtain for most ERM programs, but it is achievable. To further expand on how such benefits can be achieved, the rest of this chapter will be dedicated to program implementation planning, the steps taken, and the resources required to achieve the end results.

Figure 15.11 shows the company ERM story. The progression started from April 2018 when the creation of the ERM program was initially requested by the board of directors.

The Board of Directors' request for an ERM program was discussed internally with the CEO and decided upon during the first quarter of 2018. During this period, a presentation was made to the CEO and CFO as to the elements of the ERM program and the timeline to help set executives'

Risk Champion:	C-Suite			
Risk Owners:	Treatment Plan responsible parties			

Current Quarter ERM Activities

Risk Trend: Decreased

MXX margins has improved as the overall memory market stabilizes. In addition, business has a record breaking quarter which reduces Company's dependency on cash flow.

Risk Score Trend History

	Q2'19	Q3'19	Q4'19	Q1'20
	4.12	4.12	4.12	
	4.12	4.12		
	4.06		3.93	3.81

Actual Q4'19 risk score is better as predicted score because the record breaking quarter which lowers dependency on cash flow.

—— Actual Risk Score   — — Predicted Risk Score

Rank	6	6	10	TBD
Risk Impact ($)	$259M	$255M	$172M	TBD

Q4'19 Action Plan Status

Action Plans Due in the Quarter:	10
Action Plans Completed During the Quarter	9
Action Plans Delayed/Due Date Extensions	1

KPI Achievement

KPI	Generate PBTS EARNINGS TO PLAN for NOR and RAM			
	Q2'19	Q3'19	Q4'19	Q1'20
KPI Achievement (#prod milestone)	Not Met (96%)	Not Met (83%)	TBD	TBD

Overall Action Completion

37%
5%
58%

- Not Due: Not started
- Not Due: Started
- Due: Completed
- Due: Delayed

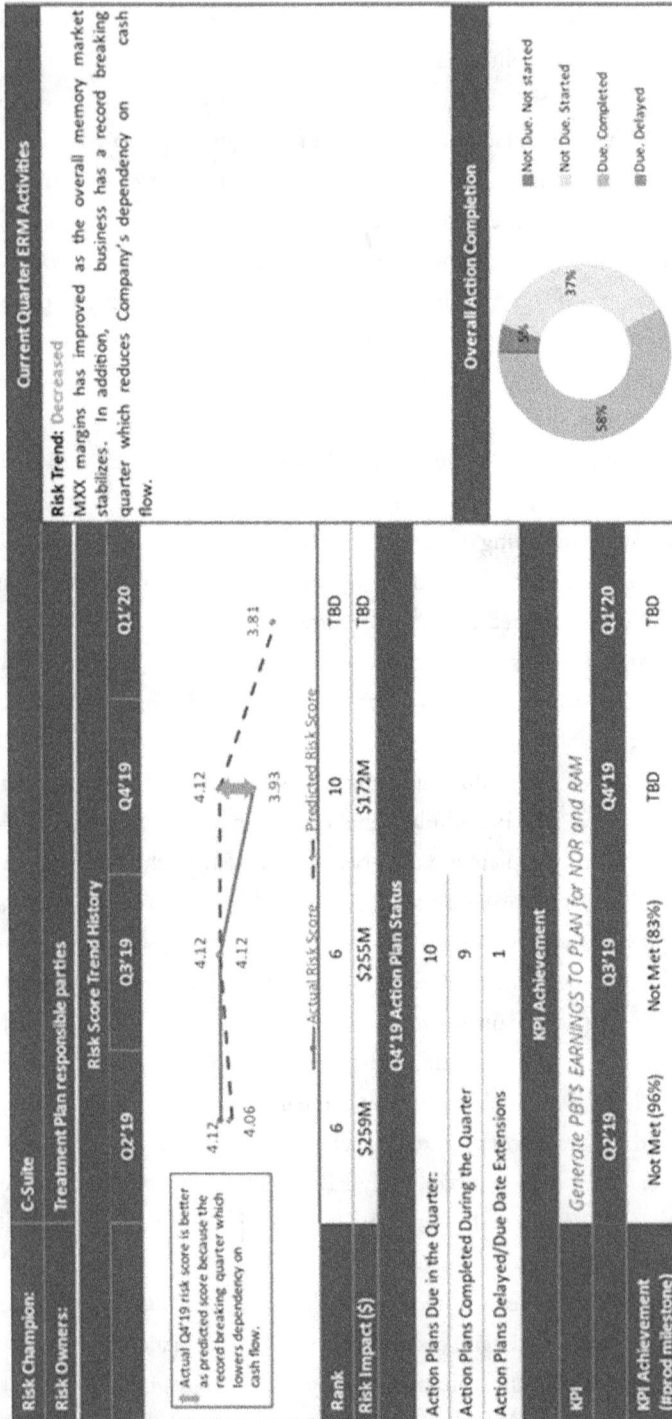

Figure 15.9 Risk performance report: #1 speed of margin and growth

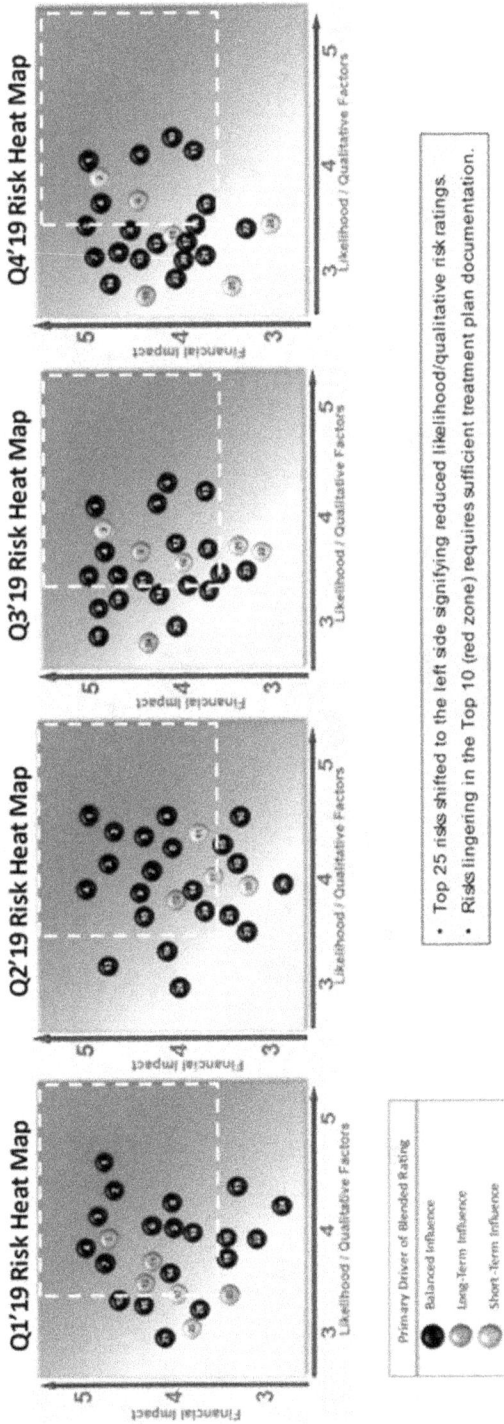

Q1'19 Risk Heat Map

Q2'19 Risk Heat Map

Q3'19 Risk Heat Map

Q4'19 Risk Heat Map

- Top 25 risks shifted to the left side signifying reduced likelihood/qualitative risk ratings.
- Risks lingering in the Top 10 (red zone) requires sufficient treatment plan documentation.

Primary Driver of Blended Rating

Balanced Influence

Long-Term Influence

Short-Term Influence

Figure 15.10 Risk heat map trend

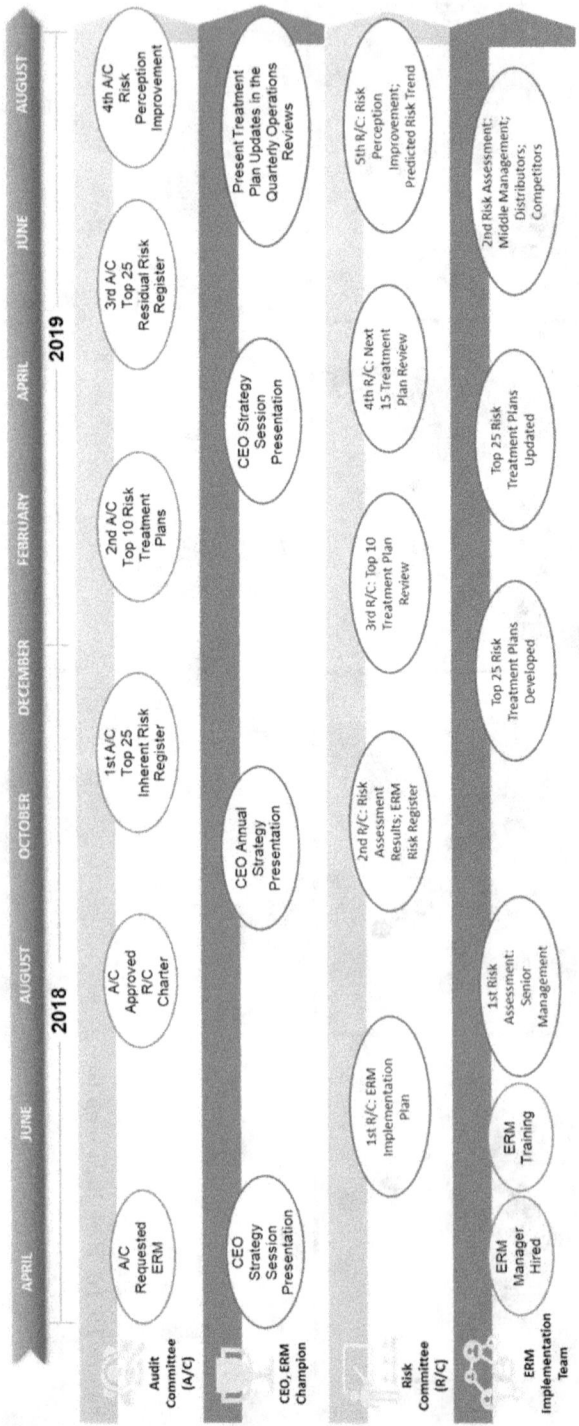

Figure 15.11 The company ERM story

expectations. Resources were hired in April of the same year to strengthen the implementation plan. During the months of May, June, and July, a large portion of the infrastructure was developed and approved for the implementation. A number of the training materials were developed as well.

In August, the Risk Committee was established, and its charter was approved accelerating the ERM program. During the same period, the first risk assessment was conducted identifying a Top 25 list of risks topics to be included in the CEO's annual strategy presentation happening in October, the same time the second risk committee meeting took place. The first ERM program presentation to the Audit Committee happened in November. This means that the full program infrastructure was put in place between April and November.

The ERM processes and training materials were created and documented. By December of the same year, the first treatment plans were developed for the Top 25 risks.

The Risk Committee reviewed the treatment plans for the Top 10 risks in depth during January the following year (2019). This progress continued focusing on the primary elements which further solidified the program. Strong executive support and a highly experienced ERM Administrative Team implementing the program ensured the sustainability of the program.

In developing the cadence for the program, the calendar shown in Figure 15.12 was created. It showed the stakeholders, including the Board of Directors and executive team, the frequency and timing of the key ERM meetings as well as other key meetings including the strategic meetings, annual operating plan meetings, and Quarterly Operations Reviews.

The key dates drive the individual actions of the ERM events to ensure the results are available for the key meetings as planned. In the lower half of Figure 15.12, there is a view of other related ERM events, one being refreshing the risk assessment in each quarter allocating time to identify any emerging risks, as well as allocating time to map the Top 25 risks to the company's 10Q and 10K risk factors. During each quarter, approximately two months were dedicated to helping risk owners develop their risk treatment plans and providing updates to the following key meetings. Lastly, time was allocated toward the end of each quarter to create the shareholder stock price analysis.

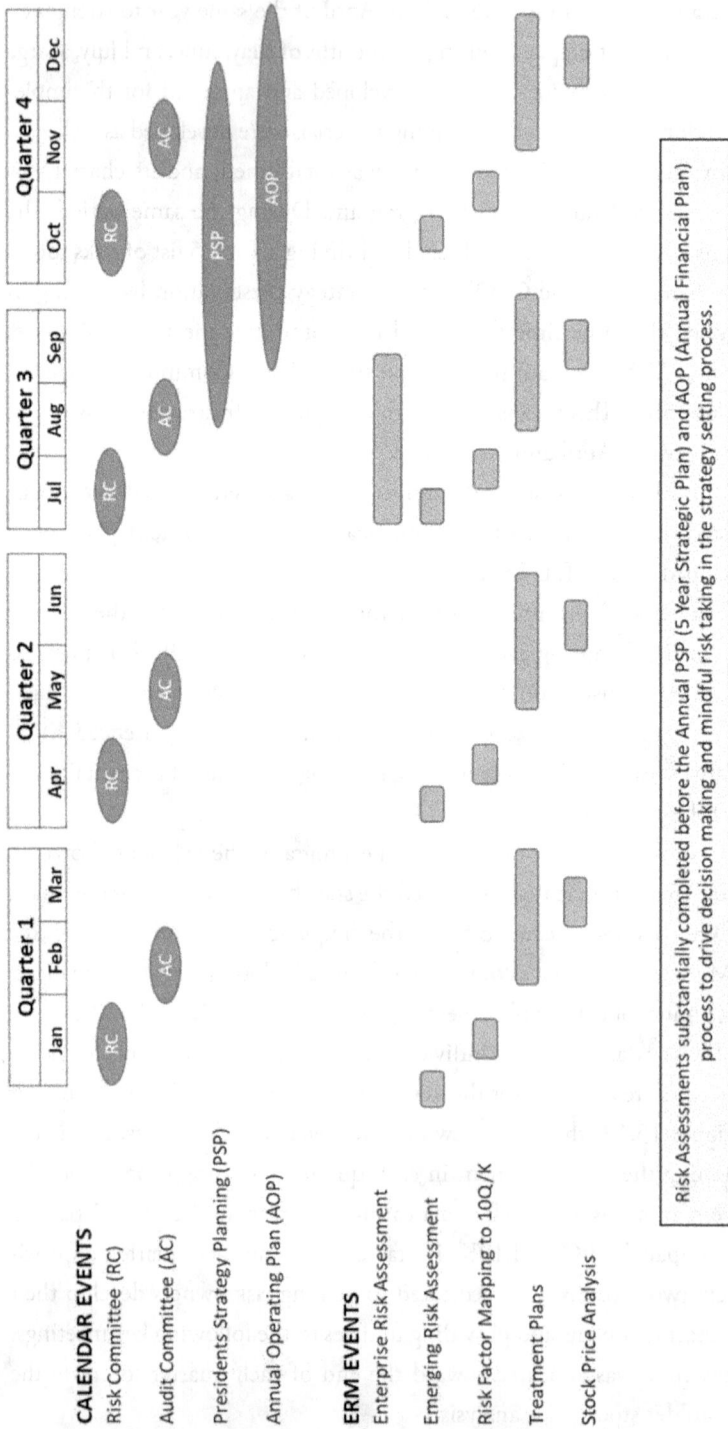

Figure 15.12 ERM calendar

A tremendous amount of work went into this short implementation period to harden this level of cadence and quality of information in a meaningful fashion. Such accelerated implementation may not necessarily be desired by all companies; however, in this particular case study, there was tremendous support from the Board of Directors, the CEO, CEO's direct staff, and by upper- and middle-level management. Much of the success was driven by including the treatment plans in the Quarterly Operations Reviews and having the treatment plan activities tied to the bonus incentive programs. This calendar was developed in the early stages to enable discussions during the training sessions, and to emphasize the importance placed on the success of the new ERM program.

Figure 15.13 shows the ERM infrastructure established at the beginning.

This illustration depicts the normal pyramid type of infrastructure that to certain extent, equates to the 3LoD, especially between the second and the third lines of defense and how each would interact with the overall risk program governance. Oversight is provided at the top of the pyramid by the Audit Committee and in some cases, the entire Board of Directors. The governance over the program is provided by the Risk Committee, which is responsible for promoting the risk awareness and evaluating the adequacy and effectiveness of the risk responses. The third tier down is the ERM Administrative Team, which is responsible for maintaining the continuous risk register, tracking the treatment plans, and reporting on the status each quarter to executive management, Risk Committee, and Audit Committee. The next level down in the pyramid is the Risk Champions, which primarily include the direct CEO's reports (also referred to as C-suite, ELT, or E-staff). The Risk Champions are accountable for the risk treatment plan execution at a high level. Figure 15.13 was developed a few quarters into the program to show the resources required to maintain the program. Note that there are 10 Risk Champions for the Top 25 risks. The risk owners who create and manage the risk treatment plans were typically senior vice presidents or senior directors. In this case study, there were 28 global risk owners who shared the Top 25 risks.

Lastly, at the bottom of the pyramid, there are the risk treatment plan Subject Matter Experts. These are the people who actually execute the risk treatment plans and are normally at director and above levels. In this case study, there were 83 Subject Matter Experts involved in executing

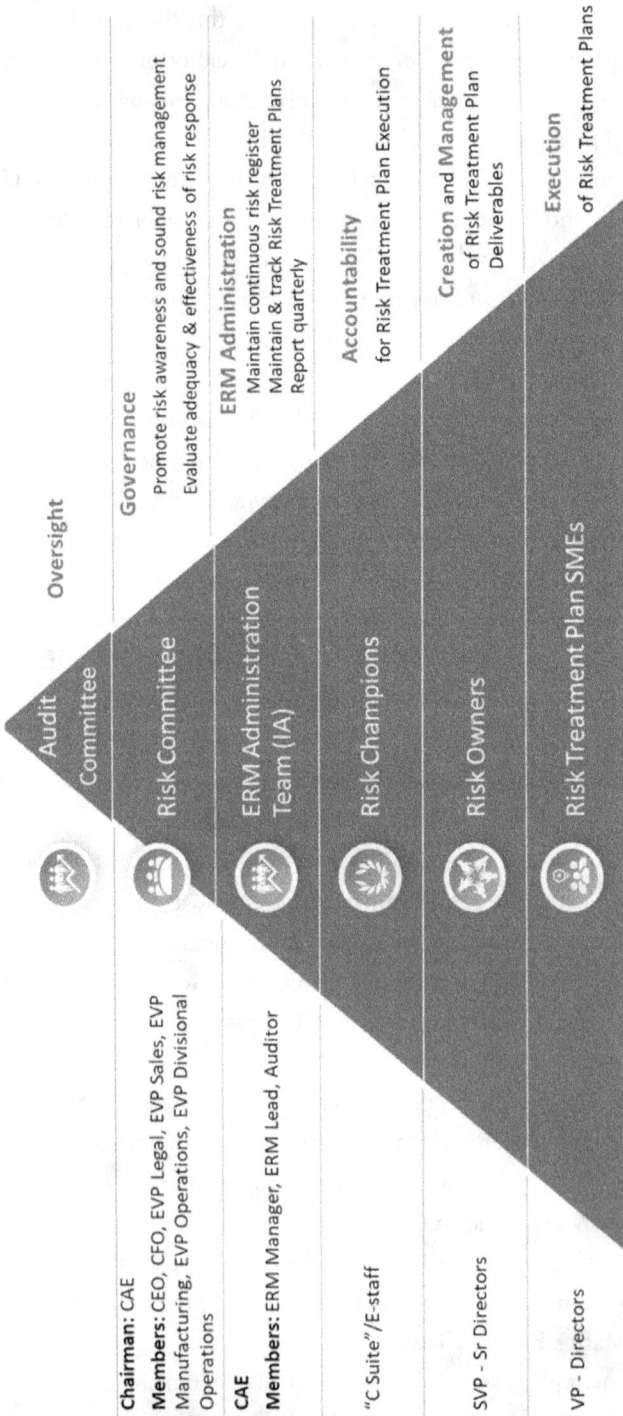

Figure 15.13 The ERM infrastructure

Oversight

Audit Committee

Chairman: CAE
Members: CEO, CFO, EVP Legal, EVP Sales, EVP Manufacturing, EVP Operations, EVP Divisional Operations

Governance

Risk Committee

Promote risk awareness and sound risk management
Evaluate adequacy & effectiveness of risk response

ERM Administration

ERM Administration Team (IA)

CAE
Members: ERM Manager, ERM Lead, Auditor

Maintain continuous risk register
Maintain & track Risk Treatment Plans
Report quarterly

Accountability

Risk Champions

"C Suite"/E-staff

for Risk Treatment Plan Execution

Creation and Management

Risk Owners

SVP - Sr Directors

of Risk Treatment Plan Deliverables

Execution

Risk Treatment Plan SMEs

VP - Directors

of Risk Treatment Plans

risk treatment plans for the Top 25 risks. While there are about 120 people in total to manage the Top 25 risks, please bear in mind that a large amount of the incremental administrative efforts was already absorbed by the ERM Administration Team. The risk owners utilize existing project management tools that are already in place and therefore, not in need of any additional resources. In this case study, there was no need for implementation of new tools or managing of the risk treatment plans' details.

Figure 15.14 shows in this case the implementation team, the ERM Administrative Team.

Figure 15.14 was developed during the second year of the ERM program to provide a view of the experience of the implementation team responsible for maintenance of the ERM program. The program was led by the Head of Internal Audit and the Manager of ERM. There were five members in the pool of internal auditors for this company, and each of those five people contributed only a part of their time to the ERM program. Some of the team contributed more than the others, which depended on the other projects that were ongoing throughout the year. It is important to note that everyone became cross-trained in the risk assessment activities. Majority of the other projects included investigations, Sarbanes–Oxley testing, internal audits, and similar internal audit related projects that surfaced throughout the year. The team member experience came from a variety of industries, and each had ERM background that substantially contributed to the success of the ERM program implementation.

Figure 15.15 provides an overview of the semiconductor business model and the departments that were involved from the beginning to the end.

Figure 15.15 shows that in this case study the ERM program included all the normal business cycle of the global organization such as product development, new product introduction, sales, operations, procurement, manufacturing, logistics, and customer support. The center hub comprised of the administrative functions such as finance, legal, human resources, and information technology.

As mentioned earlier, one of the first steps after the ERM program infrastructure is developed, is to conduct a bottom-up risk assessment. Figure 15.16 shows the parameters used for this risk identification step.

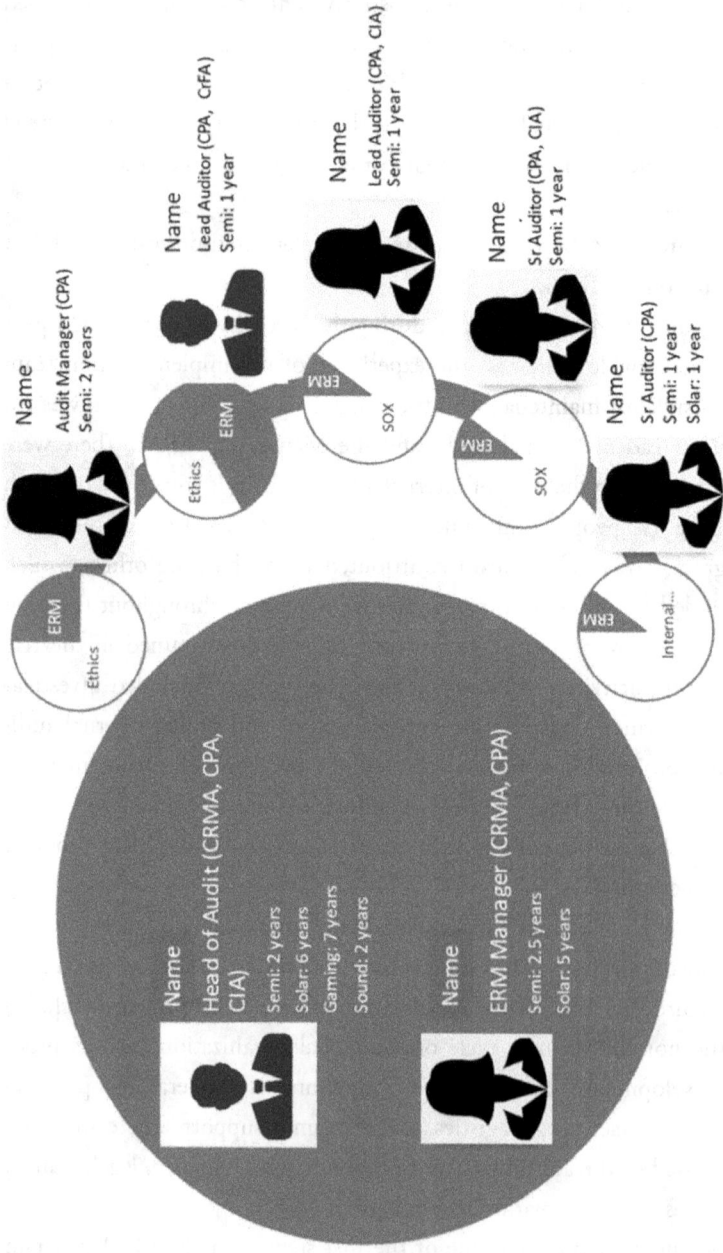

Figure 15.14 The ERM implementation team

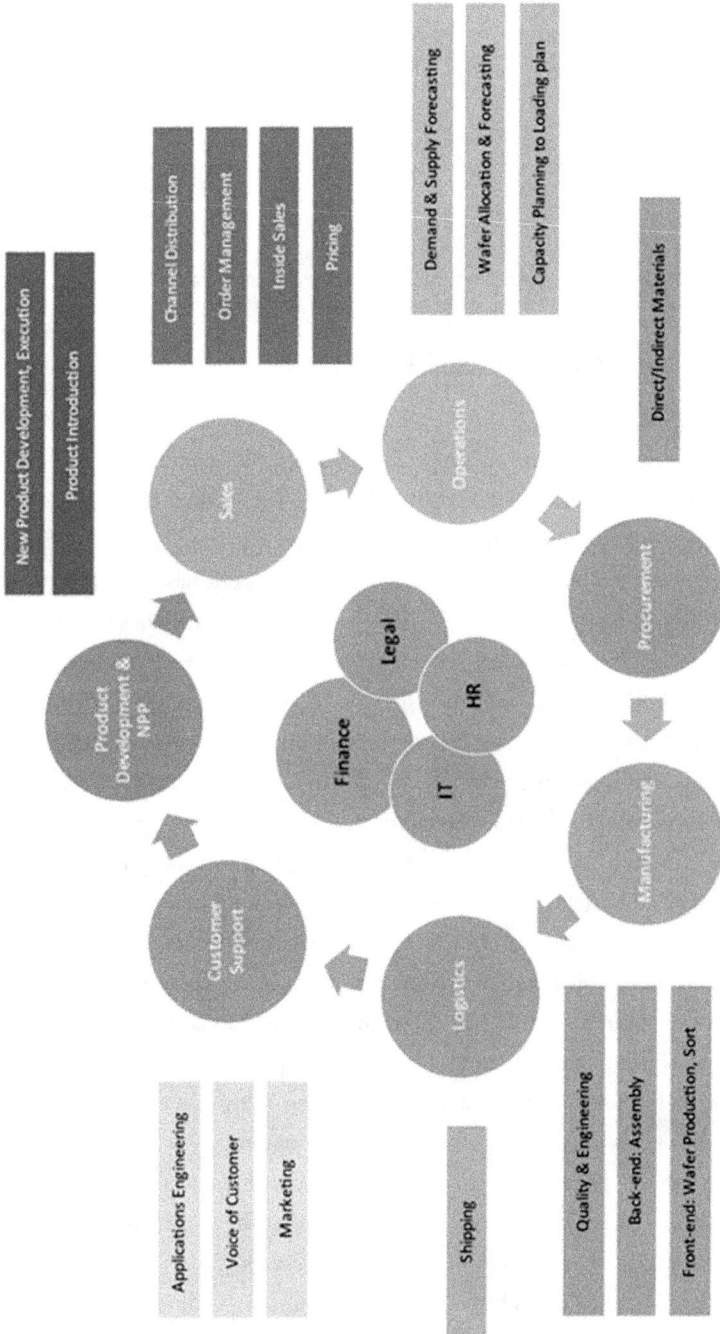

Figure 15.15 ERM business coverage

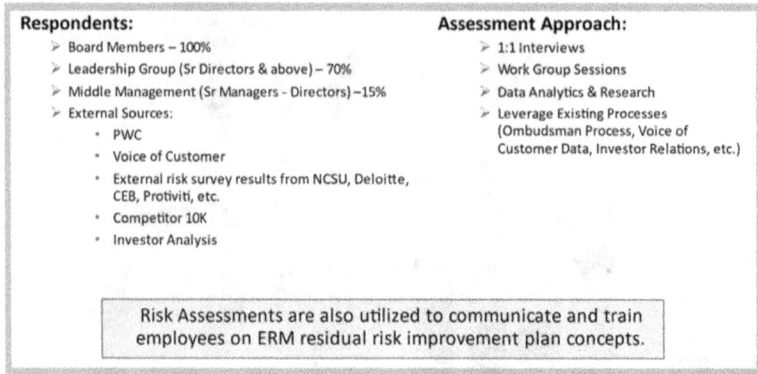

Respondents:
- Board Members – 100%
- Leadership Group (Sr Directors & above) – 70%
- Middle Management (Sr Managers - Directors) –15%
- External Sources:
  - PWC
  - Voice of Customer
  - External risk survey results from NCSU, Deloitte, CEB, Protiviti, etc.
  - Competitor 10K
  - Investor Analysis

Assessment Approach:
- 1:1 Interviews
- Work Group Sessions
- Data Analytics & Research
- Leverage Existing Processes (Ombudsman Process, Voice of Customer Data, Investor Relations, etc.)

> Risk Assessments are also utilized to communicate and train employees on ERM residual risk improvement plan concepts.

Figure 15.16 Risk identification

The respondents or participants included 100 percent of the board members, 70 percent of the leadership team (defined as senior directors and above), and 15 percent of the middle management (defined as senior managers and directors) who were specifically picked based on their particular job function related to risk management. The external sources such as external auditors, the big 4 firm, programs like voice-of-the-customer, and the competitor's 10K analysis were also included. The assessment approach was primarily based on the one-on-one interviews and lasted typically about one hour each. It is important to note that these one-hour sessions were also utilized to communicate and retrain employees on the ERM program. There were also some work group sessions particularly in manufacturing that proved to be more productive and efficient individual meetings. Data analytics and research was also utilized. In this case study, in addition to the above, there were already existing versions of risk management programs already in place throughout the company providing a very solid input to the enterprisewide level program. It is important to identify those subprograms and consider their value as it can improve the overall success of the companywide ERM program.

Figure 15.17 provides an example of the risk assessment guide questions used for the one-on-one interviews and at the workshop sessions to generate the thought flow toward risk management.

The questions focus heavily on initially understanding the company's objectives for the year, as well as any changes that are expected over the next one or two years within the business model, location, or geography.

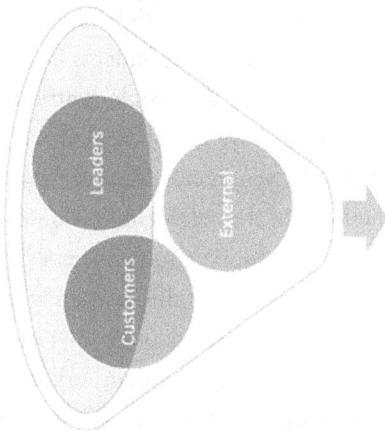

What are your organization's objectives that support Cypress mission and objectives?

Are there current activities in your group that focus on identifying and managing risks?

What are the top 5 risks in achieving your organization's objectives?

Internal strategy and operations risks (budgetary changes, reorganization, infrastructure change)

External risks (political environment, market or industry trend, competitor climate, customer behavior)

•Do we have plans to implement a new strategy?
  •What must go right for a new strategic initiative to be successful?
  •What impact might this new strategy have on our existing business?

•Are you aware of any future changes that may affect your business?

•Are you aware of potential black swans or long-term (2-5 years) risks to Cypress?

•Do you see any potential opportunity for cost containment or additional revenue source in your area?

•Are you aware of ways to enhance leveraging of data, tools and supporting systems to improve operational effectiveness?

Where is the highest potential for fraud?

Leaders

Customers

External

ERM Risk Register

Figure 15.17 One-on-one interview risk assessment guide questions

These 9 to 10 questions will generally stimulate enough conversation to obtain enough detail for highlighting the risks. Additional question and answer exchanges may create a more thorough understanding of specific areas such as the financial impact and other qualitative factors.

Figure 15.18 suggests that it is very helpful for management to look for external factors related to their department to find risks and answers about potential risks, especially when there are major changes expected within the business model, product, or territory.

In this particular case study, there were many discussions around industry consolidation and tracking competitors' acquisitions or spinoffs. There were also conversations about using various analytical models such as Porter's Five Forces or PESTLE analysis to be able to better understand other risks related to new geographies, new business models, new products, and so on. These one-on-one interviews and work group sessions were healthy conversations spurring additional thought-provoking dialogue.

Figure 15.19 shows the respondent profile for the first risk assessment that was done in the first year of implementation compared to the refresh conducted six to eight months later in the following year.

The functional areas did not change dramatically, but they did represent a very broad coverage and fair representation of all members of the business community within the organization. The previous illustration also shows the statistics of the respondents that were in each of the three primary regions (Europe, the Americas, and Asia Pacific) as well as the job titles/levels of the respondents. Maintaining this type of information is very helpful to prove the credibility of the risk identification process, as well as monitoring that the number of respondents is directly proportional to the primary business models, the people-centric activities, and the organizations that are new or have disappeared. It confirms that a representative number of people were included in the right geographic areas and in the right functions. In the risk identification process for the semiconductor industry, it was appropriate to perform a risk assessment of the distributor process. The company in this case study used an external distribution channel to sell to the end customer for a large percentage of the revenue. This step may not be applicable to other organizations, but it does suggest that one should look outside of the normal sources

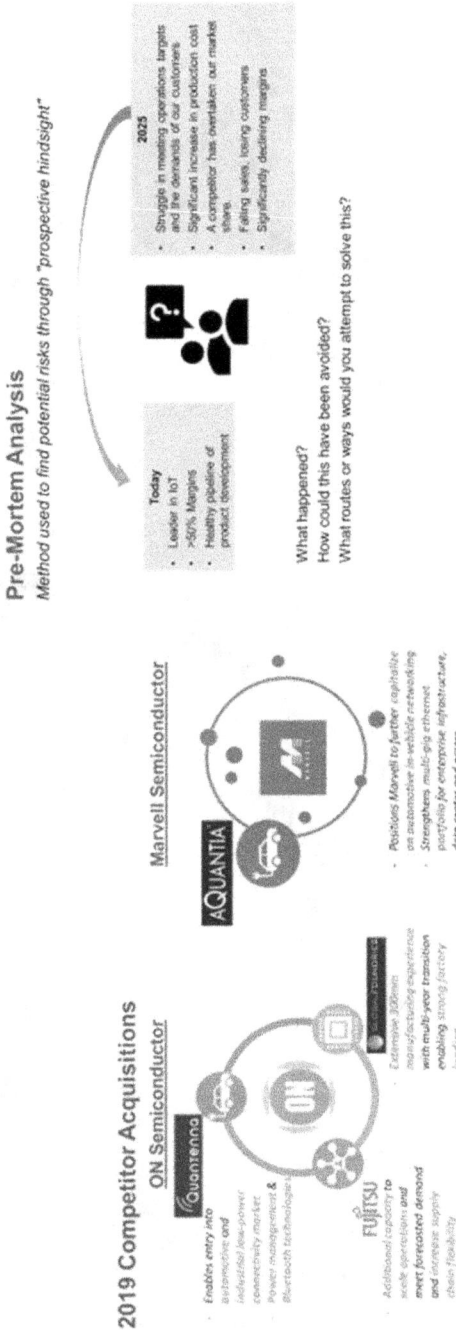

Figure 15.18 *Looking for external factors (pre/postmortem, PESTLE, Porter's Five Forces, and gaming workshops)*

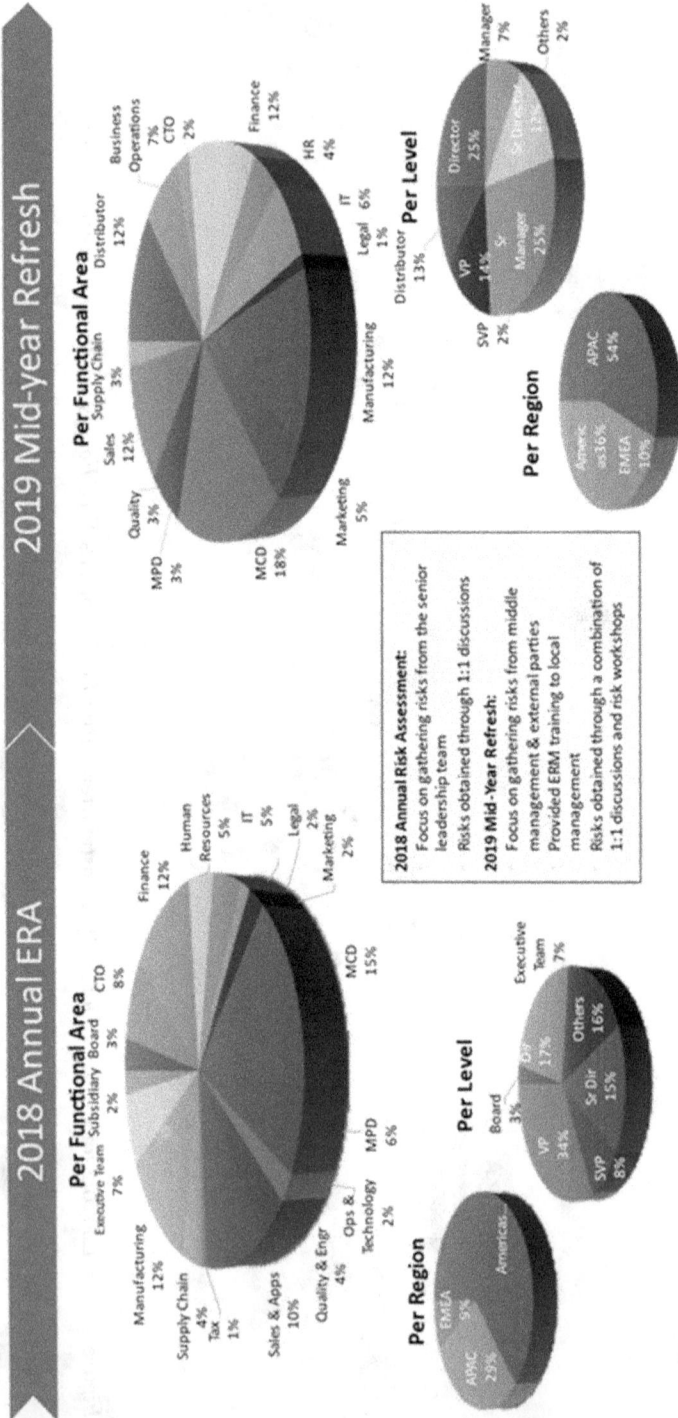

Figure 15.19 Actual risk assessment respondent profiles

that can affect the business. These other sources could also include third parties such as contractors, suppliers, foundries or original equipment manufacturers (OEMs), original design manufacturers (ODMs), joint ventures, service providers, customers, and so on.

This type of risk identification must be handled with extreme care as it involves discussing risks with third parties and customers. The best practice is just to contain the risks conversations with the distributors to the specific business relationship between the company and the customer. Conversations should center on the pain points, the differentiators, opportunities, and should include regional account executives who own the customer relationship. It is also beneficial to ensure the conversations are held with distributors' executive management to gain the bigger picture. This process was found to also be very beneficial to the relationship with the distributors because the distributors were generally impressed that the company was spending this type of time and effort in trying to improve the relationship, as well as addressing the challenges that also impacts the distributors.

Figure 15.20 shows a sample guide of questions for interviews with a distribution channel partner, and Figure 15.21 shows the results of these risk identification conversations with the distributors.

As shown above, there were specific pain points brought to light, but there were also some suggestions to improve the competitive advantage of the company's products as well as the opportunities that may increase the

What are your organization's objectives?

What are the top challenges or pain points in transactions involving Company products?

In what area is Company better than its competitors?

Do you have plans to implement a new strategy. If so, what support do you need from us for this initiative to be successful, and what impact might this new strategy have on our business?

Are you aware of emerging or longer-term (2-5 years) risks that could affect Company?

Do you see any potential opportunity to increase sales volume of Company products?

Are you aware of external risks that could adversely impact distribution or end customer sales?

Which area has the highest potential for fraud?

Are there current activities in your Organization that focuses on identifying and managing risks?

Figure 15.20 Distributor risk assessment guide questions

Top comments based on % of distributors mentioning the topic per category

Major Challenges / Pain Points	Competitive Advantage	Opportunities
Price Increase Process - Multiple price increases in the past tarnished Company's reputation with customers	**Product Portfolio** has a wide range of differentiated products	**Company Acquisition** will increase customer base and better product solutions
Low Margin Rates keep distributors from lead generation activities	**Systems and Tools** are informative and easy to use	**Expand Customer Base** by including category B customers, and improving presence in industrial and smart home markets
High Phantom Rates negatively impacts distributor rate of return and discourages build up of buffer inventory for demand generation	**Good Customer Support** from ISRs, FAEs, Product Managers	**Improve Total Solution Strategy** to play in emerging markets or products (wearable solutions, power management IC, fingerprint)
Uncompetitive Total Solution Strategy – Competitors are able to provide total solutions or more integrated solutions	**Better Product Quality** reliability and performance	**Product Innovation** to introduce new technology at competitive prices
Uncompetitive Pricing against product solutions from China or local competitors. Industrial markets are becoming more price sensitive.	**Good Relationship Management** with distributor top management	**Alliance with Bigger Suppliers** to create total market solutions
Long Lead Time need to finish this thought	**New Product Introduction Approach** has unified marketing strategy and written in both English and local language (Japan)	
Product Allocation Issues forced smaller customers to find other suppliers	**Product Innovation** at Company is good based on ability to introduce new products	
Expedite Fee charges on new products, or for new customers are unreasonable		

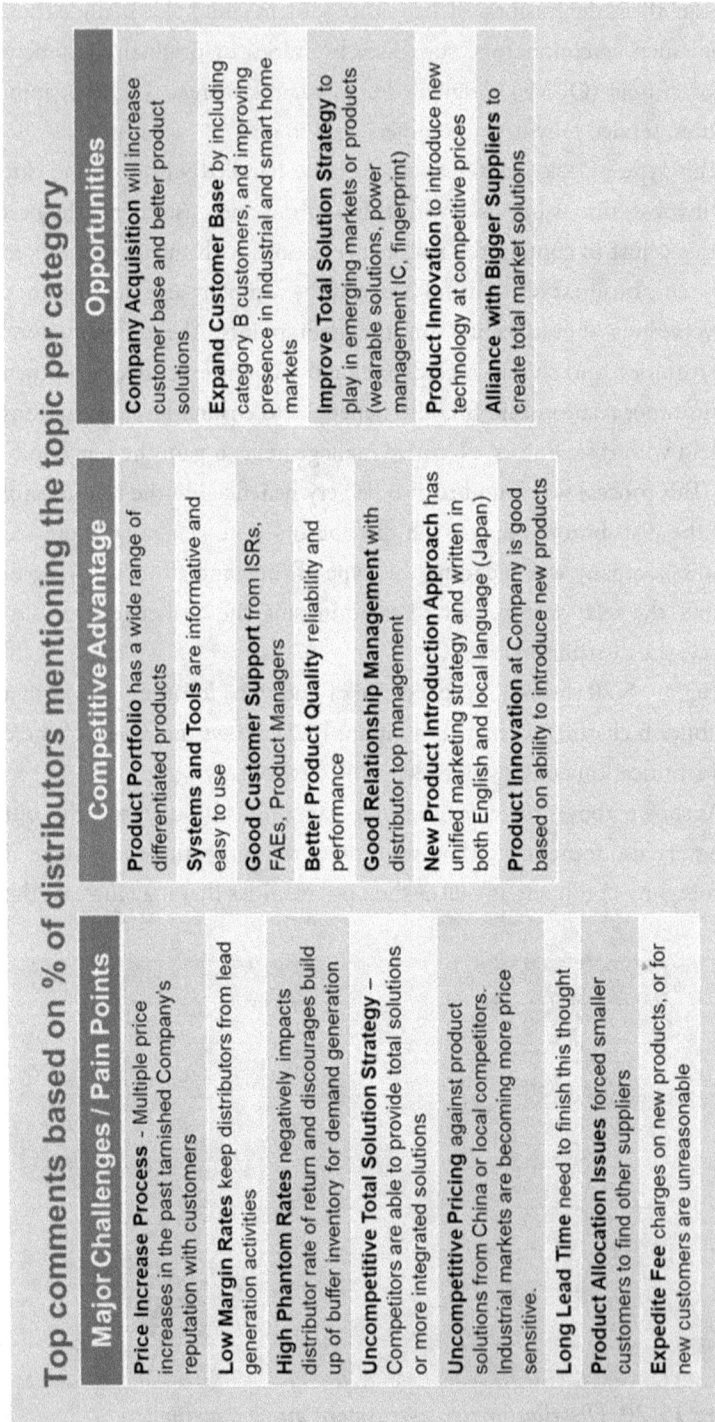

Figure 15.21 Distributors risk assessment key takeaways

business success for both the company and the distributor. This activity was taken a step further and became one of the Top 25 risks addressing primarily the challenges and pain points that were not covered in other risks.

Figure 15.22 shows the population or the risk universe for the refresh that was done in year 2 of the program after the year of implementation.

There were a few new risks identified even though they landed in Tier 4 category and ranked under the Top 25. In such an ERM Risk Register refresh, the general expectation is to identify additional completely new risks, as well as more risks related to the existing risk topics.

Figure 15.23 provides a view of comparing the frequency at which the risk topics were brought up versus last year.

The previous illustration represents a comparison of the ERM Risk Register refresh compared to the prior year. The bottom axis shows a percentage of the respondents who identified the particular risk topic, which are shown on the left-side axis. The frequency of these elements resulted from the conversations. The lighter gray bar (in digital copies—in orange) is the prior year, and the darker gray (in digital copies—blue) bar is the current year of the new refresh assessment. It is interesting to see how some of the dynamics changed dramatically, while others substantially improved. One risk topic however became a major highlight in the previously shown refresh. Nearly 85 percent of the respondents stated "employee hiring and retention" was a high risk to the company, and was nearly double that of the prior year. Although this particular risk was more of a perceived risk than a real risk, one might anticipate this topic to become the number one risk for the company. It did get on the risk register, but closer toward the Tier 3 risks group. Even if this risk topic was not necessarily a material topic in the risk ranking profile, it still shows that there is a significant perceived risk that must still be addressed. This topic may not be included in the risk treatment plan, but it must be addressed via other means such as communication and being statistically analyzed to see how severe this perceived risk is or how accurate the respondents are.

The location of the "hiring and retention risk" respondents is shown in Figure 15.24.

Each of the teardrops shows the percentage of respondents at that location, which brought up this topic as a risk. The darker gray teardrops (in

Tier	Q3 Rank	Risk Topic
TIER 1	1	Speed of MXX Margin & Growth
	2	Threat of Made in China 2025
	3	Intellectual Property Protection
	4	External Supplier Relationships & Dependency
	5	Business Continuity & Disaster Recovery
TIER 2	6	Velocity of MYY Market Decline
	7	Product Development Execution
	8	Short-Term Mindset
	9	Scalability for Rapid Growth
	10	New Product Introduction
TIER 3	11	Geopolitical Risk
	12	Continuous Pricing Pressure
	13	Inventory Management Controls & Systems
	14	Industry Consolidation
	15	Transformational Product Innovation
	16	Cybersecurity Breach
	17	Supply Demand Forecasting Accuracy
	18	Distributor & Channel Dependency
	19	Stability & Competitiveness of Fab Operations
	20	Managing Investor Confidence & Activist Investor

Tier	Q3 Rank	Risk Topic
TIER 3	21	Financial Reporting Controls (SOX)
	22	Employee Hiring & Retention
	23	Effectiveness of Procurement Activities
	24	Customer Centric Mindset
	25	High Customer Concentration
	26	Product Quality & Reliability at New Product Stage
	27	Working Capital Position
	28	Penetration into Emerging Markets
	29	Broad Product Portfolio
	30	Inventory Build Up
TIER 4	31	Data Analytics & Artificial Intelligence
	32	Product Allocation & On-Time-Delivery
	33	Brand Awareness
	34	Merger, Acquisition, Divestiture & Integration
	35	Volatility of Foreign Currencies
	36	Understanding & Alignment to New Company Strategy & Culture
	37	Employee Succession Plan
	38	Financial Planning, Budgeting & Monitoring
	39	Ethics & Governance (Fraud Risks)

Tier	Q3 Rank	Risk Topic
TIER 4	40	Environmental, Social, Governance and Sustainability
	41	Cash Flow Forecasting/Management
	42	Manufacturing Capacity & Utilization Strategy (Internal & External)
	43	Limitation on Sales & Strategic Marketing Activities
	44	COGS Optimization/Cost Reduction
	45	Compliance with External Laws & Regulations (FCPA, SEC, Labor, Statutory, Anti-Trust)
	46	Security & Protection of Private, Confidential or Cloud-Based Information
	47	Increasing Cost of Labor in Offshore Locations
	48	New Board Structure & Members
	49	Increasing Industry Litigation
	50	Credit Risk New Customers
	51	Accounts Payable Payment Process
	52	Adequacy of Current IT Infrastructure & Support
	53	Interest Rate Change
	54	Contract Management & Administration
	55	Changing International Tax Laws

New risks identified in 2019 risk assessment refresh exercise.

Figure 15.22 Refresh ERM risk register (total risk universe) in 2019

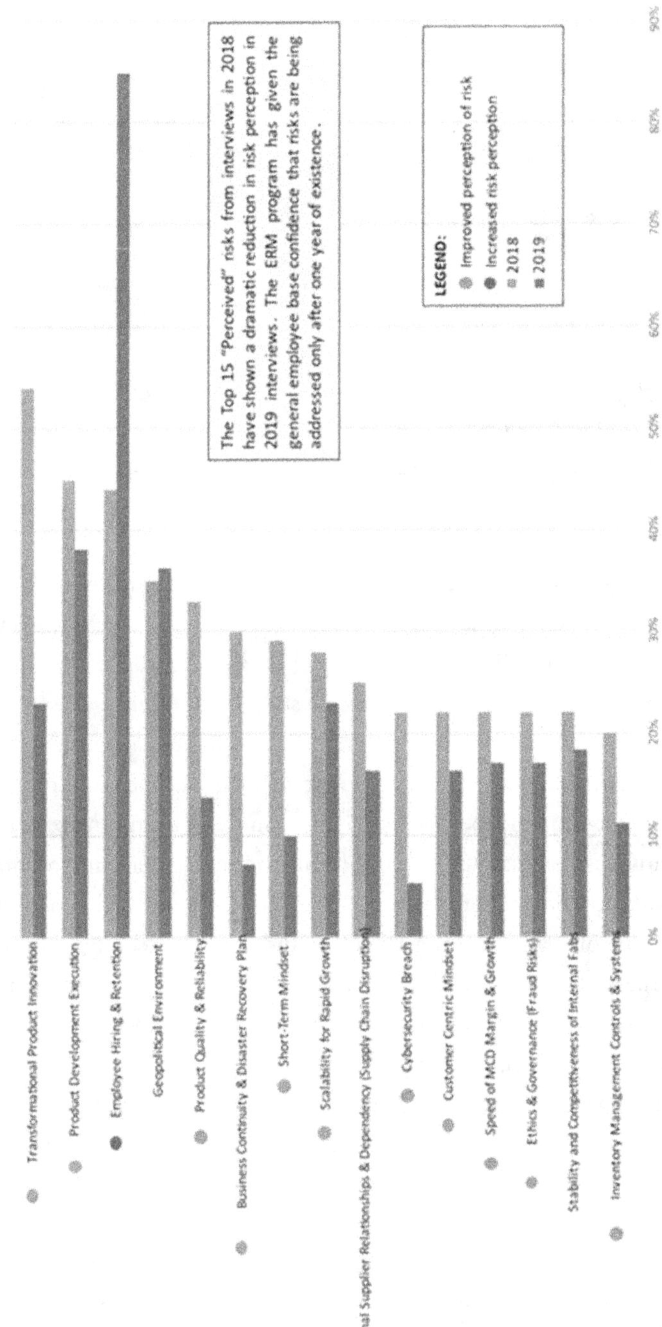

Transformational Product Innovation
Product Development Execution
Employee Hiring & Retention
Geopolitical Environment
Product Quality & Reliability
Business Continuity & Disaster Recovery Plan
Short-Term Mindset
Scalability for Rapid Growth
External Supplier Relationships & Dependency (Supply Chain Disruption)
Cybersecurity Breach
Customer Centric Mindset
Speed of MCD Margin & Growth
Ethics & Governance (Fraud Risks)
Stability and Competitiveness of Internal Fabs
Inventory Management Controls & Systems
0%
10%
20%
30%
40%
50%
60%
70%
80%
90%
The Top 15 "Perceived" risks from interviews in 2018 have shown a dramatic reduction in risk perception in 2019 interviews. The ERM program has given the general employee base confidence that risks are being addressed only after one year of existence.
LEGEND:
Improved perception of risk
Increased risk perception
2018
2019

Figure 15.23 **Risk frequency comparison with prior year**

Figure 15.24 Global mapping of hiring and retention risk respondents

digital copy—orange) indicate locations with high percentages (100 percent or so) but because they had only one or two respondents, whereas the lighter gray teardrops (in digital copy—yellow) show locations where there were many respondents, and in this case study the percentages were still concerning (still quite high). This provided executive management with the information needed to decide where to focus their communication and deep dives into the root causes. In this example of hiring and retention risks statistical analysis, San Jose, California showed 73 percent (corporate HQ location) and Philippines had 71 percent (location with a substantial amount of manufacturing facilities) and could not be ignored as a result. The bottom left shows the total percentage per region: 65 percent of respondents concerned about this risk topic were in North America, while 54 percent were in Asia and 43 percent were in Europe. These percentages indicate a startling concern, and to maintain the credibility of the ERM program and of executive management, a specific project was created and managed by the human resources department to address this risk.

After the risk identification step was completed, the next phase is to quantify the risks to generate a Top 25 profile. Figure 15.25 shows the Top 25 risk topic register with the heat map on the left side resulting from the refresh that occurred in 2019.

There are the different colors of the rating balls, each ball representing a risk topic in the Top 25 list. The black color indicates a balanced

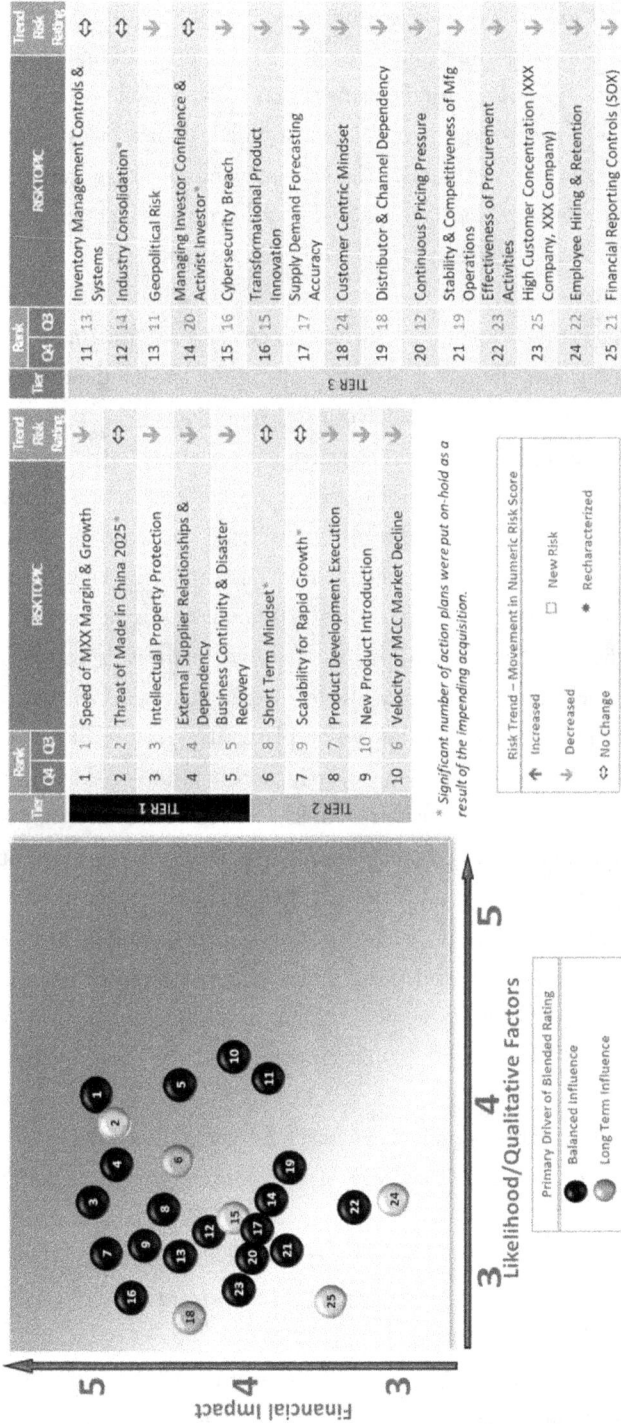

Tier	Rank Q4	Q3	RISK TOPIC	Trend Risk Rating
TIER 1	1	1	Speed of MXX Margin & Growth	→
	2	2	Threat of Made in China 2025*	⟷
	3	3	Intellectual Property Protection	→
	4	4	External Supplier Relationships & Dependency	→
	5	5	Business Continuity & Disaster Recovery	→
TIER 2	6	8	Short Term Mindset*	⟷
	7	9	Scalability for Rapid Growth*	⟷
	8	7	Product Development Execution	→
	9	10	New Product Introduction	→
	10	6	Velocity of MCC Market Decline	→

Significant number of action plans were put on-hold as a result of the impending acquisition.

Risk Trend – Movement in Numeric Risk Score

↑ Increased	□ New Risk
→ Decreased	✱ Recharacterized
⟷ No Change	

Tier	Rank Q4	Q3	RISK TOPIC	Trend Risk Rating
TIER 3	11	13	Inventory Management Controls & Systems	⟷
	12	14	Industry Consolidation*	⟷
	13	11	Geopolitical Risk	→
	14	20	Managing Investor Confidence & Activist Investor*	⟷
	15	16	Cybersecurity Breach	→
	16	15	Transformational Product Innovation	→
	17	17	Supply Demand Forecasting Accuracy	→
	18	24	Customer Centric Mindset	→
	19	18	Distributor & Channel Dependency	→
	20	12	Continuous Pricing Pressure	→
	21	19	Stability & Competitiveness of Mfg Operations	→
	22	23	Effectiveness of Procurement Activities	→
	23	25	High Customer Concentration (XXX Company, XXX Company)	→
	24	22	Employee Hiring & Retention	→
	25	21	Financial Reporting Controls (SOX)	→

Primary Driver of Blended Rating
Balanced Influence
Long Term Influence
Short Term Influence

Financial Impact
Likelihood/Qualitative Factors

Figure 15.25 Top 25 ERM blended risk heat map

influence of short term versus long term. The dark grey (blue) ones represent risks that were important, but in a much longer term influence. The light grey (green) color reflects risks that are very short-term driven. The number of short-term driven risks was higher than what is normally seen in the heat map throughout the two-year period. There were events happening in the semiconductor industry at this time, which required an immediate and a very specific attention in certain areas.

Once the risk heat map was done and the Top 25 risk list identified, the next step is to work with risk owners on creating risk treatment plans. Figure 15.26 shows the risk treatment plans in the left-hand-side section that had been in process for about four to five quarters.

The main components of the treatment plans include the risk accountability, KPIs, quantification, root causes, and high-level action plans. To supplement that, the ERM Administration Team created the individual risks scorecard, which is the center section as shown in Figure 15.26. This scorecard keeps track of the actual risk score trends versus past and versus predicted risk scores covering the last four quarters. It also showed the achievement of the KPIs over the last four quarters, which indicates the level of remediation that has taken place. If a given KPI has been accomplished for three straight quarters, the conclusion could be drawn that the risk is substantially remediated. The risk scorecard also shows the status of action plans from a completion percentage standpoint. In other words, are the risk owners on time with their treatment plans or are they delayed? Lastly, the section on the right-hand side is a result of pulling all the individual risk scorecards together and showing the corporate risk trend, which was shown in the very beginning of this chapter.

Figure 15.27 shows the actual template used for creating the risk treatment plans.

All additional project management tracking tools showing related action plans at a more detailed level should support this standard high-level template. This treatment plan template is a single-page format that would summarize all the actions to treat a particular risk topic. The same template must be used for all the Top 25 risks to create standardization in reporting and comparability.

Similarly, Figure 15.28 shows the template used for the risk performance report card.

Performance Reporting provided by ERM Administration Team

Individual Risk Treatment Plans

Main components:

- Risk Accountability
- Key Performance Indicator
- Risk Impact Quantification
- Root Causes
- High-level action plan, timeline and owner

Updates discussed by risk owners during Quarterly Operations Reviews or similar forum.

Individual Risk Scorecard

Main components:

- Risk score trend against predicted risk score for past 4 quarters
- Achievement of risk KPI for past 4 quarters
- Status of action plans (% completed that were due)
- Description of current quarter risk score trend

Overall View of Residual Risk Scores

- Shows an overall view of the risk mitigation effectiveness at Cypress
- Provided as a web chart showing a comparison between the Top 25 ERM actual risk scores versus predicted risk scores and to prior quarter risk scores.

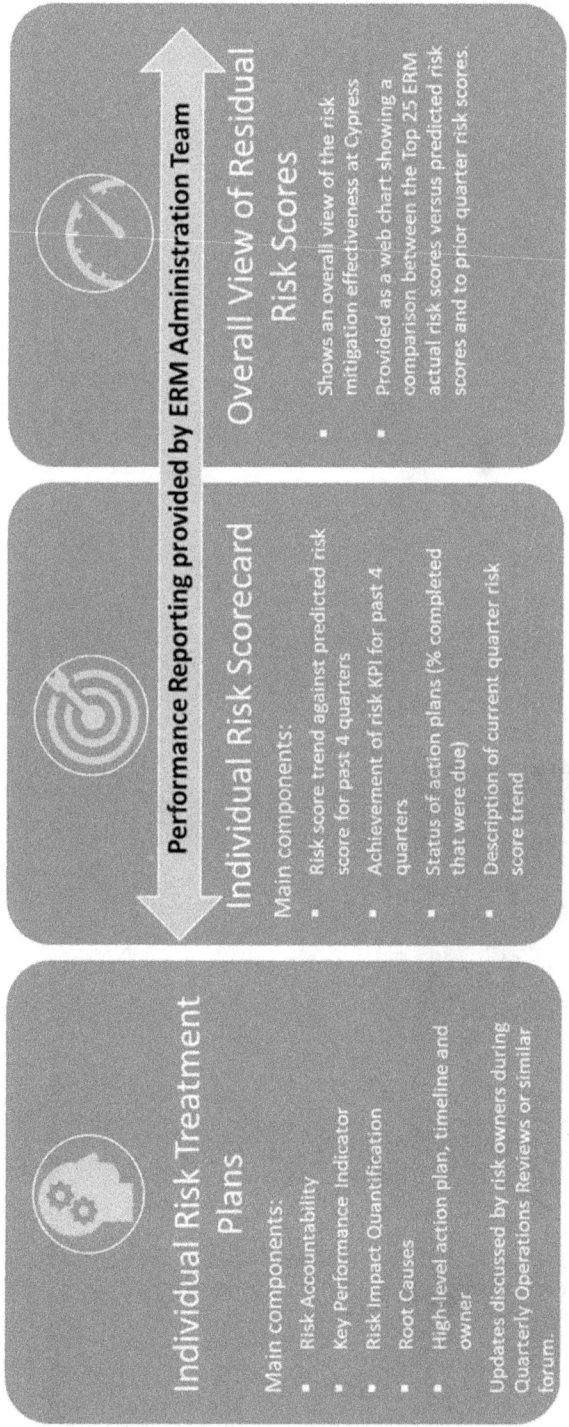

Risk Committee is accountable for promoting risk awareness and sound risk management practices across the organization. Risk responses will be evaluated on a quarterly basis to ensure that they are adequately and effectively mitigating the appropriate risks.

Figure 15.26 ERM residual risk performance report

[Risk Topic]		Mitigation Success
		KPI:
Category:	[Strategic, Financial, Operational, Legal/Compliance]	
Risk Champion/s:	[Accountable eStaff]	
Risk Owners:	[Responsible Person]	
SME:	[Subject Matter Expert]	
Impact Window:	Short-Term, LongTerm, Balanced	

Risk Condition	Root Causes	Response	Action Plans	Owner	Timeline	Status
(Process)		Reduce Transfer Avoid Exploit Accept				Not Started Launched Completed On-Going Delayed
(People)						
(System)						
(External)						
(Relationship)						

Figure 15.27 Risk plan template

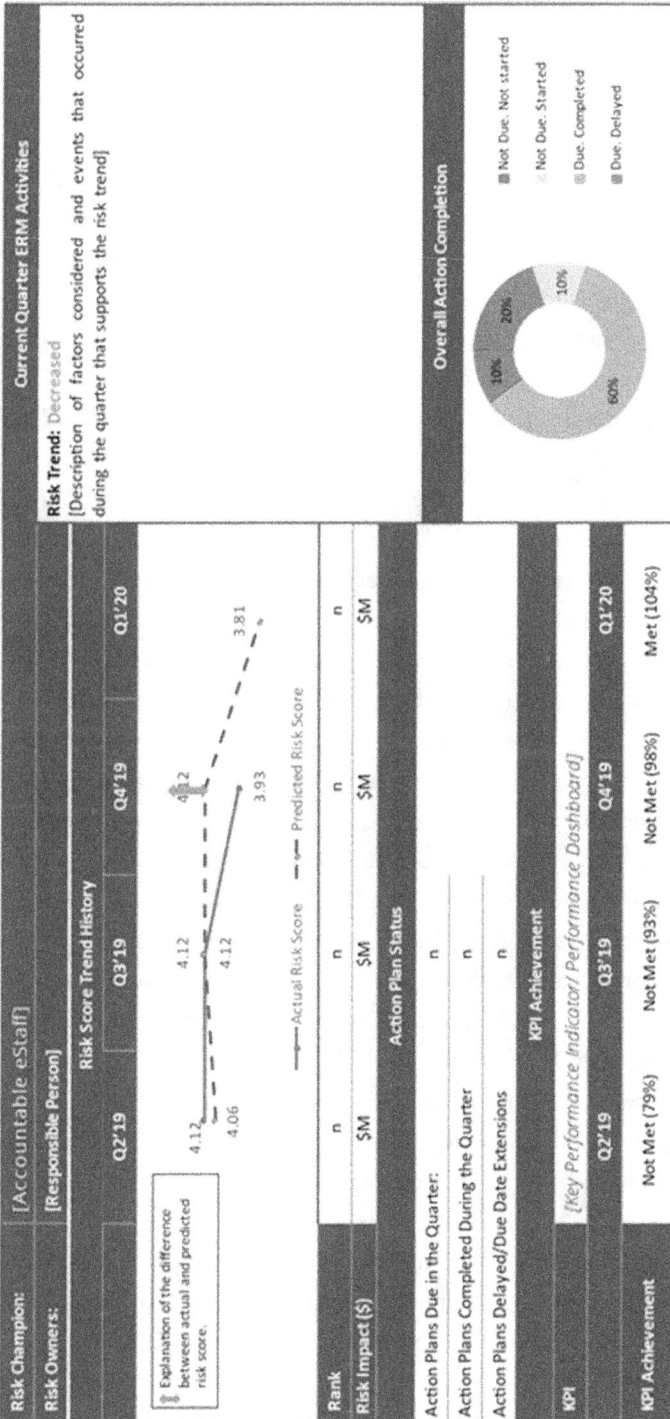

Figure 15.28 Risk performance report template

This template was used to create the score card for each of the Top 25 risks. It shows performance trend versus the individual quarter performance, and contains the narratives discussing the direction, the challenges, and the results.

The next three illustrations are similar in format. Figure 15.29 is a spiral graph that shows the residual risk performance for the Top 25 risks numbered around in the circle, while Figure 15.30 compares actual Q4 versus the predictions made in Q3 for Q4 results.

In the "Actual Q3 results versus Actual Q4 results", the grey (green) area represents an improvement in the risk ratings. Conversely, if there was a negative direction in the risk rating, it would show as a dark grey (red) gap in the graph.

The above shows that the remediation continued to be successful. There was one risk (risk number 20 titled "continuous pricing pressure") that actually declined, but by such a small amount, it was not visible in the graph.

The third measurement in Figure 15.31 is the actual Q4 versus where the risk owners predict the performance for the next quarter (Q1).

Figure 15.31 shows that all risks, except for one, are predicted to stay the same or maybe improve. Any of the risks that had a substantial change whether in the lighter gray (green) or in the darker gray (red), were highlighted with a small call-out explanation addressing the root cause. These above three graphs were viewed intensely by the CEO in the quarter reviews, as well as the Audit Committee in the quarterly Board of Directors' meetings, both of which want to be able to look forward, as well as look backward at actual results. The ability to look forward from a prediction perspective was a very positive addition to this ERM program (and it was not present in the prior example of the solar company ERM program).

Figure 15.32 shows the Top 25 risks and illustrates the assignment of the risks to specific committees of the board of directors for proper oversight.

Note that the full Board of Directors was responsible for several risk topics, while the Audit Committee was responsible for most of the others. Both the Compensation Committee and the Nominating and Corporate Governance Committee owned the oversight of one risk topic each. This element of accountability and ownership adds a layer of transparency to

Tier Q4		TOPIC	Q3
TIER 1	1	Speed of MXX Margin & Growth	1
	2	Threat of Made in China 2025	2
	3	Intellectual Property Protection	3
	4	External Supplier Relationships & Dependency	4
	5	Business Continuity & Disaster Recovery	5
	6	Short-Term Mindset	8
	7	Scalability for Rapid Growth	9
	8	Product Development Execution	7
	9	New Product Introduction	10
	10	Velocity of MYY Market Decline	6
TIER 2	11	Inventory Management Controls & Systems	14
	12	Industry Consolidation	13
	13	Geopolitical Risk	11
	14	Managing Investor Confidence & Activist Investor	20
	15	Cybersecurity Breach	16
	16	Transformational Product Innovation	15
TIER 3	17	Supply Demand Forecasting Accuracy	17
	18	Customer Centric Mindset	24
	19	Distributor & Channel Dependency	18
	20	Continuous Pricing Pressure	12
	21	Stability & Competitiveness of Fab Operations	19
	22	Effectiveness of Procurement Activities	23
	23	High Customer Concentration	25
	24	Employee Hiring & Retention	22
	25	Financial Reporting Controls (SOX)	21

LEGEND:
- ▬ 1Actual Q3
- ▬ 1Actual Q4
- ▨ Improvement in residual score in Q4.

Majority of the risks Company actively managed showed a significant improvement in Q4'19.

Improvement is attributed to the maturing level of controls put in place to increase ability to timely detect and respond to risk events.

Actual Q3 vs. Actual Q4

Figure 15.29 ERM top 25 residual risk performance (Actual Q3 versus Actual Q4)

Tier. Q4		TOPIC	Q3
TIER 1	1	Speed of MXX Margin & Growth	1
	2	Threat of Made in China 2025	2
	3	Intellectual Property Protection	3
	4	External Supplier Relationships & Dependency	4
	5	Business Continuity & Disaster Recovery	5
TIER 2	6	Short-Term Mindset	8
	7	Scalability for Rapid Growth	9
	8	Product Development Execution	7
	9	New Product Introduction	10
	10	Velocity of MYY Market Decline	6
	11	Inventory Management Controls & Systems	13
	12	Industry Consolidation	14
	13	Geopolitical Risk	11
TIER 3	14	Managing Investor Confidence & Activist Investor	20
	15	Cybersecurity Breach	16
	16	Transformational Product Innovation	15
	17	Supply Demand Forecasting Accuracy	17
	18	Customer Centric Mindset	24
	19	Distributor & Channel Dependency	18
	20	Continuous Pricing Pressure	12
	21	Stability & Competitiveness of Fab Operations	19
	22	Effectiveness of Procurement Activities	23
	23	High Customer Concentration	25
	24	Employee Hiring & Retention	22
	25	Financial Reporting Controls (SOX)	21

LEGEND:

↑Actual Q4
↓Predicted Q4

Performed better than expected

Did not perform as expected

Actual Q4 vs. Predicted Q4

10 👍 Better market condition & lesser dependency on MPD

Reduction on control deficiencies

Consistent achievement of attrition and hiring KPI's

Most of the risks showed better than predicted trend as risk owners become more confident in the effectiveness of risk mitigation and monitoring plans.

Figure 15.30 ERM top 25 residual risk performance (actual Q4 versus predicted Q4)

Tier Q4	TOPIC	Q3
TIER 1	1 Speed of MXX Margin & Growth	1
	2 Threat of Made in China 2025	2
	3 Intellectual Property Protection	3
	4 External Supplier Relationships & Dependency	4
	5 Business Continuity & Disaster Recovery	5
TIER 2	6 Short-Term Mindset	8
	7 Scalability for Rapid Growth	9
	8 Product Development Execution	7
	9 New Product Introduction	10
	10 Velocity of MYY Market Decline	6
	11 Inventory Management Controls & Systems	13
	12 Industry Consolidation	14
	13 Geopolitical Risk	11
TIER 3	14 Managing Investor Confidence & Activist Investor	20
	15 Cybersecurity Breach	16
	16 Transformational Product Innovation	15
	17 Supply Demand Forecasting Accuracy	17
	18 Customer Centric Mindset	24
	19 Distributor & Channel Dependency	18
	20 Continuous Pricing Pressure	12
	21 Stability & Competitiveness of Fab Operations	19
	22 Effectiveness of Procurement Activities	23
	23 High Customer Concentration	22
	24 Employee Hiring & Retention	27
	25 Financial Reporting Controls (SOX)	21

LEGEND:

Actual Q4

Predicted Q1

Predict an improvement in the risk score in Q1'20

Predict increase in risk score in Q1'20

Recognize return on investment

Recognizing effective treatment plan execution

Predicted Q1 vs. Actual Q4

Figure 15.31 ERM top 25 residual risk performance (predicted Q1 versus actual Q4)

Q4	TOPIC	Risk Champion	Risk Owner	Board Oversight
1	Speed of MXX Margin & Growth	C-suite	Responsible party	Board
2	Velocity of MYY Market Decline	C-suite	Responsible party	Board
3	Threat of Made in China 2025	C-suite	Responsible party	Board
4	External Supplier Relationships & Dependency (Supply Chain Disruption)	C-suite	Responsible party	Board
5	Business Continuity & Response Plan	C-suite	Responsible party	Audit Committee
6	Short-Term Mindset	C-suite	Responsible party	Compensation Committee
7	Product Development Execution	C-suite	Responsible party	Board
8	Intellectual Property Protection	C-suite	Responsible party	Audit Committee
9	Supply Demand Forecasting Accuracy	C-suite	Responsible party	Audit Committee
10	Geopolitical Risk	C-suite	Responsible party	Nominating & Corporate Governance Committee
11	Scalability for Rapid Growth	C-suite	Responsible party	Audit Committee
12	Inventory Management Controls & Systems	C-suite	Responsible party	Audit Committee
13	Cybersecurity Breach	C-suite	Responsible party	Audit Committee
14	Transformational Product Innovation	C-suite	Responsible party	Board
15	New Product Introduction	C-suite	Responsible party	Board
16	Distributor & Channel Dependency	C-suite	Responsible party	Board
17	Customer Centric Mindset	C-suite	Responsible party	Board
18	Stability of Fab Operations	C-suite	Responsible party	Audit Committee
19	Effectiveness of Procurement Activities	C-suite	Responsible party	Audit Committee
20	High Customer Concentration	C-suite	Responsible party	Board
21	Industry Consolidation	C-suite	Responsible party	Board
22	Continuous Pricing Pressure	C-suite	Responsible party	Board
	Managing Investor Confidence & Activist Investor	C-suite	Responsible party	Board
	Employee Hiring & Retention	C-suite	Responsible party	Compensation Committee
	Financial Reporting Controls (SOX)	C-suite	Responsible party	Audit Committee

Figure 15.32 ERM top 25 risk accountability and ownership

the Board of Directors and serves as a reminder that they do own these risks and that each of the board meetings should be addressing them.

Figure 15.33 is a representative illustration that shows the work of developing and comparing external or emerging risk updates.

There are several sources for identifying external and emerging risks. Those sources are generally well known but need to be developed by the ERM Administrative Team to find the organizations and the studies that are most applicable to your company and related industry. In this particular case, the top risks topics were taken from four various sources shown as follows and compared against the Top 10 risks on the semiconductor company's heat map.

- The middle column of the top risks was from a survey of "Board of Directors and C-suite" participants conducted by a university organization.
- The next column to the right lists the top threats from "Global CEOs," which was a survey conducted by a research company.
- The next column is the Top 10 emerging risks, similarly from a broader survey from a different source.
- The last column shows how those risks compared to the semiconductor company's risk ranking.

This comparison helped the executives of the semiconductor company to understand whether the semiconductor company had all the key emerging risks being addressed in their risk profile. Those were the risks shaded in lighter gray (green), which were identified as emerging risks from the three other sources, but not in the Top 25 for the semiconductor company. This generated the need for the ERM Administrative Team to do analysis and research to determine if those risk topics should be accelerated into the higher ranking.

Figure 15.34 shows yet another opportunity to confirm whether the Top 25 register is complete.

This exercise was performed periodically and resulted from a review of competitors' 10K risk factors to identify differences between the competitor's risk factors versus those of the company. In some cases, the ERM Administrative Team had to do more follow up for the risks topics that

Topic	Top Risks for BOD & C-Suites	Top Threats for Global CEO's	Top 10 Emerging Risks	ACT Rank
Ability of operations & IT infrastructure to compete against "born digital" firms	1	9	3	11
Talent Risk (Succession, Hiring & Retention, Labor Model Disruption)	2	3	1, 7, 9	24
Geopolitical Risk (Regulatory Changes, Policy Uncertainty, Protectionism, Populism, Trade Conflicts)	3	1, 2, 4, 6, 8	8, 10	7
Cybersecurity	4	5		2
Resistance to Change	5			40
Disruptive Innovation & New Technologies	6		4, 5	8
Data Privacy	7		2	27
Data Analytics & Big Data	8			36
Risk Identification & Escalation	9			NA
Customer Loyalty & Retention	10			18
Exchange Rate Volatility		10	6	39

External Sources of Top Risks / Emerging Risks:

* Protiviti & North Carolina State University (NC State) Executive Perspectives on Top Risks for 2019

** PWC 22nd Annual Global CEO Survey (1378 respondents)

*** CEB Q4 2018 Top 10 Emerging Risk Survey Report

Risks not included in ERM Top 25 Heat Map

Protiviti & NCSU: Top Risks for BOD & C-Suites

The overall global business environment is riskier in 2019; Organizations will face a lot of significant uncertainties;

Greater desire to invest in strengthening risk management capabilities;

Regulatory concerns persist, & nature of concerns vary across the globe

PWC Top Threats for Global CEO's

Expect a decline in the rate of global economic growth;

More extremely concerned about the ease of doing business in the markets where they operate than broad existential threats (terrorism or climate change);

Focus toward internal initiatives to drive revenue growth (operational efficiencies, organic growth, launching a new product or service) as they adapt to barriers between markets;

More mindful of immediate threats & more focused on what they can control as they await greater clarity on government actions & market conditions;

Increasing efforts to move aggressively on AI & data analytics for decision making, but information received from these efforts are still inadequate due to lack of analytical talent, data silos & poor data reliability.

CEB Top 10 Emerging Risk

Biggest risk is talent shortage: organizations are finding it increasingly difficult to fill positions in a tightening labor market; and critical skills become too expensive to acquire. In response, CEO's have changed talent strategy to reflect future needs and investing internally in their existing workforce.

High ranking external risks that are prioritized at a lower rank by Company: Talent Risk; Data Privacy; Resistance to Change; Data Analytics & Big Data; and Exchange Rate Volatility.

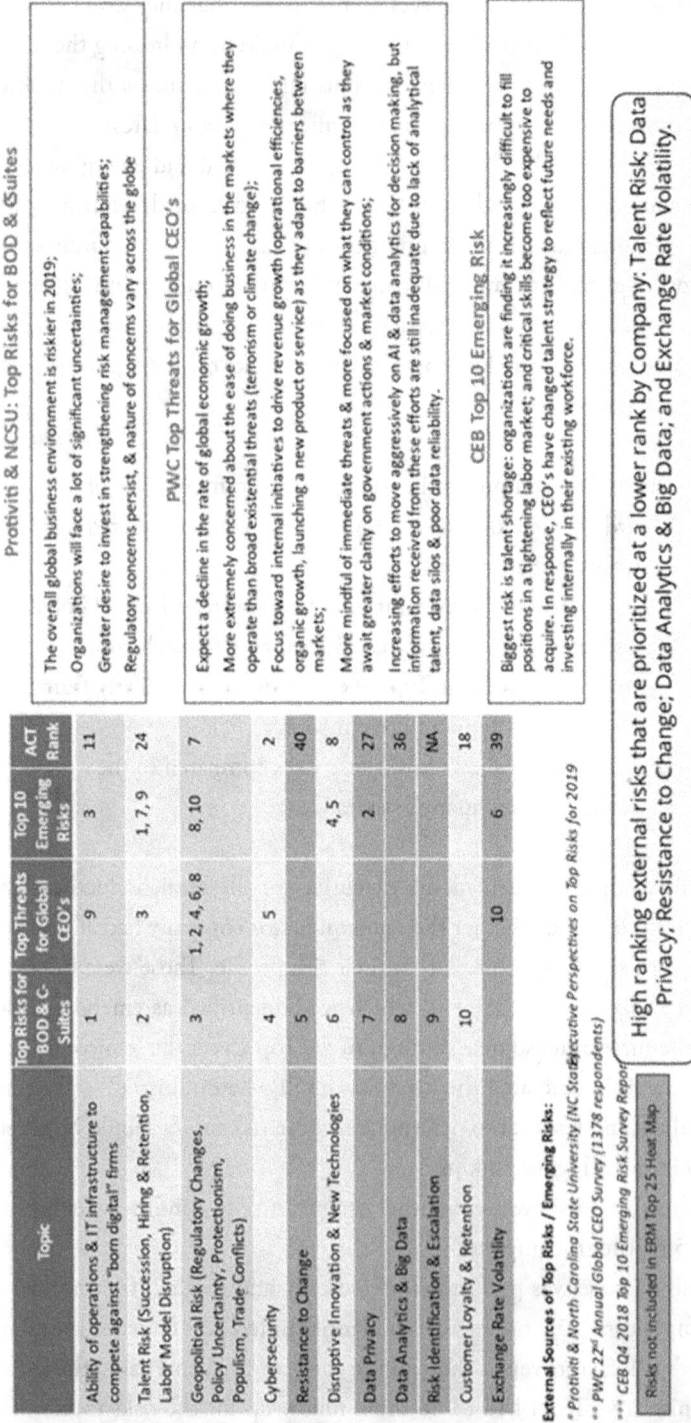

Figure 15.33 External/Emerging risk updates

A review of **ten** competitor* 10K Risk Factors was performed to test completeness of Company Risk Register (Total Risk Universe):

Most frequent risks from competitor 10K's are part of Cypress Top 25 Risk Register.

The following risks were found in competitor 10K's but not included in Company total risk register: (1) International Internal Sales Operations Risks; (2) Operating in Open Source Software Environment; (3) Accrued Pension and Severance Cost; (4) Impairment of Long-Lived Assets and Goodwill; (5) Counterfeit Products; (6) Transition to Smaller Geometry Process Technologies; and (7) Real Property Risks.

ACTION ITEM – assess in Q3 whether these are real risks for Company

The following Top 25 risks were not seen in most of competitor 10K's, and may be exploited as opportunity: (1) Transformational Product Innovation; (2) Short-Term Mindset; (3) Scalability, (4) Effectiveness of Procurement, (5) Managing Investors

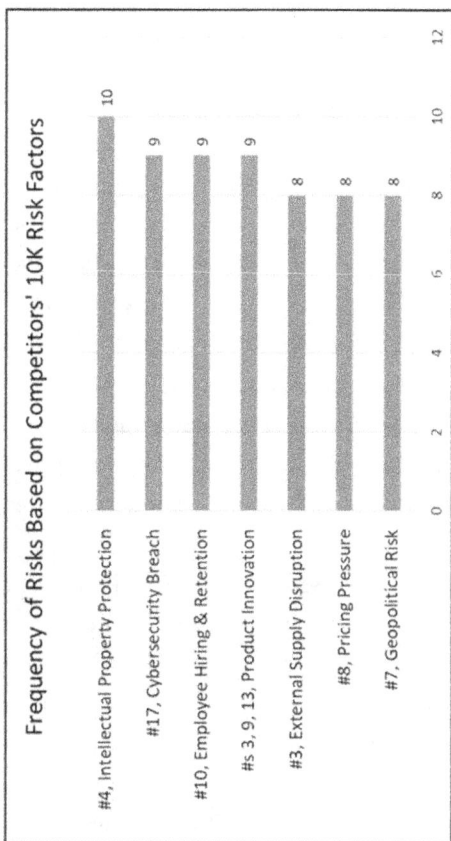

Frequency of Risks Based on Competitors' 10K Risk Factors

#4, Intellectual Property Protection — 10
#17, Cybersecurity Breach — 9
#10, Employee Hiring & Retention — 9
#s 3, 9, 13, Product Innovation — 9
#3, External Supply Disruption — 8
#8, Pricing Pressure — 8
#7, Geopolitical Risk — 8

* Competitors included in the review: Fujitsu, Marvell, Xilinx, Microchip, Micron, NXP, Qualcomm, Renesas, Texas Instruments, Toshiba

Figure 15.34 Comparison to competitor 10K risk factors

were not included in the current ERM program. The chart on the right-hand side shows the frequency of risks based on the competitors' 10K risk factors. As an example, in 10 out of 10 companies, intellectual property was listed in their 10K risk factors. The same topic was ranked as number 4 in the semiconductor's risk profile heat map. Cyber security was mentioned by 9 out of 10 companies, employee hiring and retention was also listed by 9 out of 10 companies. This comparison provided a very positive support to the credibility of the current risk topics portfolio.

The last illustration in this chapter is shown in Figure 15.35 and represents stock price trending of the semiconductor company over the period of the ERM program shown in this case study.

Since there were notable shifts in the company's share price, the ERM Administrative Team would identify (using a publicly reported information) the events that happened during this period. While this does not mean that all these activities caused the change in the share price movement, it does make the executive team think about the potential influence of key events on the share price. This analysis was well received by the investor relations department primarily and was subsequently developed in conjunction with their efforts.

In conclusion of the semiconductor case study, we would like to point out that while it was a more advanced ERM program than one shown for the solar company, it yielded a significant success only after two years of its existence. Some of the key reporting templates were shared along with information that needed to be provided to the Board of Directors and members of the organization in charge of the individual risks, but we want to remind you that these programs and processes can and should be continuously improved to increase their efficiency and to increase their benefits to your organization.

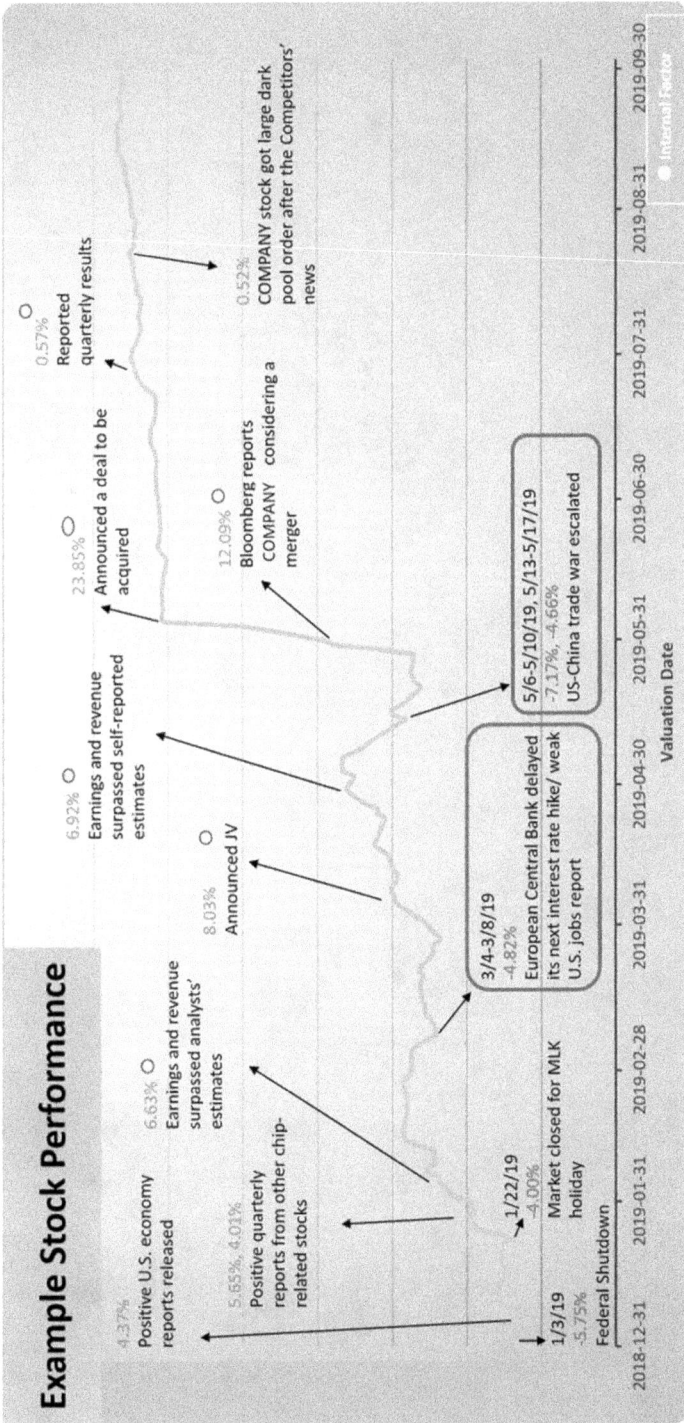

Example Stock Performance

4.37%
Positive U.S. economy
reports released

6.63% ○
Earnings and revenue
surpassed analysts'
estimates

5.65%, 4.01%
Positive quarterly
reports from other chip-
related stocks

8.03% ○
Announced JV

6.92% ○
Earnings and revenue
surpassed self-reported
estimates

23.85% ○
Announced a deal to be
acquired

12.09% ○
Bloomberg reports
COMPANY considering a
merger

0.57% ○
Reported
quarterly results

0.52% ○
COMPANY stock got large dark
pool order after the Competitors'
news

1/3/19
-5.75%
Federal Shutdown

1/22/19
-4.00%
Market closed for MLK
holiday

3/4-3/8/19
-4.82%
European Central Bank delayed
its next interest rate hike/ weak
U.S. jobs report

5/6-5/10/19, 5/13-5/17/19
-7.17%, -4.66%
US-China trade war escalated

● Internal Factor

Valuation Date

2018-12-31 2019-01-31 2019-02-28 2019-03-31 2019-04-30 2019-05-31 2019-06-30 2019-07-31 2019-08-31 2019-09-30

Figure 15.35 Stock price analysis—percent change

CHAPTER 16

Conclusion

Enterprise Risk Management (ERM) is essential for any business as it encompasses all relevant risks. An ERM Framework supports a company leaders' competency to manage the risks comprehensively, and with an understanding of the correlation among various risks. The successful business implements a robust ERM capability as part of its culture establishing a comprehensive and integrated view of a business's risks in the context of its business strategy. By doing so, the business reduces the likelihood and consequences of risks materializing. Other benefits include competitive advantage, reduced cost of capital, and better financial reporting.

In conclusion, ERM programs can be implemented in a very short timeframe or over a longer period of time and with very solid results. Regardless of the implementation period, there are certain conditions that must be met to facilitate a successful implementation of the ERM program. They include:

- Visibility into ELT and board of director support;
- Solid program infrastructure in place;
- Extensive hands-on training sessions;
- Organized and talented ERM Administrative Team;
- Culture open to change and common risk management language; and
- Mindset to refine and improve the program in a thoughtful manner over time.

Visibility Into ELT and Board of Director Support

Support from the top is the primary driver of an ERM program. The most optimal situation is when the Board of the Directors requests the program. However, it is nearly as effective and receives as much support if it is requested by the CEO. Other sources such as the CFO or the Head of Internal Audit are more of contributors in selling the program over time, but certainly have a major influence to make the program successful. Other types of support that can be facilitated by the CEO or CFO would include:

- Incorporating the responsibilities and performance of the Risk Treatment Plans into an incentive compensation program. The more specific the attachment is, the stronger the impact. Sometimes this will create the need to audit the results since it impacts compensation.
- Incorporating the reporting of the Top 25 treatment plan results in the CEO's Quarterly Operations Reviews. Sharing content at the executive level provides strong incentive to show results in a knowledgeable fashion. This process allows the CEO to probe into any level of the detail as desired.
- Incorporating the ERM progress into company goals, even if not at a specific bonus arrangement. Remediating risks to promote company goal achievement is a win for all shareholders.
- Incorporating the results of the ERM program into both short-term and long-term company strategy planning sessions.
- Incorporating the results of the ERM program into the annual operating plan budget. Many risk mitigation efforts require some investment to recognize the offsetting gain or benefit. Those financial impacts need to be transparent in the beginning.

Solid Program Infrastructure in Place

New processes and programs generally work better when the infrastructure parameters are designed, approved, and implemented early to facilitate ease of implementation, consistency in execution, and environment to sustain the program. Some examples include:

- Creating a formal Risk Committee to include key members of executive management to provide overall governance of the program.
- Developing a formal Risk Committee Charter to provide guiding principles for the program governance.
- Developing standard policies and procedures with documentation available to the general population for training and maintenance purposes.
- Determining the model for quantifying and rating risks within the risk profile for prioritization and to measure performance.
- Providing a regular reporting cadence to the various audiences needing to know such as the Risk Committee, Audit Committee, and Risk Champions.
- Utilizing standard templates for summary-level reporting to maintain familiarity of the information flow and messaging.

Extensive Hands-On Training Sessions

The amount of training required can be surprising, considering the many different levels of audiences from board of directors, to executives and upper and middle management. The level of training details varies by audience and requires periodic refresh sessions. Some of the training will be hands-on—for example, developing Risk Treatment Plans with the risk owners. Program standardization makes it easier to maintain a common risk language and reduce the complexity and frequency of training.

Organized and Talented ERM Administrative Team

The resources required to create, implement, and maintain an ERM program must be highly knowledgeable in the applicable industry, capable of learning the business, and educated in risk management discipline. The resources required to maintain the program will vary throughout the year and at each gating reporting cadence. In addition, there is a need to access other resources to complete the tasks during the peak periods of the program such as conducting the risk assessment exercise. The ERM

Administration Team's personalities must be of such ability to build relationships extending into trust and credibility. This team should eventually become a source for consultation to management.

A Culture Open to Change With a Common Risk Management Language

Modifying any business culture is difficult and can take years to accomplish. However, there are some qualities that can facilitate enough change to achieve the right mindset to build a successful ERM program, and include:

- being able to sell the benefits of the program;
- influencing risk owners to apply the needed about of attention to detail utilizing a common risk language for clarity in messaging;
- utilizing existing programs, where possible, to minimize the amount of incremental work required for the program members; and
- embedding the philosophy of risk managing into daily operations and management decision making.

Mindset to Refine and Improve the Program in a Thoughtful Manner Over Time

Once the basic ERM program is in place, the best practice is to add a new element every one or two quarters. Keep in mind that too much change may be difficult to implement at one time, so the changes made should be gradual to make it easier for everyone to digest and learn. There are many elements that can be added or refined throughout the life of the ERM program. Some enhancements might include:

- Risk heat maps at company, geographic, business model, or departmental levels;
- Increased level of focus on emerging and external risks;
- Use of automation and Artificial Intelligence in risk identification and quantification;

- Use of an automation tool reducing the administrative elements of the program;
- Shareholder Price tracking;
- Competitor comparisons and tracking for both company- and industry-level activities;
- Identify opportunities for profit maximization that are not considered risks;
- Refined risk tolerance and risk appetite application; and
- Recognition programs for remediation successes and leading practices within the organization.

The performance and even vitality of any business in today's global economy depends on managing the known and foreseeable risks. Every business must understand the level of acceptable risks in achieving its objectives as well as the type of risks that are embedded within its operations. It is vital to identify and prioritize significant risks and detect the weakest links. We hope that our book equipped you with enough excitement, ingenuity, and knowledge to create/implement/manage a successful ERM program at your organization.

Thank you for taking the time to read our book.

About the Authors

John Sidwell (Certified Public Accountant (CPA), Certified Internal Auditor (CIA), and Certification in Risk Management Assurance (CRMA)) is currently with Infinera Corporation transforming business practices and controls. Experience includes roles with PepsiCo and Coca-Cola and over 20 years of technology experience with Cypress Semiconductor (Infineon), SunPower (TotalEnergies), Electronic Arts, Dolby Laboratories, and 3COM. Past 10 years John specialized in developing robust ERM programs. He has spoken at MetricStream Global GRC Summits, Institute of Internal Auditors, and Risk Management/Internal Audit class at San Jose University, and written to blogs of companies such as AuditBoard. John has a BS Degree in Accounting from Quincy University (Quincy, IL) and is a member of Institute of Internal Auditors, Financial Executives International, Neu Group Internal Audit Peer Group, and others.

Peter Hlavnicka is currently Venture Partner with R3i Ventures (Singapore) and Founder of Phi Ventures (Singapore) specializing in risk management, Intellectual Property (IP) strategy/commercialization, and brand protection. He is also Co-Founder of SenzeCare (freelance senior care platform) and R3i IPx Trading. Previous roles include Director Brand Protection APAC (Fitbit), Director Pricing (Blackberry), Director IP Protection and Enforcement (Dolby Laboratories). Prior to Dolby, he worked at Avaya and Nortel Networks, where he established and led enterprise IP protection and licensing efforts. Mr. Hlavnicka's roles also included strategic pricing, ERM, contract management, operations, and Supply Chain Management (SCM). He is iAM IP Strategy 300 Global Leader in 2021 and 2022 and has written and spoken on a number of brand protection issues and contributed to numerous publications, including *Business Week*. Mr. Hlavnicka received his MSc in Computer Science from the Technical University of Kosice, Slovakia, and his executive MBA from the University of Western Ontario, Richard Ivey School of Business.

Index